SNAP DIAGNOSIS

CHARLES EAD

Ghost Writing Partner

Copyright © 205

By **Charles Ead**

All rights reserved.

Boston. In addition, I proudly paid all my high school, college, and graduate school expenses with my Bishop's work earnings. In other words, I came up the "hard way." I knew how to set goals. I had self-discipline.

I was a well-rounded athlete, too, and played sports through school and beyond. In high school, I distinguished myself as a cross-country and indoor track distance runner and was also named co-captain of our varsity baseball team by my coach during my senior year. Later on, I was selected to be the starting catcher on the varsity baseball team at Salem State College as a freshman.

In addition, an avid runner during and after college, I completed the Bowe Marathon in the spring of 1978 in a respectable time, despite not having adequately trained for the race. Put simply, I felt like a "somebody" and an achiever - you might even say an over-achiever. I don't believe that I was a valid candidate for involuntary psychiatric institutionalization and forced medicating. And I certainly don't think I deserved to experience the multiple horrors that befell me at the hands of rogue psychiatrists, beginning just three years after I completed Business School.

But I will let you, dear reader, be the judge of that. Thank you for your willingness to read my story.

- Charles Ead

Consider, for example, the strange and fascinating story of author Charles Ead. Analyze his life, compare him with men of achievement in this age of industry and finance, and observe how they have one outstanding trait in common - Persistence!

If you are keenly interested in studying the strange power that gives potency to Persistence, read SNAP DIAGNOSIS.

The following Synopsis of that book will provide a preview of the rare treat in store for those who take the time to read the entire story of one of the most astounding examples of the power of Persistence known to civilization.

SYNOPSIS

In mid-1982, shortly after an ambitious, MBA graduate, a former high school student returns from a five-month, physically exhausting work experience in the high heat, high humidity, Persian Gulf, a rogue psychiatrist gives him a hasty interview that does not even include a physical exam and misdiagnoses him with Bi-Polar Disorder. So begins the spiraling comedy of errors fiasco that becomes Charles' life for years to come. He is repeatedly hospitalized against his will, stigmatized in his family and community, and forced into taking harmful medications. As the nonsense eventually intensified with time, the horrifying ordeal snowballed out of control and took on a life of its own.

Charles receives a severe beating at the hands of the hospital staff in response to speaking up for both his and other patients' rights. This assault is immediately followed by a punitive, three-day solitary confinement lock-up, which was directly orchestrated by the ward head nurse who also oversaw the beating. A later attempt to forcefully administer brain-damaging, electric-convulsive shock treatment was, thank-God, miraculously averted at the last minute. The protagonist later plunges into a near-death experience from 'Neuroleptic Malignant Syndrome,' which was the direct result of involuntary and negligent medication. Charles' life ultimately descends into a living Hell that finds him alienated from friends and family, wandering homeless on the streets of Los Angeles.

Finally, Charles, through the sheer act of will and a newly developing faith, can put the pieces of his life back together and challenge a psychiatric establishment that quite simply has too much power. On the plus side, he emerges from the crucible with a new set of values and a determination to help others avoid the degradation and loss of freedom that he suffered.

The protagonist's story, paradoxically set in Massachusetts, the nation's Cradle of Liberty, casts a much-needed spotlight on the widespread Constitutional and human rights abuses that are systemically heaped upon those identified as psychiatric patients. In addition, it serves as an indictment of the saga's prime antagonist, Institutional Bio-psychiatry - a relatively unregulated wing of the medical establishment, which, with Orwellian authority, annually confines tens of thousands of Americans against their wills to mental hospitals. Research indicates that many of these voiceless, poor souls, unbeknownst to the general public, tragically suffer the same dismal fates that our protagonist did.

Though the mental health system has undergone many changes since psychiatry began, a historical review shows that its basic treatment ideology has not changed in the last two centuries. Patients are incarcerated in locked settings that mock the concept of good mental health, broken by having their privileges removed and re-earned, then forced to parrot the hospital's party line before being allowed to re-enter free society. Accounts of patients in early nineteenth-century asylums detail a remarkably similar dynamic!

On the human-interest level, this is a conflict-rich, family story in which Charles ends up being trapped by his parents' well-intentioned but misguided inability to manage his medical treatment properly. It's also a story, "Hey, this nightmare could very well happen to ME," a story anyone who has felt mistreated, humiliated, or exploited by any system, or has simply felt that their voice has not been heard, will identify with the story's protagonist.

On an inspirational level, this is a classic. Underdog, David & Goliath, Ugly Duckling, triumphant survival story of a man who endures the indignities of psychiatric institutionalization and comes out stronger, more authentic, and more socially responsible as a result of the ordeal. The shallow, do-what-it-takes-to-make-a-profit value system that Charles developed in Business School morphs into a much more empathetic understanding of the world, the development of a strong social conscience, and an abiding faith in his Maker, who personally saw him through his multiple travails.

The compelling theme of this saga is that despite being put through the ringer and having his insides kicked out, the protagonist never gave up and quit—just the opposite. With God's always present help and support, he picks himself up and fights his way back, overcoming ill health, long suffering, scorn, shame, and injustice. Charles' story should also be viewed as a traditional morality play as well as a cautionary tale and a rallying cry.

TABLE OF CONTENTS

Drunk, but not with the wine. Thus says the Lord, your God who defends his people. See, I am taking your hand the cup of staggering, the bowl of my wrath you shall no longer drink. I will put it into the hands of your tormentors. Those who said to you bow down then we may walk over you. So you offered like the ground, like the street to walk on.

"Nobody is ever defeated until defeat has been accepted as a reality."

-Helen Keller

"The only thing that allows evil to flourish is for good men to do nothing."

-Billy Graham

ACT I: THE BACKSTORY

Chapter 1:
My Proud Pedigree

They say that nothing happens in a vacuum. The details of our lives are inseparable from the tapestry into which they're woven. I'd like to share a bit of my tapestry with you, if you'll indulge me. I think that it will help you to understand my life in a richer way.

I am a third-generation descendant of Lebanese immigrants. My grandparents on my father's side emigrated right after each other around the year 1920 from the sprawling city of Dier-El Kamar in the heart of central Lebanon to Lawrence Massachusetts, an equally bustling (at the time), multi-ethnic, and densely populated mill town, often later referred to in the 1940s and '50s as "the friendliest city in America."

My grandmother - Mary (Zaidy) Ead, painfully buried her husband and three of her four young children, who all died from starvation when the locust famine hit her native Lebanon in 1919. Following these horrific events, in which she helplessly watched three of her kids die in her arms, one right after the other, she somehow summoned enough chutzpah to get on a boat in the capital port city of Beirut with her only remaining living child, an 11-year-old girl named Elma. Together, they bravely crossed the turbulent Atlantic and successfully arrived in America, full of hopes to start all over again and, against all odds, build a new life for the two of them.

Grandma and young Elma faced severe obstacles from the very start. They didn't know a soul in this country, didn't speak a word of English, and didn't have a penny to their name the fifty, U.S. dollars with which my grandmother left Lebanon with to start was stolen from her purse while she and Elma were docked in Marseilles, France. Thus, the two Zaidy gals arrived flat, broke in a new world and were forced to navigate life with absolutely nothing at all to start with. It all must have seemed so overwhelming and daunting to them when they finally arrived in Lawrence - the mill city that would become their abode for the remainder of their lives.

My grandfather Khalil (Charlie) Fad, also emigrated to America from Dier-El-Kamat, along with his younger brother, roughly two years before grandmother did. My grandparents had never met in Dier-El-Kamar. His plan was to work five years in prosperous mills here in Lawrence and then return home to Lebanon with enough money to provide a good life for him, his wife, and the three children he had left behind. Sadly, after busting his hump for three years, working twelve hours a day in the Wood Worsted Mill Grandpa learned through a Western Union telegram that his wife and three children had also died of starvation from the same deadly locust famine dur took my grandmother's family.

Somehow, after stoically digesting this news, the man decided not to return to Lebanon as he had planned and instead to stay here in America and try to build a new life for himself. He initially lived alone in a shabby rooming house downtown, continuing to plug away at his mill job. His faith and persistence paid off he met my grandmother a year later in Lawrence. The two realized they had a lot in common, fell in love, and later on married in 1924. Theirs, unlike today's loose standards, would be a marriage that was happily harmonious and would last a lifetime.

3

These two soulmates were further blessed with two new children - a girl they named Elsie and a son they named Farid (Fred in English) my father. These two offspring, along with my step-aunt Elma, are all married and in turn provided my grandparents with eleven grandchildren. My grandparents always spoke to us grandkids of their strong faith in God as being central to their success in putting the past behind them and rebuilding their shattered lives here in the States.

And not once can I recall either of them ever burdening us grandchildren with the travails and losses they went through. They kept it all to themselves. Sithoo and Jidoo's hearts, despite what they were forced to endure, never became small, bitter and/or self-pitying. They instead displayed only love for their new family and their neighbors and always expressed gratitude for being blessed with so much plenty in the new land of opportunity. They did this even though they lived by today's lofty standards anyway, in severe poverty.

All they could initially afford for living quarters was a fourth floor, cold-water flat on Elm Street in the poor, Lebanese section of Lawrence. They had no steam heat and no hot running water in their apartment. In order to heat the house in the winter, my grandmother was forced to throw wood in the oven/stove. Ice to cool the refrigerator had to be carried up four flights of stairs by the ice man three times a week. To wash themselves, on Saturday nights, Grandma would boil water on the stove and fill the tub so that she, my grandfather, my father, and his two older sisters could take turns bathing. They all used the same water, even though it was often still dirty from whoever had used the tub before. None the less, despite these adversities, I often heard Grandma say:

"Thank God for America. This is the Promised Land. May God bless America."

Grandma, who never learned much English, was forced to work only menial, low-paying jobs all her life. I recall that she worked for many years as a cook in the Lawrence High School cafeteria. And the best my grandfather could do for work was to hold down a job all his life at the Wood Mill for a paltry two dollars week, barely enough to pay the rent and put food on the table. After his retirement from the mill, he occasionally (and reluctantly) told kids horror stories of how he had slaved twelve hours a day in a dungeon-like setting where there was no central cooling. It was always oppressively hot in the mill during the summer months and conversely very cold during the late fall and winter months.

Rats ran rampant in the mill, too, Grandpa told us, and they would often eat his bagged lunch if he was forgetful enough to leave it on the floor and not hang it on a nail. Jidoo (the Arabic word for Grandpa) walked two miles to work at six o'clock every morning - rain, snow or shine, in the pitch dark, and walked the two miles back home every night at seven p.m. after he clocked out. Seeing sunshine was a rare occurrence for this man.

My father told me he worked just one summer in the Wood Mill, right alongside Grandpa, after his sophomore year in college. Jidoo had gotten him the job. Dad said that this brief, three-month work experience was so discouraging and traumatizing that he resolved never to work in a mill again. In fact, the experience Dad said provided him with the motivation to finish college and "better himself." Despite their hardships though, my grandparents always spoke well of this country and made it a habit to thank the Higher Power daily for what they saw at least, as their many blessings.

They knew they would never be rich, or even reasonably well-off, but they contented themselves with knowing they and their three kids at least had sustenance and shelter. Unlike most of today's Baby Boomers who were blessed with a strong post-war wind at their backs to launch them into lives of spoiled plenty, my grandparents' main aim in life was just to survive. They were willing to sacrifice and work hard for the little they had, confident and more financial success, better lives, and richer blessings would come to them were willing to sacrifice and work hard for the little they had. confident that children and their grandchildren in the following generations. They, perhaps rightly so, saw their wealth as being in their family.

People in the Lebanese community often spoke of Sithoo grandmother, as a "Bonafide saint." She walked to church and attended Mass faithfully every morning. She had an especially strong devotion to the Blessed Mother and to the Rosary. And, because of her strong faith, she would often be asked by others in the Lebanese community to come to their homes and anoint them or their sick family members with oil and quite often, they'd quickly get better. She was also a skilled midwife and helped bring many children into the world. And she'd also often chanted for the dead at wakes. The woman did it all. Furthermore, as legend has it, and as was the case with Mother Teresa, many folks who met up with Grandma even claimed they noticed a halo that surrounded her.

In addition, Sithoo was generous to a fault, often giving of what little she and my grandfather earned to the church or to others on Elm Street who were in need. She never refused anybody who came to her for financial or other kinds of help. Moreover, she would always go to her stove and cook up a meal for whoever came over to her house to visit, even though she had little food in her refrigerator or cupboards. Somehow, she always found a way to scrape together a dish or two for her prized guests. And yet her frugality was also legendary. Right after she died, my aunt Elsie, who managed her finances, handed each of us eleven grandkids in her name, a government bond for 125 dollars.

Grandma had evidently scrimped and saved a little of her meager income every week and then saved from her Social Security checks after she retired from work. She did so, my aunt said, in order to leave us "a little something to remember her by" after she died. It wasn't much, and many of us were doing well and didn't need the meagre 150 dollars, but it was an indication of the woman's strong devotion to her family and her character.

In addition to her many other virtues, my grandmother was considered to be utterly fearless. Like King David, her Biblical hero who courageously sling shotted the giant, the woman was known to be "afraid of absolutely nothing and nobody." The following story, as told to me by my father, evidences this. It goes as follows:

As an eight-year-old boy, my dad and my grandmother were picking blueberries together in a local forest in nearby Methuen. My grandmother would pick the berries and sell them to others on Elm Street to make ends meet. While Sithoo was doing her picking, my father noticed a large, multi-colored snake in the tree in front of her. He was sure it was poisonous and quickly yelled out in Arabic:

"Ma there's a snake right in that tree; watch out!"

Sithoo immediately located the snake on the tree, and without hesitation, grabbed it and crushed its head with a rock she had picked up, instantly killing it. She then threw the dead reptile to the ground, turned to my awestruck father, and said with a straight face also in Arabic,

"There's no snake here, son. Where do you see a snake?"

Let me say plainly, I don't consider myself, or any of my siblings or cousins, despite our accomplishments in life, to even be in the same league with my grandparents. They remain in a class by themselves. News anchor Tom Brokaw had it right when he named my grandparents' generation "Our Greatest Generation." I can't even buy the shoe polish to begin shining these two truly amazing folks' shoes.

In addition to coping with their own immense losses and family struggles, they had to endure - one right after another, the great Influenza Epidemic, World War One, the Stock Market Crash of 1929, the ensuing, ten-year Great Depression, World War II, and then finally, the Korean War. Even my father, who, as you will later see, was a great man in his own right, and who courageously faced many uphill battles in his life, once confided in me that if he could be "half the man" his father was, he'd "be something."

And how's this for awesomeness? My grandparents, in the mid-1930s, despite their paltry incomes, somehow managed to save up to three thousand dollars and buy a one-acre plot of land in the nearby rural town of Methuen, apple and peach trees, and potatoes. My grandmother also reserved a small which they turned into farmland, planting vegetables, corn, blueberries, plot on the "farm" for her beloved flowers. She loved nature and the innate beauty of a flower.

My grandfather, for his part, had an excavator dig a fifty-foot well in the middle of "the farm" for irrigation purposes and for drinking water, and later built by hand and by himself a one-room red cabin for him and my grandmother to live in.

Each spring when planting season arrived, the two of them would leave their city apartment in Lawrence, move up to the farm and plant and reap all day. They would then sell the produce at a makeshift farm stand to passersby on the sidewalk they built in front of the farm. My grandparents would also often invite one of us grandchildren up to the farm to spend the weekend there with them. We all took turns doing this and looked forward to it.

There was room for only one large bed in the cabin, and we all slept in it. The place had no running water, shower, or toilet, and we were forced to make use of the outhouse my grandfather had built right next to the cabin when duty called. All of us, including my first cousins, found this practice unpleasant and humiliating and we often voiced our disapproval amongst ourselves.

My grandmother would usually arise early in the morning and make blueberry pancakes for breakfast on the wood stove, which, like the bed, was located in the main room of the cabin. She used fresh blueberries she picked at the farm. The pancakes were delicious. We would always wash them down with a cup of hot chocolate that Grandma made for us in a black metal pot on the stove.

Somehow, my Jidoo - a man of slight build who weighed a mere 150 pounds, amazingly managed to dig large boulders and rocks out of the ground and build, by himself, a huge wall that encircled the whole farm. Using only a simple lever and a large shovel, he dug them up, as large and heavy as they were, and then moved them all, then stacked them carefully, by hand, one on top of the other. To this day, it's a mystery to all of us within his extended family how he was able to accomplish this remarkable feat by himself. The wall stood there for thirty years as a living testimonial to this amazing man whom we all greatly admired.

To his further credit, making use of his strong will power, Grandpa managed to keep himself out of the half dozen or so Elm Street coffee houses where many other, less disciplined Lebanese men his age could too often be found gambling their weekly pay checks away. The man was always quick to share words of wisdom with us too, often taken directly from the Bible. For example. I still remember him pulling me aside as a young kid and telling me,

"Remember Chuckie: when you give something to somebody else who needs it more than you do - especially money, - 'Just throw it in the ocean' and don't brag about it to anybody else, and above all never ask for it back either. Then God will see what you did 'in secret' and will reward you."

This advice was drawn directly from Jesus' Sermon on The Mount. Grandpa for sure, knew his Bible. I also remember him telling me, when I was about twelve years old, something that has stuck with me and benefitted me throughout my whole life:

"Grandson, when you know you're in the right, don't take a backward step for anybody!"

And, I also remember him saying to me more than once:

"Chuckie, there's no right way to do the wrong thing."

Jidoo was clearly a man of high moral principle and was fond of watching morality play westerns on TV. He loved stories that were simplistic and easy to follow, and where good people and bad people clashed openly with one another. He confided to me several times as a boy that his favorite such gunslinger flicks to watch were the 1960's thriller - 'The Magnificent Seven' which starred one of his favorite actors - Yule Brenner, and which he viewed and reviewed many times on his home TV, and the 1940's classic - 'High Noon' which starred the legendary Gary Cooper - another one of his favorite actors. And he was always overjoyed when, as in both movies, the "good guys" prevailed in the end.

He could also always be seen carrying around his Arabic, holy, prayer book and continually reading dutifully from it. And I'm still deeply honored that my father named me after my Jidoo. My grandfather's Arabic first name -Khalil, translates in English into my name -"Charles." That's why most of the folks in the Lebanese community called Jidoo 'Charlie.'

On a more humorous note, as the story was told to me by my dad. One-time Jidoo travelled to Chicago to attend a funeral. While at the funeral hall, a strange man approached him and asked him where he was from. My grandfather responded:

"I'm from Massachusetts."

The man then inquired:

"Whereabouts in Massachusetts sir?

Apparently wanting to put his best foot forward and not appear to be just another nobody from nowhere, Jidoo responded:

"Oh, I'm from Boston."

The stranger then asked Grand Pa:

"Boston, is that anywhere near Lawrence?"

As you will see, the faith and resiliency I inherited from my grandparents would resurface and shape later events in my own life. These traits would also rub off on my older cousin Lenny and inspire him to leave a comfortable, well-paying job as a tax examiner at the IRS, against his father's strong objections and enter the priesthood at age forty, and for considerably less pay I might add.

Now, a little history on my parents. My mother, Rose Hashem Ead, left her family in the secluded, Christian, mountain village of Ahoura, Lebanon, to get on a boat alone at the tender age of 18 and cross the Atlantic to settle in the United States. She is a member of the large and highly esteemed Hashem family in Lebanon and throughout the Middle East. In fact, the current king of Jordan I has been told is a Hashemite. I'm extremely proud to say, we Hashems have traced our roots all the way back to the seventh century Muslim prophet Mohammed.

And moreover, an ancestry trace done on my younger sister Pamela several years ago, evidenced that my family has ten percent Jewish blood in us. I suspect that it came from my father's side of the family which my grandfather told me once roamed alongside the nomadic Jewish tribes during the Israelites heyday in the valley all the Semites knew back then as only Pheonicia.

So maybe we Ead's in fact, proudly carry some Jewish blood in us as well. I'd be a very proud guy if that eventually ended up being true. I'd even like to think of the distinct possibility that our partial, Semetic blood line actually traces itself all the way back to Israel's beloved King David or even better, maybe even much earlier; employing a little imagination,

12

even possibly to all the way back to our spiritual father and "God's friend" - the Patriarch Abraham himself, who was known to roam Pheonicia (the land known as Cannan back then) some four thousand years ago. The Hebrew folks are God's "Chosen People" aren't they? Enough wasteful speculation though about a subject that probably can never to be documented and/or proven.

Now back to Ma. A day after her arrival at Ellis Island in New York, Ma took a train to Dover, New Hampshire, where she met up with her aunt Mary her father's sister, and her uncle Simon, Mary's husband, both of whom had emigrated from Lebanon some thirty years earlier. Aunt Mary sponsored Ma to come to America. Mary and Uncle Simon ran a successful grocery store in downtown Dover. Years after my mom's arrival, Simon was tragically hit by a train as he crossed the railroad tracks in downtown Dover and was killed instantly. None of us ever found out why he was walking along the tracks by himself on that fateful afternoon.

My mother, who had only a sixth-grade education, was a stunningly beautiful woman with such a great figure that folks often referred to her as the Sophia Loren of Lawrence. In addition, she was a virgin - innocent, pure, and loaded with class. She was a very religious woman too. Her father - Yahoub, the moral leader and "Godfather" of Ahoura, had emigrated from Lebanon as a teenager and worked the railroads out west in Wyoming and Montana for fifteen years, along with his younger brother Saba. He loved America.

Yahoub eventually returned to Lebanon with a large bankroll and bought a ton of real estate with it. He married there and had three children - a son, Nemer; a daughter, Nemra; and

13

then my mother by his first wife - Christine. Christine died from a mysterious illness one year after my mother was born, and two years later Yahoub married his second wife - Filamena. They together had seven more children, proudly adding to the Hashem family. Jidoo Yahoub saw enormous potential in my mother and wanted desperately to gain a foothold for his growing family in America, should throughout her younger years, to emigrate to the U.S. After Aunt Mary, at they later choose to emigrate here. And so, he repeatedly encouraged Ma, her, that she'd sponsor her to come here. Ma discussed the move with her brother Yahoub's request, sent my mom a letter from the U.S., informing dad. got the green light and came to Dover. Shortly after arriving there, at the behest of her aunt, she enrolled in English classes at the local high school and in only six months' time spoke perfect English with only a faint accent.

Lebanese American who spoke fluent Arabic, which he had learned as a child My father, Fred Ead, meanwhile, was an American-born, first-generation from his parents who only spoke their native language to him during his pre-school years. Dad was athletic, outgoing, good-looking and an extremely upbeat, positive, and humorous guy. Not surprisingly, he became quite a ladies' man when he got older.

To his further credit, while in high school and then later while he was on home leave from the Navy, he would go dancing on Saturday nights with his older sister - Elsie, often at the huge ballroom at Canobie Lake Park where famous band leaders like Artie Shaw, Bennie Goodman, and Tommy Dorsey would sometimes show up and play along with their orchestras. Dad in fact was such a great dancer and such a beloved figure on the dance floor that I'm told the girls would line up sometimes ten or even twenty deep and wait their turn just to get a single dance with him.

14

Dad ended up graduating with an accounting degree from Suffolk University under GI Bill after a three-year stint in the Navy, where he functioned as a medic. After his service duty and education were complete, he held a good job as a cost accountant in Lawrence. He was five years older than my mother. When my much less educated and more introverted mother met my father through relatives at a Labor Day Lebanese festival in Lawrence - the Mahrajan, she became infatuated with him at once.

Speaking English to her, which she now fully understood, Dad "quickly swept her off her feet." My father, meanwhile, was blown away by my mother's engrained Lebanese persona, her native beauty, and her child-like purity and innocence. As the story goes, despite Dad's many prior female escapades, he had never encountered a woman is beautiful and charming as Ma. She took his breath away and wept him off HIS feet.

Soon after they met at the fall festival, my father started driving thirty miles from Lawrence, where he was still living with his parents, to Dover, NH. every weekend to see my mother. At the onset of their relationship, Dad needed to first needed to win the approval of my mother's uncle Simon, as was the Lebanese custom back then. Making use of his great people skills, he quickly accomplished this feat with ease.

Ma's one-year "visit visa to the U.S. eventually expired, and Dad instructed her to return to Lebanon with the paperwork he had filled out at the local immigration office. He told her to take the papers to the main immigration office in Beirut and request they issue her a "permanent" visa. In short order, Ma got on a plane and flew hack to Lebanon. Dad, meanwhile. eagerly awaited her return to the States

15

After spending three months in Lebanon, Ma returned to the States with her new permanent visa in hand. One year later, still very much in love, the two got married in Saint Anthony's Matonite Church in Lawrence, then moved in with my grandparents in their fourth-floor, cold-water flat on Elm Street. After living on Elm Street for about a year and a half, my parents, no doubt seeking breathing space, moved into the first-floor apartment of a three-decker on Hampshire Street that Dad purchased with the help of a low-interest GI loan- one of the many postwar perks awarded to him by the federal government in exchange for his pre-college, three-year service in the Navy.

I was told by my mother when I had grown up that the twenty-five dollar a week rent received weekly by my parents on each of the two top floors above us fully paid the mortgage on our house by themselves. Thus, Dad and Ma were spared having to chip in even a penny of their own money to pay the ongoing debt to the bank who financed our family abode.

My grandparents followed them a year later. They left their cold-water flat and moved in with my parents on Hampshire Street. In direct contrast to the Elm Street apartment they had all left, the first floor on Hampshire Street had steam heat, four, good-sized bedrooms, two bathrooms both having hot water and a shower, an air conditioner in the kitchen window and a gas stove electricity, a TV and a washer and dryer. Quite apparently, they had all moved second or third-generation American will often proudly confide to you: up in the world. So that's my proud pedigree. As I'm sure many a reflective, "We Stand on the Shoulders of Giants."

Chapter 2:
My Wonderful Childhood

Unfortunately, my parents' marriage got off to a rocky start, at least for my mother. You see, both my grandmother and my dad's older sister, Elsie had wanted my father to marry an American-born, Lebanese girl - preferably from Elm Street and preferably a mate they could have pick out themselves, and not my immigrant mother. Maybe I'm being too hard on them, but they likely wrongly regarded my mom as an "inferior" who wasn't "worthy" of Dad.

Simply put, I reasoned after hearing Ma's side of the story several times that my mother was a clear affront to their Americanism. Grandma and Elsie, I think, were good people with a bad motive. Luckily for my eventual existence on this earth, Dad was highly opposed to complying with their wishes and went ahead and married Ma anyhow. As you might guess, intense friction and resentment later developed between these three strong-willed ladies.

The two busybodies, feeling slight, teamed up and retaliated out of spite. So, in order to get back at Dad, for what they most probably viewed was his clear miscue, they took out their resentment on Mom, repeatedly demeaning, and emotionally abusing and the poor woman with the sole intent of making her life as miserable as they could, perhaps hoping that she would eventually get totally fed up with the situation and leave Dad.

This behavior has always seemed totally out of character, not so much for my aunt, but most especially for my grandmother, who, as I mentioned earlier, was regarded by many who knew her as a saint. Also included in the negative

17

mix was a bit of well-hidden jealousy by my aunt towards my mother because Ma was by far much better looking. It was a twisted soap opera I still haven't been able to fully get my arms around, even to this day.

To make matters even worse for Mom, when she complained to Dad about this abuse, he would typically dismiss her complaints and side with his mother and older sister. Alone in a new country and far away from the family and support system she had left behind in Lebanon, Ma often felt isolated and betrayed in her marriage.

Drawing on her strong faith and her commitment to the marriage vow, she had taken, however, Ma eventually weathered the storm and stayed loyal to Dad. Before you knew it, she had given birth to five kids - my sister Marion, then me, then my younger brothers George and Mark, and then finally my younger sister Pamela - all of us roughly two years apart. Mark and I were the closest of the bunch. Mark idolized me as his older brother and I, in turn, loved him to death as my kid brother. And he was the apple of not only my eye but both my parents' eyes too.

Mark loved me so much, in fact that he would often leave the bunkbed he shared with George at night and come sleep with me in my twin bed. Mark was also by far the brightest of us kids. He'd come home with 100s on his math and English tests when the rest of us could only manage 80s. He was so brilliant, in fact, that the nuns at St. Rita's School wanted to give him a double promotion in the only the second grade. Mark loved playing with rockets too and, at only the age of eight, mind you, confided to us that his goal in life was to work as a rocket scientist for NASA.

In the meantime, my father proved himself to be a responsible and loving provider. He worked a full time, 9 to 5 job as a cost accountant at Bolta Products in Lawrence and later as a cost analyst at Avco Defense Corporation, in Wilmington, Mass., always moonlighting at night as a waiter at Bishop's Restaurant in Lawrence to earn extra money to keep the family going. And he saw to it too that all of us kids attended parochial school at nearby St. Rita's, where the Catholic nuns taught. There was no way he or my mother would allow us to be educated in the supposedly subpar, public schools.

My mother, for her part, worked part-time here and there when she had time to spare, but mostly played the dutiful housewife, staying at home and raising us kids. My grandparents eventually left our apartment. In early 1960, right around the time Mark was born, they began to feel they needed their own space, so they moved into a federally subsidized apartment in the elderly housing complex that was located on Hampshire Street, just five blocks from our house. My father, who knew just about everybody in town, was good friends with the mayor of Lawrence at the time - John Buckley - and secured the apartment with his help. My grandparents, in fact, were the first residents to move into the newly built, hundred-unit apartment complex.

Dad as well, religiously took all of us kids to Saint Joseph's Melkite Church, just a half mile or so up the street from us on Hampshire Street on Sunday mornings for church services. After Mass, we'd all head over to our grandparents' apartment and have lunch with them. My grandparents seemed to be in heaven when we came over. "Thut-burnee," (my sweethearts), my grandmother, would greet us with kisses as soon as we opened the door from her hallway and entered her kitchen. My grandfather, I was told years later, was especially thrilled to see me come over, his namesake, "Young Charlie."

19

When I was between the ages of nine and eleven, Dad would wake me up early on the weekend mornings and take me with him to Merrimack Country Club in Methuen to caddy for him. I greatly enjoyed doing this and excelled at it. Dad would pay me five bucks for my services - a king's ransom in those days, and in addition to the generous fee he paid me for my all-day caddy services would treat me to a cheeseburger, fries, and a soft drink in the "nineteenth hole" clubhouse right after we finished the round.

I always looked forward to this lunch with Dad throughout the entire day of golf whenever I caddied for him. Moreover, we would often sit and eat with other players. What a huge thrill this was for me as a young kid like me to rap with and observe these successful older fellows. It was at about this time that I began to idolize Dad and his interpersonal skills to such a level that I almost viewed him as God Himself walking on earth.

When I was nine years old, my younger brother George and I came home after school one afternoon sporting bloodied faces and embarrassingly told Dad we had just been beaten up by bullies in the schoolyard. Dad responded by promptly phoning his friend - Norm Salem, an ex-collegiate wrestler who, but for an untimely back injury, would have made the National Olympic Team. Retired from active wrestling, Norm, a first-generation Lebanese - American like Dad was, selflessly volunteered his time to run a wrestling class at the Lawrence YMCA.

In order to comply with Dad's request and teach George and I how to defend ourselves, Salem agreed immediately to accept us into his class, which consisted mostly of Lebanese - American kids from the Greater Lawrence area. The wrestling class proved to be a great experience for my younger brother and me. We practiced on Thursday nights and Saturday mornings. Dad would drop us off at the Y and then pick us up after practice.

After doing some calisthenics as a group, we boys would pair up with each other by weight and, under Salem's supervision, practice wrestling holds for a short spell and then free - wrestling with each other. After we did this, Salem would lead all of us upstairs to the small running track above the old gym, where he had us run a mile around the oval, asphalt circle to get our wind in shape. The track was small in size too as thirty-two often boring laps around constituted a mile.

Every couple of weeks or so, George and I competed in wrestling tournaments, some at the local YMCA and others at various Ys across New England. With Norm Salem always present to coach us and cheer us on, we won just about every one of these tournaments. My younger brother and I brought home numerous first-place trophies, which we as soon as we got home, proudly placed on a wooden shelf in our TV room.

I recall Salem taking our whole wrestling team to the Kane School gym in South Lawrence several times to put on wrestling exhibitions in front of hundreds of spectators, who sat in wonderment. We'd start the exhibition off with exercises we learned in class. One exercise the spectators especially liked was when about ten of us would fall back and land on our heads, uninjured, on the wrestling mat. My brother George and I were especially skilled at this. We'd then follow the exercises up by pairing up and demonstrating the wrestling holds we learned in class. For a ten-year-old kid, hearing a huge crowd cheering your every move was larger than life and highly esteemed building.

In addition, right after practice one Saturday afternoon, Salem treated our entire wrestling team - all twenty-five or so of us, to a full lunch of Lamb on the Stick, French Fries and Salad at the old, Bishop's Restaurant on White Street, - all at his expense. There can be no argument here. This Norm Salem guy was a class act.

When he was a youngster, Dad was a catcher on the CYO baseball team. He later caught high school ball, American Legion ball, and four years of college ball at Suffolk University. He prided himself on being a great defensive catcher with a quick release to second base and told me he more often than not threw out runners who dared to attempt to steal second base on him.

He claimed he was a good hitter too; not a homerun or power hitter, but a "bingles guy" - singles and doubles mostly. He also said he was a fast runner and stole a lot of bases. Dad introduced George and me to baseball as eight and nine-year-olds, teaching us both how to hit, throw, catch, and run the bases at the Howard Playground, which was located just two blocks up the hill from our house. We accordingly made our respective Little League teams at Howard, the Red Sox and with Dad as our coach and mentor, won the league championship two years in a row.

More than anything, Dad wanted me to follow in his footsteps and be a catcher too. Toward that end, he bought me a catcher's mitt at age eight and then taught me how to catch at the Howard, throwing me pop ups and showing me how to block balls in the dirt with my body. He freely admitted he was reliving his prized youth through me. Under Dad's tutelage, I eventually developed into a good catcher, and at age 12 was selected to be the starting catcher on our league's all-star team, which was earmarked to play in the upcoming State Little League Tournament.

There were fifteen of us, blessed with enormous talent on the team, who happened to come together, improbably, at the same time - just like our Founding Fathers did, and we proceeded to slug and scrape our way to thirteen straight wins across the state. The local newspaper - The Lawrence Eagle Tribune, diligently followed our exploits, and we regularly read stories of our games and saw pictures of ourselves in the daily sports section. What another thrill it was for a young kid to make the paper like that! We eventually found ourselves playing Parkway National out of the Boston suburb of West Roxbury for the state championship. The game took place on a Sunday afternoon in August, in front of three thousand passionate fans in Worcester Mass.

We had first earned our way into that final match with Parkway by defeating the team from the Massachusetts, suburban, bedroom town of Oxford the afternoon before - 1 to 0, in a ten inning, pitching duel that pitted our mound ace at the time, as well as our best clutch hitter - Mike Takovrian ("Tak"), against a highly talented Oxford pitcher as well.

Tak, who later went on and played his college ball for top notch USC and but for a career ending, knee injury that occurred during the tail end of his senior year season, was sure bet to be drafted into the majors after graduation. From what I have been told, no less than a half dozen major league teams had expressed a strong interest in him to his coaches before that untimely injury. All of us on our team, as a matter of fact, greatly looked up to our star pitcher as our right-handed throwing, version of the Hall of Fame - Sandy Koufax.

23

During the tenth inning of that same Oxford game, our big man - six foot two, 220 pound first baseman Jim Trotochaud, rose to the occasion as he, batting from the left side, golfed and pulled a 3 and 2, - two out, outside pitch that arrived to the plate a good two inches below his knees, twenty feet over the right feel fence to break what had been up to then, a 0-0 tie and secure an electrifying, walk-off, solo, home run victory for us.

Unfortunately, our two coaches had made the fatal mistake of taking all of us out bowling and then later after to that to wax museum in downtown Worcester that Saturday night before the following day's scheduled championship game and for reasons that I still can't recall, we ended up hanging around the museum much longer than we were supposed to and resultingly failed to return back to our downtown, living quarters until two in the morning. Not surprisingly, we awoke to have breakfast at six a.m. the next morning to find our entire team to the man, thoroughly exhausted, and still physically spent.

When game time with Parkway National arrived later on that fateful Sunday afternoon, we were all fatigued and out of synch, which resulted in our making seven uncharacteristic errors in the field. I myself can claim responsibility for two of them - a rare, passed ball and a third base-throwing error.

Although our pitcher that day, the six-foot tall and impressively built, twelve-year-old - Bobbie Berndston, who I went to grammar school with, pitched a two hitter, our miscues in the field sadly sealed our negative fate. Berndston wasn't his usual invincible self on the mound either and as I'm sure he'd admit if questioned about it today, that although he pitched a two hitter, it was definitely a subpar game for him as he threw several, untimely, wild pitches which in turn resulted in two unearned runs for Parkway. The fatigue affected our bats too.

Hitting all the way down the line up was usually our forte, but for the first time in the month and half long tournament and due exclusively to our mutually depleted condition, our Louisville Sluggers remained dead silent throughout the day.

Needless to say, we lost that do-or-die final game to Parkway National, (a team we all knew we were much better than), by I believe a score of 6 to 1 as best I can now recollect. Had we instead, managed to pull out a win that day, we would have flown straight to Williamsport, Pennsylvania to play little league baseball teams from all across America and the world in the nationally televised, Little League World Championship tournament - every eleven and twelve-year-old boy's dream. As you might imagine, our team was so shocked and distraught after that unanticipated Sunday afternoon loss that you could literally hear a pin drop on the darkened bus ride back home to Lawrence that Sunday night.

Cushioning the blow for me at least, the coach at the next rung in the playing ladder, the local Babe Ruth League team (made up of 13-, 14- and 15-year-olds), began "courting" me during the state tournament. Coach Dave Mullens would come to my house on Hampshire Street in repeated attempts to recruit me for his team and in so doing became good friends with my father. Mullens followed our all-star team's run and told us he desperately wanted me to play for his junior league team the following year. More than once, he presented my family with framed, colored pictures he had taken of me catching at our state tournament games.

I ended up playing for Mullens, - a tall and stocky, single man for the next three years. Right after practice on Saturday mornings, this great guy would often take three or four of his favorite players (which usually included me), to Fenway

Park in Boston, at his own expense mind you, to take in a Red Sox game. And we didn't sit in the cheap grandstand seats, or even in the more expensive box seats, we sat instead, in the glass - enclosed, much more expensive, sky-view seats which overlooked the park.

Coach Mullens always went first class too and treated his kids like rock stars. He would spring even further and buy each who accompanied him to the game, a couple of hot dogs, an ice cream sandwich, and a Coke, all with his own money as well. Equally as impressive, very often after a league game, he'd treat the whole team, all fifteen of us, as well as his assistant coaches, to Jim Dandy sundaes at Friendly's.

Moreover, right after our Saturday morning practice, he would also selflessly stay alone with me for an extra half hour, grab his fungo bat, park his feet at home plate alone with me and hit me ball after ball of super high popups which were often subject to shifts in the wind just so I could get the hang of catching them. Mullens, who we all wondered why being so faithful to young kids so much, never married and fathered children of his own, spared no effort or expense for his players, all of whom he treated like as if they were his "adopted" children.

Interestingly, I had the opportunity to hook up again with former coach Mullens after many years over lunch last year. During the middle of our stimulating conversation, and well aware of my dad's influence on me as a youngster from first-hand experience, he cut our discussion short to make what he apparently felt was an important point:

"Chuckie, your late Dad made you into the man you are today." Amen to that Coach!

In addition to the wrestling and baseball success I enjoyed as a youngster, Dad began taking me along with him to the Merrimack Valley Golf Course at age ten to receive golfing lessons from the pro there - Billy Max, who himself had done a three-year stint on the PGA Tour. After five or six lessons, Max, a scratch golfer, built up my ego even further by telling me that I had a great swing and great natural golfing talent and that if I stayed with the game and practiced religiously, I could very well make the PGA Tour when I became of age.

Under Max's and Dad's tutelage, I eventually shot 40 for nine holes one afternoon while playing along with Dad, as only an eleven-year-old. At around the same time, my Aunt Elsie began taking me to the YMCA, where they had an Olympic-sized pool, for swimming lessons. In six-week's' time, I became a good swimmer as well.

All this youthful, athletic success served to boost my self-image. During this period, Dad was nothing short of the greatest, most loving and involved father a kid could have - a "man's man," and was loved and admired by everybody it seemed who came in contact with him. He was "the straw that stirred the drink" - the Ben Cartwright of Hampshire Street. I remember for example, my sixth - grade home-room nun at St. Rita's walking up to my desk and saying to me:

"I met your father at our PTA meeting last night Chuckie. What a kind and charming man he is. I hope you realize how blessed you are to have a father like him.

In addition, around noontime on Sunday afternoons during the summer, Dad would load the whole family into his green Chevy "beach wagon" and take us to Aunt Elsie's Lake front, summer camp on Arlington Pond which is located in nearby Salem, New Hampshire. The other kids in our neighborhood I could tell envied us because they had to remain in the city and endure its sweltering summer heat. Along with Elsie's children - my first cousins - Lenny the oldest, his younger brother - Michael, and the youngest of the family, their sister - Paula, we'd often spend the whole afternoon swimming in the lake together, water skiing on the back of my cousin Michael's speed boat, and row-boating with my cousin Paula - a highly attractive "tomboy" back then.

My first cousins were always very welcoming of us. as they seemed to greatly enjoy having us there with them. Late in the afternoon after we had finished swimming and boating, we would all sit out on the picnic table and enjoy a cookout. My grandparents would join us whenever they could, as would my aunt Elma and her Mexican - born husband - Uncle Louie. Dad, a skilled chef too, always manned the grill. He cooked hamburgers, hot dogs, chicken wings which were his specialty, and sausages for us. We'd all have a feast.

I remember on many occasions, just before our cookout, venturing off by myself and swimming across the lake and back, about a mile in total length, much to the thrill and amazement of my Aunt Elsie who, as I mentioned earlier, had prepared me for this endeavor by taking me for swimming lessons. I also remember also, Aunt Elsie telling me one day at the camp in front of everyone, right after I had just finished one of my swims across the lake,

"Chuckie, the gods have fashioned you for greatness. We're all expecting big things from you. Make sure you don't let us down."

Clearly, the bar was raised very high for me very early on in life.

And something else I remember about my dad was his great sense of humor. As an example, one night while all of us in the family were eating supper together at the kitchen table, my brother George's best buddy from the neighborhood - Johnny Pensak, unexpectedly showed up at our house. Sadly, Johnny's Dad had abandoned his family a few years earlier, and my brother's friend had no male adult role model to guide his steps. Wearing the uniform of our Red Sox Little League team, he complained to Dad, whom he now looked up to as his adopted father and mentor, "Mr. Ead, why is it that Chuckie and Georgie get hits and I can't get hits?"

Without missing a beat, Dad promptly answered him with:

"Johnny, do you eat Syrian bread?"

"No Mr. Ead, I don't." Pensak answered

"Chuckie and Georgie eat Syrian bread all the time."

Dad then took a round, flat loaf of Arabic bread from a plastic bag that rested on the kitchen table, handed it to Johnny, and said, "Well, eat this, Johnny." We then all watched the bewildered kid dutifully gobble it down. That night, at our Little League game, Johnny for a change got two hits. He went home that night after the game and told his mother to start buying Syrian bread. Next, he followed this up by showing up at our house the following night while we were all having supper a second time, and immediately upon his arrival, grabbed a loaf from the plastic bag and ate it, as he proudly told and thanked Dad for orchestrating the feet he had accomplished the night before.

In addition to coaching our Little League team, Dad would with regularity, show up at St. Rita's schoolyard after supper on nights we didn't have games or practices and throw a football to all of us boys in the neighborhood, directing us to run pass patterns in the yard. Dad never lost his strong throwing arm. Because of selfless acts like this, he was beloved by every kid in our neighborhood.

My parents' generosity extended to family members in the old country as well. For example, in 1967, they sponsored Ma's younger half-sister - Lorice Hashem, her husband - Joe, and their two small kids to emigrate to Lawrence from Lebanon. This gesture was repeated in 1971 when Ma's older sister - Nemra, and her husband - George Hashem, again at my parent's behest, emigrated here along with their eight young kids, ages 4 to 13. In addition to orchestrating the sponsorships, my folks helped these folks get settled and, on their feet, here.

For example, Ma and Dad moved the new arrivals into the second-floor apartment of our three-tenement, Hampshire Street house, where they lived rent free for as long as they needed. My folks also got the elders jobs and got their non-English-speaking kids into public schools. These youngsters eventually grew up, married, and later sponsored other relatives to come over here, and so on. Before you knew it, we had half the town of Ahoura living here in Lawrence. Although it was invigorating to have all my new cousins here with us, I likened it at the time to a British invasion.

Us Ead's, our extended family members, and our many neighborhood friends were one big, happy family. And, although we didn't have a lot of money to brag about, we were still living full-tilt the "American Dream" and, with Dad around to glue us all together and lead us on, life was full and rich, we all felt that these joy-filled days would never end.

Chapter 3:
An Unexpected Tragedy Strikes My Family

And then suddenly, on a late Friday afternoon, on or around June 21st, 1968 - just a week after presidential candidate Bobby Kennedy was shot dead by the Arab gunman - Sirhan-Sirhan in Los Angeles, the immense force of a nuclear bomb unexpectedly struck our family. While crossing the street near the Howard Playground two blocks from our house, just after he left school, my younger brother Mark, at the tender age of only eight, was run down by a drunk driver.

This happened only the day before Dad had planned to bring Mark to the golf course and initiate him into caddying so he could take over the mantle from me. We later learned that Mark was heading to the Howard Playground fully expecting to hook up with me and my younger brother George, whom he incorrectly presumed were playing baseball together. Mark was struck in the head by the automobile. Five minutes later, an ambulance arrived and rushed him to the nearby Bon Secours Hospital (Now named: Holy Family Hospital). The prognosis was awful - death or brain damage. We were told the next day by the attending neurosurgeon - Dr. LeMaitre, that if Mark miraculously somehow managed to live, he'd be reduced to must being a "vegetable."

Thankfully, three days later, Dr. LeMaitre ordered the nursing staff to turn off the machine that was artificially keeping Mark alive. They followed orders, and my youngest brother quickly succumbed. My family was horrified, but at the same time we were greatly relieved as well. No one wanted to

31

see this brilliant and very likeable young boy living a hollow shell of a life.

The tragedy shook the whole city, especially the Lebanese - American community, and even sent shockwaves to our many aunts, uncles, and cousins who were still living in Lebanon. The wake was held at the Dewhurst Funeral Home in Methuen and was packed with a two hour long waiting line snaking around the building. Mark's casket was an open one, and he was laid out in his navy-blue, cub scout uniform. I remember being appalled by the fact that the guy who ran him down didn't even have the decency to show up and say he was sorry to our grieving family; though I suppose he may have feared for his life; and with good reason too.

Even more dispiriting was our learning that no charges of drunk driving or vehicular homicide were going to be leveled at the man. The jerk was getting off scot-free. This angered both me and my father to no end. We had justice and revenge on our minds. My mother, meanwhile, although obviously hurting deeply, kept her pain inside and seemed to accept what had happened to Mark with serenity and stoicism, just as the Blessed Mother did at the Foot of the Cross.

Several days after the funeral, when we were all visiting my grandparents' home, I approached my father:

"Dad, you know the head of the Lebanese Mafia in Methuen (I won't divulge this man's name, because his whole family was then, and still is today, very dear to me.). Give him some money and tell him to hire one of his hitmen and have him knock this unrepentant prick off."

Dad responded by telling me that he didn't need a hit man, that he had a revolver in his drawer and would finish the guy off himself. My grandmother, overhearing this alarming remark, drew upon her deep faith, stepped in, and told my father she knew what it was like to bury a child. She said he should forgive and then forget about this man - ASAP and instead focus on employing his energies on bringing up his other four kids. She urged him not to get his hands dirty and to instead to:

"Let God take care of this guy in His own way and in His own time."

"Vengeance is mine, says the Lord," quoting Romans 12:19. "then she went on even further: "Leave room for God's wrath. It's HIS to repay!" she concluded with.

Dad however, initially refused to heed Grand Ma's wise message. So, the next day, the Chief of Police in Lawrence, who knew my father very well and who had found out through the grapevine that he was gunning for this man, called Dad into his office:

"Fred, if you finish this guy off, you'll go to jail for the rest of your life. Is that what you want? What the Hell's the matter with you? Pull your head out of your ass for God's sake and start thinking straight, will Yah? If you spend your life in jail, who will bring up your other kids? So go home right now, get that gun, bring it back here, and turn it into me before something really bad happens."

Dad, thank God, finally saw the light. He left the chief's office, drove home right away, took the revolver out of his closet, brought it back to the station, and handed it over to the chief. Thankfully, the potential nightmare ended without escalation. Somehow, with the spiritual guidance of my grandparents, who knew firsthand the tragedy of losing children, we all summoned the courage to put Mark's death behind us as best we could and soldier on with our lives. But it was hard - painfully hard.

As you might imagine though, Mark's death permanently altered my family's lives, especially my father's, as we all struggled hard - sometimes unsuccessfully, to deal with it. Often at the kitchen table when we were all eating dinner, Dad would suddenly burst into tears. Someone would ask why. He would then point at Mark's empty seat at the table and rage; "that's why!"

My mother, on the other hand, showed little emotion. She rarely even talked of my kid brother. Instead, she just kept it all inside. Dad, who before Mark's death loved playing golf at Merrimack Country Club on the weekends, especially with his first cousin and closest friend at the time - Freddie Corey, was so distraught at Mark's passing he refused to pick up a golf club or even step foot on a golf course again for the next ten years. Now, with no ride to and from Dad's golf course, I was forced to give up playing the game I excelled at and had come to love. So much for "PGA potential."

And, on top of everything, my eighth-grade home room teacher - Sister Edward Louise, a truly sadistic, Catholic nun, launched a personal crusade against me for reasons I still can't fathom. She would constantly pick on me and demean me in class for the least little thing. It was obvious even to my classmates, that for some unknown reason, she hated me intensely. Her attitude apparently was:

"I don't care that your brother was killed last summer and how much it hurt you Chuckie; I'm going to hurt you even more and make your life even MORE miserable."

Only thirteen at the time and still grieving Mark's death, I didn't need nor expect that kind of treatment from her, a "Catholic" nun, mind you. I didn't view her as a true Christian. Looking back, she was more than likely a sexually frustrated and psychologically damaged person and I'm sure she had a strong influence on my questioning of religion during my later teen and early adult years.

In January of 1969, six months after Mark was killed, and during the middle of my eighth-grade year, coach Norm Salem held a wrestling tournament at the Lawrence Y in honor of my deceased brother. It was fittingly called 'The Mark Ead Memorial Tournament,' and it proved to be the wrestling event of the year, as midget wrestling teams from all over New England showed up to participate. I won my first four matches, two by pins, but then had to wrestle a much tougher and stronger wrestler than me who came from North Adams, Mass. for the 110-pound weight division championship.

My younger brother George had just a short while earlier sewed up his 100-pound weight class championship. I was losing my match 4 to 3 with about a minute to go, and the other wrestler had me on my back and was poised to pin me and thereby ended the match. Coach Salem kept yelling at me though, while at the same time kneeling down and thumping the mat:

"Chuckie, get up off your back! Turn this guy over!"

I tried hard but just didn't have the wherewithal to accomplish what Coach Salem wanted done. For some still unknown reason, I then quickly closed my eyes for about five seconds and saw my dead brother, perhaps now in heaven, passionately staring at me directly into my eyes and I said to myself:

"Lord, please give me strength. I've got to win this for Mark."

With just about thirty seconds remaining on the clock, I somehow summoned a "strength beyond myself" to avoid the pin, get up off my back, throw the other wrestler to the ground, put him on his back, and then jump on top of him for a two-point conversion. I won the match 5 to 4, and my weight-division championship as well, matching George's earlier weight-division win. Our Lawrence Y wrestling team, as was usually the case, took the team championship that day as well.

The following Sunday afternoon, Coach Salem summoned me, George, and my father to the Lawrence Eagle Tribune offices, where we all had our picture taken while seated together, with George and I holding our first-place trophies in front. I remember it was the same cold, wintery, January Sunday afternoon that the highly confident Joe Namath's miracle, Jets' team upset the more highly favored Baltimore Colts for the Super Bowl Championship. Our photo and wrestling story appeared the following day in the sports section of the paper, just below the Super Bowl, summary article, along with a detailed writeup of Mark's abbreviated life.

Chapter 4:
My Super High School Years

At the beginning of my freshman year at Central Catholic High School, Dad refused my repeated requests to sign for me to play freshman football. He claimed that at five feet tall and only 110 pounds, I was too small to go up against the much bigger 250-pound linemen and linebackers and would probably get hurt, so I reluctantly ran freshman cross-country track instead.

As part of our training, twice a week our coach, Central brother - William Cowey, would have our whole team run "quarters" up at the Lawrence Reservoir. It went like this. The whole team would line up at the starting line of the rectangular-shaped pathway surrounding the reservoir and pricking a timing watch which held in his right hand, Cowey ordered us to run, full speed, for a full quarter of a mile around. He would then instruct us to slowly jog the quarter mile back to the starting line and then immediately run another quarter mile around, again at full speed.

This dynamic continued until we had completed ten such runs around the reservoir. I can still recall that this workout was so demanding that after only about five or six such laps around, some of us complained that we felt like we were literally going to drop dead. The workout literally tore at a runner's lungs and often caused him to buckle over and occasionally even throw up. Don't kid yourself, pal. Cross Country is definitely not the sport of wimps, whatever you might have been led to believe.

One day, during the fall of the following year when I was a sophomore at Central and a member of the J.V. cross country team, Dad took a couple of hours off from his job at City Hall (he now worked as a tax assessor in Lawrence) and showed up at the finish line of a two and a half-mile race I was running in at my school's home course which encircled a local cemetery. There were three schools, including mine, competing and roughly thirty-five kids in the race. I felt exceptionally good that afternoon, and after the first mile and a half, I was comfortably stationed in third place, about thirty yards behind the leader who belonged to a competing school.

With about a half mile to go in the race, I experienced a sudden burst of energy, passed the second and first place runners, and took the lead and held it right up until the finish. What a thrill it was for me to see Dad standing there applauding me as I crossed the finish line in first place and a full fifty yards ahead of the second-place finisher. After the race, several of the other runners on my team admitted that they were envious of me because their fathers had not showed up to watch them race. That's what kind of a loving and supportive father God blessed me with.

During that same sophomore year, Dad bought a ping pong table and put it in the cellar. In addition to his many other talents, he was a great ping pong player and had been the champion of the entire base where he was stationed during his three-year stint in the Navy. My brother George and I, of course, began taking ping pong lessons from Dad - the master. He taught both of us how to serve, volley, and slam. After a successful slam, Dad would proudly yell things at us like:

"Take that one to the dance with you!"

Within six months, under Dad's tutelage, George and I became so good at the game that we'd even often beat Dad and yell out:

"Take that to the dance yourself Dad," whenever we slammed one by him.

The three of us would go down cellar after supper and play for a full hour and a half, sometimes even longer, three nights a week. Win or lose, paddle in hand, Dad always seemed like he was in his parental glory.

Later that same year, wanting to instill a work ethic and a spirit of self-reliance in me, Dad took me down to the newly built Bishop's Restaurant which was located just five blocks down from our house on Hampshire Street in downtown Lawrence. A three-hundred seat, nationally known eating place that made its name serving great food and large portions and whose many customers felt it had "the best french-fries in the world," the restaurant was so well regarded that high-ranking members of the Saudi Royal Family, who often flew into Boston to receive medical care at the city's world - renowned hospitals, would stop in for a bite whenever they came to town. Well-known television actor, comedian and fellow Lebanese American - Danny Thomas and his actress, daughter - Marlo also frequented and ate there whenever they made it into town as well.

NBC national sports broadcaster Curt Gowdy was a regular at the restaurant too, most often showing up for lunch. He owned and operated the Lawrence radio station - WCCM, at the time. Dad knew the owners of Bishop's - the Beshara family very well. They had grown up next door to him in a four-tenement house that abutted his own on Elm Street. They were as close as brothers to Dad, he often confided to me.

The day he took me into Bishop's, Dad talked directly for a couple of minutes with his lifelong friend - Abe Beshara. Abe, without ever having met me before, and solely on Dad's urging, hired me on the spot to be a busboy. Grinning from ear to ear, the Lebanese restaurant owner then told me to show up for training the following afternoon.

I did so and soon find myself working Wednesday and Saturday nights and Sunday afternoons. I was making roughly a hundred dollars a week as a fourteen - year - old. That was great money for a high school kid back then in the seventies. I can still recall that many of my fellow broke classmates at Central who wanted to work but weren't as lucky as I was to find a job, used to hit me up for lunch money in the school cafeteria.

I most always felt bad for them and would more often than not hand them a couple of bucks to buy a sandwich and a Coke from the vending machines in the cafeteria. I'm proud to say that I paid all of my high school tuition at Central - $500 per year at the time, and bought all my school supplies, clothes, shoes, and even a late-model used car when I turned sixteen and a half and got my license. I felt like a rock star because I always had a buck in my pocket.

I thoroughly enjoyed and exceled at every facet of the busboy job. I still maintain to this day that although it was very hard work - you were so busy at the job that you couldn't stop for even a minute or two to have a smoke that it was the best job I ever had. I most often worked for Sam Khoury, the most demanding of Bishop's waiters. Although a very nice man with a great sense of humor, Sam was a slowpoke and would often lean on his busboy to get his coffees and desserts from the kitchen and occasionally to pick up his food orders from the chef's station.

Understandably, none of the other busboys wanted to do these extra chores and so, when asked, refused to work for Sam. I, on the other hand, welcomed the challenge and found that I loved working for the man. He brought out the best in me. The other waiter who shared Sam's station with him - Pewee Assad, would often complain openly to Sam that I was his busboy too; that Sam was "hogging me" for himself, and that I should be helping him out with extra waiter's duties too. Pewee's critical comments seemed to have absolutely no impact on Sam as he most often just completely dismissed them from his mind.

Sam would additionally often serve members of the Boston Bruins hockey team, who from time to time showed up at the restaurant like Derek Sanderson, Johnny Mackenzie, and Ken Hodge, and players from the Boston Celtics, like Johnny Havlicek and Bill Russell, as well a horse trainers and jockeys he knew from nearby Rockingham Racetrack. One Wednesday night in fact, Carlton "Pudge" Fisk, - the longtime Red Sox starting all-star catcher, showed up with his family and sat at one of Sam's square tables. A catcher myself, and an ardent admirer of Fisk for years, I made sure that I chatted with him and got his autograph.

Sam too was a heavy gambler who went to the racetrack early just about every morning and had breakfast with all the jockeys and trainers, naively hoping to get tips from those who had finished working out their horses. Many of these guys frequented the restaurant at night. Among them was Bruins goalie Gerry Cheevers, a horse lover, owner, and a top racing executive at Rockingham who came to Bishop's often. He always sat at Sam's station along with his wife and a few of his friends, aimlessly chewing on an expensive Cuban cigar while holding a glass of Chivas Regal scotch in his right hand.

Sam sucked up to these track people and waited on their hand and foot falsely thinking they would reciprocate and help him pick winners at the track the next day. I remember one Saturday night my father came to pick me up after my work shift was over and he chatted briefly with Sam before leaving. I heard Sam tell Dad:

"Cappy (my father's nickname among his many Elm Street buddies because he voraciously read Captain Midnight magazines as a youth), 'this kid of yours (referring to me) is the best to ever put on the jacket. He buses with his heart. Got any more like him at home?"

Working with the much older waiters, waitresses, and kitchen help was thrill for a young, high school kid like me. Bishops proved to be a fascinating world within itself. Nearly everybody in the restaurant loved the racetrack and gambled on the horses daily. The buzz of the day in the kitchen when I came into work at four o'clock was often:

"Hey Chuckie, do you by any chance know who won the fourth race at Rockingham today?"

I wasn't especially attracted to the racetrack and gambling but I do remember making my way to Rockingham Park one summer afternoon an hour before work and betting $10 on an eighty-to-one long shot. My horse miraculously came from all the way from last place to win, and I collected a neat eight hundred dollars for my wager. Trust me. Cashing in a longshot at the racetrack is the greatest thrill one can ever experience. It's an even a better rush than sex is. I didn't press my luck though. Right after the race, I left the track and went directly to work and have rarely shown my face at Rockingham since then. I guess always felt that betting on horses was a losing proposition. I mean, the house always wins in the end - don't they?

I learned a lot about life and the intricacies of human nature from the people at the restaurant, especially the waitresses, who helped me break out of the introverted shell I'd been in since grammar school. Believing that I was ugly, I was especially hesitant to interact with girls. In eighth grade at St. Rita's for example, I'd been one of two boys in our class who didn't have a girlfriend.

And later on, as a freshman in high school, I worked in the coat room at Friday night dances along with my older cousin Billy Zaidy, who was a year ahead of me at Central and who got me the job. I was so shy, I literally quivered in my shoes whenever a girl, especially a good-looking one, would check her coat in and begin a conversation with me. And I was too fearful to venture out onto the dance floor like my more outgoing cousin Billy and the two other guys who worked in the coat room with Bill and I did whenever they had a break. I just stayed hesitantly hunkered down in the coat room all night.

Being around the more mature waitresses who reinforced that I was good-looking and intelligent and who even courted me a bit, made me feel better about myself and unleashed my personality. One waitress - Janet B. in fact, who was married back then to the head chef - Andy, even told me once she wanted me to live with her when I got older. I'm not sure however, how Andy would have felt about that prospect.

The head honcho in charge of all the waiters, waitresses, and busboys at Bishop's was a stern, female taskmaster named Bobbie C. - a painfully thin, blonde, chain-smoking, middle-aged woman who was always well-dressed and well - groomed but quite unattractive. For reasons that I still don't understand, Bobbie ran roughshod over everyone who worked under her, except me. Maybe it was my no-nonsense work ethic that won her heart. I still don't know.

I was inarguably the apple of the sullen woman's eye. In Bobbie's eyes, I could do nothing wrong. The positive chemistry between her and me was easily noticeable to everybody at the restaurant, prompting a fellow busboy to ask me, point blank, for one Saturday-night shift:

"Chuckle, be honest with me. Are you banging Bobbie?"

I stayed happily employed as a busboy until I turned eighteen, old enough to serve drinks, and then with part owner Abe's blessing. I became a waiter at the restaurant just like my dad had been. When he became old enough, my younger brother George also became as a busboy at Bishop's, and my two sisters, Marion and Pamela, manned the cash register with co-owner Vickie. My mother even worked in the coat room three nights a week for a few years. Thus, the restaurant, and the Beshara's, financially sustained our whole family throughout the entire seventies and were a great blessing to us. And the connections ran deeper than employment.

For example, Abe's mother and restaurant founder - (Saada), whom everybody in the restaurant referred to affectionately as "The Chief," spent hours chatting on the phone with my grandmother every night. My family members and I often said to each other, "What kind and wonderful people the Beshara's were my family all thought, (from Abe, his older brother - Charles ("Bishy"), his youngest brother - Joey, a super guy and the perpetual playboy in the family, all of the brother's older sister Vickie, and finally his mother, the Chief. And how lucky we are to work in such a great restaurant, only a mile or so from our house. Bishops was so close to us in fact that we could all walk to work, and we often did just that."

My younger sister Pamela's work experience at Bishop's was not quite as smooth as mine was. She was a very attractive young girl who often complained that I was ruining her social life when we both worked at the Restaurant often on the same shift. You see, word got out to all the busboys, waiters, and male kitchen help that if they tried to score with Pam, they'd have to answer to me.

I looked out for my younger sister at the time as I believed an older brother should, and I still have no regrets. Bishop's back then was a literal Peyton Place where everybody was making it with everybody else and there was accordingly a lot of drama and heartache. I didn't want that lifestyle for Pam. But she didn't understand where I was coming from and would often voice her complaints openly to my father when she got home from work:

"Your son Chuckie is ruining my social life, Dad. So, tell him to knock it off."

On an even more unpleasant note, I'm sorry to have to report that an older male cousin of mine/Mike, in the bedroom of his family's summer camp when no one else was at lakefront summer camp, initially overpowered me, then threw me onto my back on his bed, unzipped my pants, pulled down my underpants and then proceeded to orally, sexually molest me. The one-time incident was traumatic to say the least, and I still suffer a few lasting, emotional scars from it to this day.

But however, I'm pleased to report that for the most part, I soon after the incident took a page from my grandmother's spiritual playbook, forgave my cousin, and tried my best put it behind me. So, I'm proud to say that I refused to allow this ordeal to ruin the rest of my life as I'm well aware that most other sexual abuse victims often do.

45

Now, back to some good stuff again! My best friend in both grammar and high school was Ronny Karcz. He lived just two blocks from me on Hampshire Street. The two of us were inseparable. We'd often hang out in Ronnie's yard and shoot basket balls through the rimmed net that hung from the side of his house when we were in the seventh and eighth grade together. Later on, I got Ronny a job with me as a busboy at Bishop's, so we both always had extra money in our pockets. We'd spend some of that money going to the movies together once a week.

I'd meet up with Ronny at his house and we'd walk the three miles together, across the Merrimack River that divided the city of Lawrence into North and South, to the Showcase Cinema in South Lawrence. In addition to going to the movies each week, Ronny and I would bowl candlepins twice a week at Lawrence Rec, another local establishment. We'd walk to the Rec after supper and hit the lanes, and over time became good bowlers, often finishing our strings with scores of a hundred or more, which was very respectable for candlepins.

We also discovered the game of chess together when the young, flamboyant, Jewish-American, grandmaster - Bobby Fischer, fresh out of New York City, upset the much older and more highly favored Russian, grandmaster - Boris Spassky for the world championship during the late summer of 1972. The two played a series of non-televised matches in Reykjavik, Iceland. Fischer's unexpected victory was a monumental David-vs.-Goliath upset that shocked the entire chess world and even had Cold War implications. During the Fischer-Spassky matches, Ronny would come to my house after supper and we'd watch the reconstructed, move-by-move analyses of the games provided by the then accomplished grandmaster Shelby Lyman on Public Television.

46

The young Fischer's innovative, over-daring, and swashbuckling style of play revolutionized the game and deservedly won the hearts and admiration of chess enthusiasts around the globe. Fischer broke the chess mold and almost single-handedly put the game on the map, especially in the U.S. where very few people, including Ronny and me, had given the game much thought before.

Right after the Reykjavik matches, due solely to Fischer's impetus, chess clubs sprang up all over the country. Not surprisingly, I played a lot of chess with Ronny that summer. Since then, I've read a lot of 'how to' chess books and have become a pretty decent player. Playing the game regularly has kept my mind sharp and given me a tremendous amount of enjoyment over the years.

At Central Catholic, I studied hard at Dad's insistence, kept up with my schoolwork, and played catcher on the freshman, J.V., and varsity baseball teams during the four years that I was there and I was further given the distinct honor of being named co-captain of the varsity team at the beginning of my senior year. Life was good again!

Chapter 5:
Dawning Manhood

People repeatedly told me I was the spitting image of my very good-looking mother, so I no longer saw myself as ugly and began to develop confidence with the opposite sex. I had a number of girlfriends in high school and later on in college. I was also popular and well liked at my all-boys' high school too, and I hung around and ate lunch with the other favored kids in my class - the "hot shits," as we were called by the other students.

I recall one particular girl in my junior year - Carol M. who was a junior at Lawrence High - a coed school just three blocks from Central Catholic. A natural blonde, Carol was a knockout and could easily have become a super-model if she had aspired to. She also could have gone out with any guy she wanted to be at Lawrence High or Central, even the prized quarterbacks of the football teams if she chose to, but our good friend Carol wanted me instead!

She found out through the high school grapevine that I worked at Bishop's and personally phoned owner Abe Beshara himself who I was told her family supposedly knew well and boldly asked him for my phone number. Abe acceded to her request, and she phoned me shortly thereafter. I agreed to take her out.

And so, Carol would often come, along with her girlfriends, to the Friday night Central dances, which were held in the spacious school gym, meet up with me there, and follow me like a lost sheep around the dance floor. Being seen with her by all my high school male buddies fed my ego like a protein shake. ("How did Chuckie manage to score a bombshell like that?" I heard them several times ask each other."

On Friday nights, I always wore my navy blue, bell-bottom, Landlubber jeans, my shin high, Frye boots, and my prized, black leather, Fonzie jacket, all of which I had proudly bought downtown for eighty dollars with money I had earned at Bishops. I remember one Friday night, before the dance, I went out drinking beer with a bunch of my buddies. We did this about twice a month. It was a test of manhood for Lawrence boys back then - how many Schlitz beers can you pound down and how many Marlboro cigarettes can you inhale during the night?

I wasn't a big beer drinker and would usually drink just one or two sixteen-ounce cans of the famed beer. But that night, perhaps to impress my friends, I put away a full six-pack of sixteen ounces which was way above my usual limit and arrived at the dance staggering and totally blitzed out of my mind.

Carol, as was usually the case, met me there. She seemed to get a kick out of seeing me in this sordid state, poked gentle fun at me, and led me to the gym cafeteria where she plied me with three or four black coffees until I sobered up. Before doing so, I recall throwing up in front of her and her girlfriends.

For reasons I can't recall, though maybe she still can, during that following summer, we somehow drifted apart and broke up. Not too long after, I met another very attractive Kathy C., a Lebanese - American, girl by the name of Kathy C. who seemed to have had a lot more depth to her than poor Carol did at a summer function at Canobie Lake Amusement Park. A junior at Lawrence High, she was the younger sister of Charlie C., - a fellow busboy of mine at Bishops. Kathy eventually became my senior-year flame.

Charlie C and his father, also named Charlie, both thought the world of me, and I was always treated well by Kathy's family whenever I visited her at her home. I recall talking with

Kathy on the phone for an hour or more after baseball practice every spring afternoon. We bonded closely during those phone conversations and her and I seemed to hit it off very well.

I was so fond of Kathy at the time that I often thought of marrying her when we both got older. I took her to my senior prom, and she came to the graduation party my parents threw for me at our house. At the tail end of the party though, Kathy leveled this bombshell on me:

"Chuckle, I'm only a junior. I'm too young to be having sex with you. Plus, my family and I are devout Catholics. I don't feel comfortable doing it with you anymore; so, I'm breaking up with you."

I was devastated to say the least. Throughout that spring semester, Kathy and I had a babysat most Friday nights at her neighbor's house. After the kids went to bed, we'd "fool around" on the living room couch for a spell. We never went all the way though. I enjoyed this immensely and thought Kathy did too. If I had known that it bothered her so much though, I would have knocked it off before it gained any steam.

During the winter of my senior year, I gave up the butts and went out for the indoor track team. After seeing me run, first year coach William Perry told me I was one of the best long-distance runners in his stable and in turn asked me to run the very difficult 600-yard event for him. This event was rougher than the one mile or two-mile races, which were run at a slower speed and allowed you to slow yourself down pace a bit.

The 600 was instead, "balls to the wall." Running the race severely tested your wind capacity, speed, stamina, and mental toughness. Knowing beforehand what I was getting myself into, I took on coach Perry's challenge and ran the 600 that year for our indoor team, making the coach happy and often finishing in first place, another nice boost to my growing self-esteem.

In the later part of high school, I began to become independent thinker, too, which enhanced my self-image even further. Let me explain. At the tail end of our senior year, my fellow classmates voted me "Most Radical," mainly because of my outspoken disagreement with what I viewed as outdated teachings of the Catholic Church as well as my ardent opposition to the Vietnam War. I wasn't shy either about expressing my views openly in class. Remember, this was a Catholic School and although I didn't post them to the Church's door like the latter-day Protestant church reformer Martin Luther did, I had about ten specific complaints with the Church.

They included:

(1) The Church's staunch opposition to birth control. Do they really still want young couples, struggling in a tough economy, and especially in the impoverished third world, to have to financially support ten kids? Moreover, how in God's Name did the totally ineffective and silly "rhythm method" gain any credence in the Church? What numbskull I ask was responsible for giving life to that?

(2) The Church's antiquated views on euthanasia. I just couldn't wrap my head around the idea that someone who chose to end their life because they were suffering excruciating pain from for example, terminal cancer would be severely punished by a "loving and compassionate" God only because Christ himself suffered on the cross. Later in life, I came to view the much maligned, 1980's figure, Dr. Kevorkian, as a courageous, free-thinking, pioneer who was centuries ahead of his time.

(3) The Vatican's outdated notion that sex outside of marriage, which I believe could be highly natural and therapeutic, is also a grave sin punishable by the flames of Hell as well.

(4) The Church's strong opposition to priests being allowed to marry. Why not? What is the harm in it? Tell me Holy Father.

(5) The Vatican's irreversible view that women were not "qualified" to become priests. So, I guess that means that Mother Teresa, Joan of Arc, and the heroic martyr, - Perpetua to name just three examples, would be "spiritually unqualified" for priesthood? Ridiculous.

(6) The Holy See's contention that homosexuals and masturbators - (the latter of which included virtually every thirteen-year-old boy back then in America) were also Godless sinners that were going to be severely punished too. Regarding the gay issue, didn't the Church always teach us that we're ALL, loved children of God? A little bit of disconnect here, don't you think?

(7) I also had problems with the Church continuing to teach Creationism and defying Evolution Theory. Catholics needed to grow up and look at the scientific facts as laid out by that brave nineteenth century free thinker and scientifically sound, pioneer - Charles Darwin. Science and religion are not antagonists, they're sisters.

(8) The notion that all Protestants and all other non-Catholics were going to Hell, when they died and the even more absurd contentions of several of my grammar school nuns that if you as a Catholic kid, dared to befriend a Protestant kid, he'd "poison you" and thereby take you to Hell with him.

And finally, (9), the long-outdated idea that every story or event in the Bible should be interpreted "literally" instead of "figuratively." For example, the obvious fables of Noah's Ark and Adam and Eve in the Garden, which I felt were allegories, crafted and invented by highly insightful and creative Bible writers to teach humanity moral and spiritual lessons.

I don't mean to appear anti-religious or anti-Catholic. I'm not. In fact, I'm presently a 24-7 Catholic and am very proud of it too. Regarding the evolution issue, for example, I don't mean to suggest that God wasn't involved in the stream of creation. On the contrary, I believe firmly that He was and that He oversaw and guided the evolutionary process every step of the way.

The theories of Creationism and Evolution I feel aren't mutually exclusive; you can believe in both. I think that it's high time the Holy See started coming around to this more scientifically sound, and more plausible, twenty-first century explanation of how life began and developed. It's vitally important for future generations to get this subject right.

I viewed my "Most Radical" honor as even more precious than being voted Best Dressed, Handsomest, or Most Likely to Succeed. I received a purple ribbon on stage in the high school theatre about a week before graduation. I'm still proud of being given that award, which evidenced traits of critical thinking and open mindedness on my part as well as a willingness to challenge conventional authority - personality traits which, as you will see later, have thankfully remained with me to this day.

Now, regarding the Vietnam War, I didn't buy the utter horseshit being spewed out by know-it-all Secretary of Defense - Robert McNamara, a Ford Motor Company alumnus who was strictly a numbers, guy and felt in way over his head geopolitically, and by the equally inept President Lydon Johnson, to justify our involvement over there - the notorious "Domino Theory" which claimed that if we didn't stand up to communism and more secretly to a people's justified right to self-determination in little Vietnam, these two supposedly dangerous virus would spread to and infect all of South East Asia.

It's widely accepted now in intellectual circles that because we felt that since the end of WW-II we were the new imperialist power in the world (replacing the fast-fading British Empire), that we had a "divine right" (a Manifest Destiny) to exert hegemony over all other nations under the guise of liberty, freedom and democracy. And we're still unjustifiably meddling in other countries' affairs today. But that's a highly provocative subject that is to be best left for another book.

I had learned years earlier from studying the history of the issue a little bit that the imperialist French had been in Vietnam during the mid-fifties, had summarily gotten their asses kicked while there, and had repeatedly warned us not to make the same mistake that they did and stay the Hell out. From my partial knowledge of global events back then, and from reading what well-respected columnists in newspapers were writing and listening to what anti-war activists like Noam Chomsky, Bobby Kennedy and Martin Luther King were saying, I came to view the controversially divisive stalemate which was occurring in in Vietnam as nothing more than a minor civil war in an inconsequential country, brought on by a courageous leader - Ho Chi Minh in the North to unify and bring self determination to his people. Conversely, I saw the U.S. backed, puppet leader of South Vietnam - Mr. Diem, to be nothing more than a weak-willed and corrupt dictator who was not even worth the time of day.

On an even more disturbing level, I saw frequent reports on the evening news that the North Vietnamese soldiers were akin to the Japanese soldiers who fought in World War II; they never gave up or surrendered. Rather, they were brutal and fought to the death. They were also highly skilled and trained in jungle warfare, while our soldiers weren't. Also, with the campaign being waged on the enemy's "home court," I saw the war as an unwinnable mismatch from day one.

I further dishearteningly learned from the anti-war movement that President Johnson's sole motivation in prolonging the battle was his petty wish not to be remembered as the only American president to have lost a war. All of this weighed greatly on my mind back then, especially when I saw the multiple body bags coming home every night on the evening news while at the same time my impending draft date was quickly approaching, and so, I wasn't shy about informing my classmates of my views. History, I believe, has already proven the validity of my convictions about our unjustified over-reach in Southeast Asia.

What also bothered me about this stalemate, however, was the dismissive attitude that the overly self-righteous, anti-war folks too often displayed towards our soldiers when they returned home. They called them "baby killers." For my part, I conversely viewed these brave young men who had traveled halfway across the world and risked their lives in the oppressively humid and snake infested jungles of Vietnam as noble patriots instead.

True, the war had for too long been a dismal effort, and many had died for naught. But I felt our young men should be respected for their unselfishness and patriotism. They killed as I saw it only as they were trained and commanded to do and/or by superiors, in order or to defend their lives. Many of these poor young men returned home with lifelong ailments such as Agent Orange poisoning, as well as grievous emotional scars and other psychological disorders. Many were never the same again. To blame and shun them just wasn't right.

The war hit close to home during my junior year in high school. A great cross-country and middle-distance runner who was a year ahead of me and ran for Lawrence High - Jim Kent was a guy I greatly looked up to and idolized. He and his cross-country team used to come over and practice with our Central JV and varsity teams from time to time at our home course in Lawrence.

Tall and spectacularly built, Kent ran with a grace, speed, and innate skill that even the best distance runner on our team - Mike Buckley could scarcely emulate, and we all believed he'd eventually crack the four-minute mile. I remember, as a young sophomore, watching with awe as the young Kent lapped everybody in the race and won the two-miler in record time at the indoor state championships held on a makeshift, wooden, indoor track at the famed Boston Garden.

In the middle of his senior year, Kent sadly learned that his older brother Greg, who'd been a track star at Lawrence High before him, had been killed while fighting in Vietnam. Young Jim couldn't handle the news. He promptly quit running, cracked emotionally, started shooting heroin, and barely managed to hold on to graduate from school later on that year.

Decades later, I was walking into my father's tax preparation office on Essex Street, - Lawrence's main downtown drag, when a disarming voice spoke out to me:

"Hello Sir! I'm Jim Kent. I'm down on my luck, homeless, and hungry. Would you have a few bucks you can give me so I can get myself something to eat?"

I turned to the man in shock. Recognizing the name but not the face, this one time giant of a young man was now reduced to a severely gaunt, disheveled, and shell of the guy I once knew in high school. For old times' sake, I without hesitation reached in my pocket, pulled out a twenty-dollar bill and handed it to the poor soul. As I did so, I asked myself:

"Can this really be Jim Kent standing here in front of me?"

I later learned that Kent sadly never straitened himself out and died of a heroin overdose in just his mid-forties, just a brief why after I had met up with him on Essex Street. He was living when he overdosed, completely homeless and without any hope at all to offer resurrected life on the unforgiving streets of Lawrence. Without question, this stupid, fucking war had clearly claimed many victims beyond the official, dead body counts. Did you get Mister Lyndon Johnson and Mr. Robert MacNamara?

Chapter 6:
My Up and Down College Years

During the tail end of my senior year at Central, I applied to two colleges - Merrimack in nearby North Andover, Mass. and Salem State in Salem, Mass. - some thirty miles away. I eventually chose Salem State because they had a baseball team and I wanted to play college baseball. My father strongly recommended that I follow in his footsteps and study accounting as he did in college, insisting that accountants were always in demand and that because of it, I'd never want for a job after graduation. Not really knowing what I wanted to do in life looking back now, perhaps political science would have been more up my alley, but I listened to Dad, who always seemed to rightly guide me, and signed up in the business program.

During my freshman year at Salem State, I took a sabbatical from working at Bishop's and carpooled with three other guys, - Joey Nassar, John Beaudoin, and Charlie Goia, all former classmates of mine at Central, for the commute to school. Every day we drove from Lawrence to Salem, and down the treacherous Route 114. Only a two-lane road back then, 114 seemed to cough up an auto accident every other day, especially during the winter months when there was snow and ice on the road.

Many times, it seemed like we were on the dodgems ride at the nearby Canobie Lake Amusement Park. My accounting buddies and I got up early in the morning when it was still dark, showered, dressed, shoved down some breakfast, then picked each other up and drove for an hour or more down the treacherous road to make our eight o'clock morning classes.

Right after we all finished classes at about four o'clock in the afternoon, we'd again meet up together again and drive for over an hour on 114, in rush-hour traffic to get back home. We were so tired from all this driving that we often found ourselves too washed out to even eat supper or do our homework at night. Somehow, we managed the commute, kept up with our difficult accounting classes, and all performed fairly credibly in class.

In the early spring of that freshman year, I went out for varsity baseball and impressed the coach - Joe Lavachia, during tryouts. One day at spring practice, with Lavachia coaching third base and me at bat, I drove an outside pitch the opposite way down the right field line, past the right fielder and into the right field corner. After rounding first and second, I slid head-first into third just in time to beat the throw from the right fielder for a triple. Lavachia - standing in the coach's box at third, looked down at me and yelled, "Chuckie, you really want to make this team, don't you?" Needless to say, I became the starting catcher on opening day. When I joined the team, I started commuting with former Central classmate - Tommy Ferris, who made the varsity team that year too, as a pitcher. Now battery-mates again as we had been at Central, Ferris and I didn't get home at five o'clock. No, we dragged our butts in our doors at nine or ten at night after our afternoon practices or games were over. Sometimes we'd play doubleheaders with other college teams around the state, and we wouldn't finish playing until well after dark.

I would then stay up alone in the house until one or two o'clock in the morning, doing my time-consuming accounting homework. When burning the midnight oil like this, I often asked myself whether playing baseball - a kid's game - really, was worth all of this. I somehow kept up with my studies though, and finished with a respectable, although not a dean's list grade point average of 3.0 grade at the end of my freshman year.

College life was a refreshing change from high school. First of all, unlike at the all-male Central Catholic, there were plenty of girls around, and good-looking girls to boot. Also, to my liking, we were often visited at school by prominent social or antiwar activists which included among others the famed MIT professor and social critic - Noam Chomsky, all of whom spoke in the main hall of the Student Union Building.

In addition to Chomsky, one of my favorite speakers of the bunch, was the white-bearded African - American - Dick Gregory. He like Chomsky, spoke of how "immoral" the Vietnam War was, and additionally, of the possible role our CIA might have played in the JFK Assassination. These revelations fed my then already cynical, political mindset. Strongly against the war, as I mentioned earlier, and also believing Lee Harvey Oswald didn't act alone, as clearly evidenced by the infamous Zapruder clip. I greatly looked up to and admired this outspoken man for having the courage to speak his mind publicly and invite potential retribution from our then big-brother-style government.

Things seemed to be going very well for me. Then, suddenly, one night during the fall semester of my sophomore year, while studying in the kitchen at home, I became embroiled in an argument with my younger brother George, who was a senior at the time at Central Catholic. The issue, as I recall, was that George was playing his hard rock, Black Sabbath music so loud in our bedroom that I couldn't concentrate on doing my homework at the kitchen table. Several times I asked George to lower the music, but each time I did so, in defiance, he turned it up even higher.

A little history: George, at the time, had somewhere taken a wrong turn and wandered off the straight path caused by started hanging with the wrong people at school, and become a pothead and dealer in the process. In fact, my parents were called to his school principal's office two weeks before graduation because George had been caught selling marijuana to some of his classmates. The principal told Ma and Dad that he was getting ready to throw George out of school if he didn't quit this practice immediately. Dad came home after the meeting and displayed some tough love, put it right to George:

"If you don't stop your drug-dealing at school, you can get your ass the Hell out of this house."

Instead of denying he was selling the dope, George confessed and with repentant tears, promised Dad he would stop. And he did. But he still had that rebellious streak. - like his older brother did to, I guess.

After asking George a third time to turn down the music, I realized diplomacy wasn't the solution to the problem, so, I proceeded to punch him three times in the head; not my proudest moment. After the final punch, George dropped to the floor, unconscious. My mother, having followed us into the bedroom and witnessed the fiasco, went to the kitchen and returned with a pot of cold water, which she poured over George's face and forehead.

After coming to, George quickly got up from the floor, went into the kitchen and returned with a butcher's knife and started waving it at my head:

"I'll fucking kill you, Chuckie."

I immediately grabbed George's knife-wielding wrist with my left hand and with my right hand punched him in the face two more times, knocking him out cold again. This time, when he came to, he didn't get up. Instead, he just lay there on the floor, crying like a baby. I then went back to the kitchen table and tried to study, but I was so emotionally distraught by the incident that I couldn't concentrate. I ended up going to bed early that night, totally exhausted.

The next morning, I awoke to find George had gone from the house. He had packed his bags and moved in with his best friend, Johnny Pensak, whose father had abandoned his family years earlier. Johnny's mother, a kind and gentle woman, welcomed George with open arms and let him stay in their house rent-free. George lived there for about a month before he and I reconciled, and he moved back home.

The incident with George marked the beginning of a downward spiral for me. That fall, I moved into the dorms at Salem State to be closer to school and avoid the long commute. I was assigned to the second floor of Marsh Hall, which housed mostly business majors like me. My roommate - a quiet, studious kid from nearby Peabody, Mass., was a nice enough guy, but we had little in common. Most of the other guys on my floor were from the Boston area, specifically Hyde Park, and they were a wild bunch - heavy partiers who smoked pot, drank beer, and played poker all night in their rooms.

Soon I was staying up into the early hours of the morning with these guys, smoking and playing poker, joke telling, and bullshitting aimlessly. For the first time in my life, my self-discipline broke down and I neglected to attend to my studies. My aggressive poker play, coupled with my outspoken views, gave me an additional nickname: "The Cool Hand Chuckie of Salem State."

I was so tired in the mornings I couldn't get up for early classes and in turn skipped nearly all of them. I would often stay in bed till twelve or one o'clock in the afternoon. Often on weeknights, when we didn't feel like playing poker and when we should have been studying, a bunch of us would load ourselves into two cars and travel down Route 1 to Revere and bet the dogs all night at Wonderland Park Raceway. On other evenings, we'd "socialize" all night with the girls from floors one and three who'd come to our floor's spacious recreation room, often throwing themselves at us while we listened to rock music. I learned then that a lot of girls are often attracted to guys who break the mold.

Not surprisingly, that semester I did poorly academically and finished the half-year with only a 2.2 GPA - down markedly from my 3.0 of the previous year. The following spring semester proved to be even worse. Still hanging with the Hyde Park guys by night and missing classes by day, I was forced to pull "all-nighters" during finals and with the help of fellow accounting majors on my floor, cramming to learn everything I'd missed during the semester.

To my dismay, when I got my grades - which were mailed to my home in Lawrence right after the spring semester was over, I found out that my "cramming strategy" had failed to produce its desired results. Securing one C, three Ds, and an F that semester, I finished the year with a cumulative 1.8 GPA. A sobering letter from the Business School's dean, which arrived "Certified Mail - Return Receipt Requested," stated that due to my pitiful performance that year, and my pitifully low cumulative grade point average, the dean was actively contemplating suspending me permanently from college which more specifically meant that if this became a reality, that I'd never to be able to return to school again.

As fate would have it, the day after I received the letter from the dean, my Uncle George Faris came to our house to visit. Uncle and Dad were close and got along well together. As soon as I sat at the kitchen table to join them, my uncle, without even knowing about my grades, or the dean's letter, snapped at me out of nowhere:

"Chuckie, you better start getting serious and 'buckle down'!"

Something mysterious had caused Uncle to say that. Perhaps seeing the cigarette, I was smoking clued him in to some type of deterioration in me and prompted him to speak up; I don't know. All I know is that I suddenly realized my very entire future was hanging by a thread and I needed to act quickly and decisively.

So, the next day, I called the summer extension program's office at Merrimack College and requested a listing of all their summer courses. I signed up for four business classes that were being offered that summer, hoping to resurrect my academic life. Away from the negative influences of my hapless Salem State dormmates and determined to do better, I attended my summer classes on time each day and did my homework religiously every night.

Moreover, two weeks into classes, I quit smoking cold turkey and joined the YMCA and started running around the Lawrence Common, across the street from the Y thereby a bad habit with a good one. I started off running one mile a day and was quite windy from my smoking. By the end of that summer though, I was jogging three miles a day and wasn't out of breath anymore. After working out at the Y each weekday, at around three o'clock, I would head home, have a bite to eat, catch a little of the evening news on TV and then get to my studies right away.

64

At the same time, I was working as a waiter at Bishop's on Saturday nights and all day on Sundays - an exhausting twelve-hour shift. Happily, I was netting around two hundred bucks each weekend, which was good money back then. After the summer courses had finished, I received my grades from the dean's office. They indicated that I'd earned an A and three Bs. Feeling a renewed sense of achievement and self-confidence, I treated myself to a good used car from my Bishop's summer earnings.

Meanwhile, I liked the Merrimack campus much better than I did the Salem State one, it was homier, more spacious and much closer to home and I was eager to stay the Hell away from my negative associations at Salem. About a week before the fall semester began, I petitioned the dean of the Merrimack business program - James Lee, to allow me to transfer to Merrimack as a full-time student for the upcoming semester. With the help of my uncle - Ernie Montella, who had been and still was a math teacher at Merrimack for over thirty years, I secured a speedy interview with Lee.

"Dean Lee, I know I screwed up big time at Salem State. But I know I'm better than that. If you just give me this second chance, I promise you I now mean business and will do much better."

The dean responded:

"Something tells me young man that you will. On top of that, my good friend - your Uncle Ernie, tells me you're a quality kid. So, I'm going to break the protocol and authorize the transfer. Welcome aboard, and I hope you'll do well and prosper here with us."

Dean Lee didn't have to allow this. With my grades as low as they were, he could easily have told me to take a hike. I was ecstatic, like a prisoner who is miraculously released from jail after being handed a lifetime sentence. "Wow, what a fantastic break I just got," I said to myself over and over again while driving home that day. Although I failed to fully realize it back then, somebody up there was unarguably looking out for me.

Chapter 7:
Innocent Days of My Youth Are Cut Short

The first month and a half or so of the fall semester went very well. I was running around Common just about every day, working as waiter on weekends, attending all my classes, studying hard at night, and preparing for the upcoming midterms. My life felt like it had all the makings of a major comeback. Then, like Mount Vesuvius erupting without warning and pouring lava down on the helpless residents of Pompei, something personally devastating and totally unthinkable took place.

To this day, some forty-five years later, I still struggle at times to fully comprehend exactly what happened back then. I considered omitting the humiliating details of the humiliating ordeal from this manuscript, but upon reflection realized that to do so would not be fully forthright. So, here it goes in its full ugliness:

On or around the third week of October, my mother approached me one night after supper while I was doing my homework at the kitchen table:

"Chuckie, I'm not happy anymore living here with your father," she said. "Will you move us out and into our own apartment?" I answered:

"Ma, I'm sorry to hear that. I thought you and Dad were getting along okay. I want to help you but I'm 'full out' with school and work right now. Can't it wait until summer when I'm out of classes and have more time to help you with that?"

"No Chuckie; I want to move out NOW! Tell me; are you going to help me or not?

"No, Ma, I told you I can't right now. I'm too busy."

What followed was purely punitive:

"Okay, Chuckie, if you won't help me out, I'm not talking to you anymore."

And she meant it. The old silent treatment. Full tilt. "Hello, Ma. How are you this morning?" I'd say.

Nothing. Not even a word back in response. Not even a glance in my direction. You no longer exist to me, she was saying with silence. You are no longer my son!

As the days passed, the ignoring treatment started to put heavy stress on me. To be the victim of silent resentment from anyone you care about is bad enough, but for that person to be your own mother, the person who carried you in her womb and nurtured you as a baby, is exponentially worse.

Finally, after about a week of Ma's childish behavior, I was forced to rethink the situation. I was highly conflicted. Things were going so well at school and in my life in general, I didn't want to upset the apple cart by taking on this additional burden. But at the same time, I desperately wanted Ma to start speaking with me again. So, just to get her to talk to me again and end the emotional and psychological impasse, I followed my emotions instead of my intellect and relented; not always a great strategy it turns out.

"Okay, Ma; Let's do it."

With the ice between us now broken, I soon found myself calling random real estate agents from the yellow pages each day after I got home from the Y, to see if there were any suitable apartments available for rent. This took my attention away from my studies, which in itself created a new level of stress. After three days of persistent effort however, I finally hit upon a two-bedroom apartment for what seemed to be a reasonable rent ($500 a month, without heat and hot water though) at the Clover Hill Apartments in nearby Methuen, and just three miles from our home Hampshire Street.

Shortly thereafter, together with my friend and fellow Bishop's waiter - Mike Abodeely, I rented a U-Haul truck and moved all of Ma's belongings along with some house furniture she wanted to take, out of our family house and over to the Berkeley Street complex. My older sister Marion, seeing all the furniture Mike and I were carrying out of the house, including our bran new refrigerator, quickly called me to account:

"Chuckie, where the Hell are you and Mike going with all of our furniture? If you and your friend don't stop what you are doing this instant, I'm going to call Dad at City Hall and tell him what you're doing. So, leave all of our god-damn stuff just where it is."

Undaunted by Marion's remarks, I just ignored her and kept doing what Abodeely and I had commenced doing from the start. Ma and soon I settled into our new two-bedroom abode together and I was glad that the ordeal was finally over so that I could focus again on my studies, which I had let slide during the moving process. As soon as I arrive back at the apartment around three o'clock each afternoon from school, however, Ma would be sitting at the kitchen table, just waiting to unload her pent-up dissatisfaction at Dad on me. I would often sit down at the dining table and passively listen to her complaints, hoping she would eventually burn herself out and stop.

Why, I thought to myself, was this woman complaining? How bad could things really be? Dad had always been a good provider and a great father to her kids, and he had never, ever assaulted or physically abused her. What was she looking for in a husband - Saint Joseph? After about a week of listening to what I considered to be total self-pitying malarky, I had had enough and finally spoke my mind to her:

"Ma, I know Dad isn't the perfect husband. There is no such thing. But try to see the glass as half full, will you? Dad's a super guy; one in a million. He's given you and the rest of us a great life. I really don't like hearing these negative things said about a man I adore and respect. So, knock it off, will Yah. If you're so unhappy being married to Dad, maybe both of you should go see a marriage counselor."

The infamous Nazi propaganda information minister and Adolph Hitler confidant - Joseph Gerbels was known to have stated:

"If you're going to tell a lie, tell a big one for if you tell a big lie over and over again, people will eventually believe it." Just ask our good friend - Donald Trump about this.

Or consider this quote from renowned author Napoleon Hill from his landmark book Think and Grow Rich: "If a person repeats a lie over and over, the lie will eventually be accepted as truth. Moreover, it will be believed to be the truth. Each of us is who we are because of the dominating thoughts which permit us to occupy our minds. Thoughts which we deliberately place in our minds (or which we allow to be placed there by others - my addition), and are encouraged with sympathy, and with which one or more of the emotions are mixed direct and control our every movement, act and deed."

Instead of ceasing her verbal attacks on Dad's character after my rebuttal, Ma intensified them over the ensuing weeks. Undaunted by my repeated complaints, she barreled on nonstop:

"He stuck me in the house every night with you kids and went out and had a ball for himself with his friends and who knows who else. And he never stood up for me when your Aunt Elsie and your grandmother ganged up on me. Instead, he always took their side."

And on and on the pity, party went drip drip drip. Maybe my father had or still was still cheating on Ma, but it still seemed to me - a neophyte back then on the subject of marital relations - that Ma was suffering from extreme and unjustified ingratitude. But I'm not a psychologist or a therapist. I know that there are two sides to every story and each side should be listened to. Maybe my mother did have some legitimate complaints against Dad at the time, who knows.

Throughout the entire following week (week four of her unending attack on Dad), she really turned up the dissatisfaction flame and now, as thug Gerbels and author Hill predicted would happen, I actually started to 'believe and sympathize' with the distraught woman. I remember thinking to myself after week four of Ma's mind-poisoning:

"Wow! Maybe Ma's right. Maybe Dad isn't the good man me and everyone else thinks he is after all. Maybe he's just like she claims - "a wolf in sheep's clothing."

Through some strange phenomenon of mental chemistry that I still can't explain, as week four came to an end, I became "convinced" that dad was indeed a truly bad egg. Accordingly, early one Saturday afternoon in late November, a day that will live in personal infamy for me even long after I've exited this planet, I decided to drive over to Hampshire Street and confront the great man. Before going to Dad's house, however, I drove around Lawrence for a full hour, thinking about what I was going to say to the guy about whom my opinion had unjustifiably shifted 180 degrees.

71

Not as an excuse, but keep in mind that I was taking five very tough business classes at Merrimack, running and exercising five days a week, working late on Saturday nights and twelve-hour double shifts on Sundays, and burning the midnight oil on weeknights, often studying until early morning. In addition, that particular week, restaurant manager - Bobbie had called me in for an additional night's work the night before (a Friday) because she was short as a waiter, and I had worked till twelve. And so, that early following Saturday afternoon, I felt extremely stressed out, emotionally drained, out of synch, and very much not like my usual clear-thinking upbeat self. I understand full well that none of these excuses what was about to happen. There is no excuse for my behavior that day - period; but it puts it in a bit of context.

I finally arrived at Dad's house in a charged and disillusioned state. I hadn't seen or spoke to him in the four weeks that my mother and I had been out on our own but, true to form, the once-cherished head of the family was seated at the kitchen table alone, innocently sipping a cup of coffee. Then, right after I boldly entered the house without knocking, Dad got up from his chair and, totally unaware of the horrible fiasco that was about to unfold, greeted me with his typical disarming smile, and reached out to shake my hand in apparent friendship.

"Hello, son. How have you been? And how's your mother? Take a load off. Sit down and have a cup of coffee here with me."

For reasons that have eluded me my entire subsequent life, I ignored Dad's welcoming statements and without explanation, became devoid of my senses and "lost it." Without provocation, I began punching the man in the head. After about twenty seconds of this, I saw that Dad was bleeding from the nose and forehead, and I thank God came to my senses and stopped hitting him before things got even worse. What had come over me? Why in Hell had I needlessly and mercilessly harmed the man I had loved and admitted all of my life?

In order to get away from me, Dad, now in total shock and horrified disbelief, gathered himself together and quickly ran out the kitchen door, through the hallway, and out onto the sidewalk in front of our Hampshire Street house. I was left in the kitchen alone to reflect on my despicable actions. *What the Hell did you just do, scumbag? What kind of coward physically attacks a defenseless, old man twice his age? And his own father to boot?* I had long before memorized the Ten Commandments in Catholic grammar school while a Saint Rita's and the sixth one suddenly arose to the surface and drilled into my mind: It commands:

"Thou shalt honor thy father and thy mother."

I stood there stunned for three or four seemingly endless minutes. Nobody had to tell me I had just fucked up big time. The question was why It had all happened so fast and was totally unpremeditated. I had gone over to Dad's only to 'talk' to him. What the Hell happened here? To this day, I still don't have a plausible explanation. All I know is that I felt like a wordless piece of shit in the aftermath, and despite the many years that have gone by, since sometimes I still do when I think about it although time and a heartfelt confession has lessened the pain.

As I left the house, I saw Dad, still shocked by the ordeal, sobbing on the sidewalk and nursing his head wounds. I can't recall why, but I didn't go over to him right away and say I was sorry. Instead, probably because I was too ashamed and frightened to face the man, I got in my car, now crying too, and drove back to the Berkeley Street apartment in a spirit of shock and disbelief. Unfortunately, my mother wasn't home when I arrived there as I desperately needed to vent emotionally to somebody about what had just taken place.

About two hours later, right after my mother arrived back home, two Lawrence police officers showed up at our apartment and told me I was being arrested for assault and battery on my father. Per their request, I followed them out to their cruiser parked outside on the street and without incident willingly did as they instructed and got in the back seat. The cops then drove me to the Lawrence police station, which was located oddly enough, right next door to Bishop's Restaurant, booked me, escorted me down to the cellar of the station, then shoved me into an empty cell and locked it behind me.

I spent the rest of the day and the whole night locked up by myself in the station's freezing and only cell. Around eleven o'clock that same night, right after he finished his evening shift at Bishop's, fellow waiter and great friend - Sam Khoury came to visit with me in my cell and brought a large wool blanket for me. News of what had transpired between Dad and me was already all over Bishop's, as I had not shown up for work that evening.

"Chuckle," Sam said to me, "don't break your parents apart. Mend what's broken. Bring them together."

"Thanks for the good advice, Sam," I said. "Where were you early this afternoon when I could have used it?"

The following morning at about ten A.M. Sunday, the officer on duty finally released me from jail and I took a cab back to my mother and I's Berkeley Street apartment. To my utter amazement, my mother seemed totally unfazed when I

74

told her where I had spent the night. She acted as if nothing major had taken place. The following afternoon, I ripped open the local paper to look at the Police Log on the second page, and there it was staring at me in capital letters, along with some superfluous, additional commentary:

"LOCAL MAN BEATS UP OWN FATHER! - CAN YOU BELIEVE IT?"

Within two days, the entire Lebanese community and everyone else throughout the Merrimack Valley who knew either me and/or my family had found out about the incident. The busy-body, older, Lebanese women of the city had made sure no phone was left undialed and I knew full well that my name was now dirt in Lawrence.

After looking at the paper, I phoned Dad at home to see how he was doing and to offer an apology (for what little it was worth), but he wasn't ready to talk to me yet and without even responding, hung up the phone on me. That was the first time in my life my father had ever rebuffed me. It shook me to my roots and felt indescribably abandoned and terrible. My mother, meanwhile, despite being shown the police log, failed again to grasp the magnitude of what had taken place.

"Oh, it isn't a big deal Chuckie," she said. "It'll all work out. Don't you even bother yourself about it anymore?"

I then promptly went alone into my bedroom, laid down on my back on my bed, and began bawling my guts out. The following night - my scheduled night off from work, I somehow summoned enough courage to show my face at Bishop's in order to speak with the only person in the world I thought could make some sense of all this, my close friend and fellow waiter - Teddy George. While I was speaking with Teddy, a good friend of my father's and mine - Ray A., and a one-time admirer of me, walked into the kitchen, saw me talking to Teddy near the cash register, strode up to the two of us and whispered in my ear, in a quiet but firm voice:

"PUSSY!"

This one word - the most demeaning thing you can call a guy, rendered me completely naked, penetrated deep into to my joints and marrow, gnawed at my manhood and by itself, rendered all the self-esteem I had built over my lifetime null and void. Instantly, I felt like I was a disgrace to humanity, which I'm sure was Ray's intent in voicing that word to me. Co-owner Vickie Beshara, who was manning the cashier's booth right next to us as she always did, apparently heard the word that came out of Ray's mouth and glared at me with a look of both pity and disgust. As she did so, I could see tears flowing from her eyes and down her face.

Right after Ray quickly departed us, I told Teddy that I was ruined, that I couldn't face my father, my brother and sisters, my relatives, my fellow employees at Bishop's, or my friends at the Y any longer, and that I just wanted to drop out of school, quit my job, and get the Hell out of town as fast as I could. I also confided to him that I'd even had thoughts of just "finishing myself off" and getting as I said: "the whole fucking thing over with."

Much to my surprise, Teddy laughed at this confession, which actually took some of the pressure off of me, then true to form, told me:

"We're all just made of clay, Chuckie. We all fuck up from time to time, and don't let anybody tell you differently. But you can't just cut and run or do yourself in. That's not what a real man does when he faces a challenge."

"Yah right Teddy, some real man I am," my mind silently responded. Teddy then went on:

"Tough this out for a spell and give it a chance to blow over brother. A year from now, I promise you, no one will even remember it. The next few months are going to be a test of your mettle. Maybe now we'll all see what you're made of."

Over the ensuing weeks leading up to my assault-and-battery hearing in District Court, I tried several times, per the advice of the parish priest at St Anthony's, to pray to God for mercy and forgiveness, I concluded, however, that if there really was a God (I wasn't sure in those days if there was, as I had left the faith), He would likely view me as a coward, and, as the axiom goes: "God hates a coward." so I in short order, abandoned this approach.

It seemed everyone I encountered at the Y, at Bishop's, or on the street now looked disparagingly at me, if they looked at me at all like I was Charles Manson, not Charles Ead. This only made me feel even worse about myself than I already did.

Now keenly aware that I had become radioactive, I phoned my good friend Cliff Jourdi, a Lebanese - American man who was five years older than me. Cliff knew my whole family well and had been like an older brother to me growing up. He'd always held me in high esteem. A highly talented basketball player, he had taught me how to shoot layups with my left hand when I was just in the eighth grade:

"Cliffy, I just fucked up big time. I've become a laughingstock. What the Hell do I do now?"

"Yah Chuckie, I heard all about it."

Jourdi, to his great credit, stood by me right then and throughout the entire year following the calamity. To keep me from buckling during the psychological onslaught that he knew was coming, my loyal friend sternly warned me:

"You're still a good kid. Don't let anyone look down on you or shit on you. Whenever they try to, just repeat the following words from the Holy Book over and over to yourself. They'll help soften the blows. Those words were:

- Let he who is without sin throw the first stone.

- First, take the BEAM out of your own eye and then you will see clearly to take the SPLINTER out of mine.

- This too shall pass.

Jourdí continued: "You're a bright hombre cousin (all Lebanese guys affectionately call each other "cousins" even if they aren't). You're going to get through this, I know you will. And know that I'll always have your back. Call me anytime you need to talk."

I tried my best to adhere to Cliffy's wise advice, and it helped to some degree, sure. Looking back now, though, I don't know how I even survived the first few months of the ordeal without cracking up or ending it all. It was a real pressure cooker to say the least. In just twenty, misguided seconds, I had gone from being the city golden boy to being the city goat.

About a month after the late November incident took place, I was forced to appear before Judge Paul Perrochi in Lawrence District Court to face the charges my father was bringing against me. I was represented at the hearing by my mother's Jewish attorney - Henry Malice, who initially hadn't provided me with much hope of a successful outcome. Outside the courtroom, just moments before the hearing, he pulled me aside and said,

"Kid, I'm afraid there's no way I can spin this in your favor. If your father goes ahead with the charges, I'm obligated to tell you; you're going to jail!"

My mother was present in the courtroom and sat with Malice and me on the defendants' bench, unperturbed and seemingly still oblivious as to the gravity of the situation. Upon hearing the charges leveled against me, Judge Perrochi addressed me with a deeply penetrating look:

"Young man, this is without question the lowest thing I've seen in my thirty years on the bench, and furthermore you're the most decrepit and despicable person I've ever come across. My body chills just looking at you. So, with your dad's permission, I'm going to exact a pound of flesh from you and send you to the county jail to teach you a much-needed lesson.

I knew the county jail he was talking about - the medieval, dungeon-like building located in the five-acre lot adjacent to my alma mater, Central Catholic High School. With barbed wire encircling it, the low-level prison was held over from the Civil War days and had no running water and no toilets, forcing the prisoners to shit in cans. I remember as students at Central, we'd often stick our heads out of our classroom windows and mock the prisoners who congregated for exercise in the prison yard directly below us.

I knew very well the possible fate that awaited me. I also knew that my fellow prisoners-to-be had fathers of their own and would probably beat me to a pulp every day for what I had done, perhaps I further thought - "they might even finish me off." And also, on the back of my mind, was the haunting thought that the gay prisoners would most likely pass me around like a lit joint.

After hearing Perrochi's threat of impending incarceration, for the first time in my life, I started to get scared. Dad then boldly took the helm, spoke up, and like the compassionate and Prodigal Son Christian man he was, assuaged my fear:

"Paul (Dad knew Perrochi on a first-name basis.), I know my son better than anybody; better than he even knows himself. He's a good kid, and despite what he did, I still love him and I forgive him. He's never done anything like this before. This was an aberration. I have no idea what transpired that led up to this. I do know that if I send him to jail, I'll destroy the kid's life. If he's lucky enough to keep himself alive in there, he'll never be the same again whenever he gets out. I don't think I could live with myself as a father if I allowed that to happen."

"So, after much prayer and reflection, I've decided to go against the grain here and do what I believe both my God and my loving mother said she that wants me to do, to choose mercy over justice and give my son a mulligan. So, as of right now, I drop all the charges that I initially lodged against him."

Now highly dissatisfied with Dad's pronouncement, my father's attorney - Ignatius (Iggy) Piscitello - a close friend of Dad's since their soccer-playing days at Suffolk University, vehemently tried to talk my father out of his decision. Iggy was known as an emotionally charged lawyer who could be rather theatrical in his style. I had run into him on Essex Street in Lawrence a week earlier. I hadn't met or known the man prior to our brief encounter that day. Apparently, Iggy knew who I was though, because right after he angrily greeted me, he spat on the sidewalk and called me a "RAT." In front Judge Perrochi, Dad, my mother, and my lawyer Malice, he protested:

"Freddie, you're wrong. Chuckie's not a good kid. In fact, let me tell you the truth. He's fucking garbage! Just look at what he did to you. If you do the dance, you've got to pay the piper. We need to hit him hard here!"

I would later find out as the years passed that despite Dad's attorney's rough and tumble, outer exterior, (probably developed as a sort of defense mechanism), in reality, he was instead, a highly generous, easy to get along with notice. Evidencing this, after the dust had settled years later, the two of us, now having a chance to really get to know each other, eventually became good friends.

Without words, Dad shook his head from side to side several times, indicating he wasn't going to budge on his decision. Iggy wasn't alone in his opinion of me. I was saddened to learn, in the weeks leading up to the hearing, that my Aunt Elsie Faris, her husband George, and their three children were also gunning for me and, like my father's attorney, had whenever they had the opportunity to, lobbied Dad to send me to jail as well.

Aunt Elsie in fact, I feel never fully forgave me for the one-time incident and accordingly held a strong grudge against me for the rest of her life. Her three kids, Lenny, Michael, and Paula, - my first cousins, with whom I had spent many happy days at my Aunt's summer camp with when we were all much younger, softened up a little more than Auntie did as the years passed but never really, fully welcomed me back into their lives either. Perhaps they were just plain scared that someday I might turn on them and beat them up as well. I believe the thinking went that if this guy is willing to beat up his own father, what might he do to me?

Although I am still pained when I think of the stance Iggy and the Faris' family took toward me back then, I can fully understand their feelings, especially my Aunts being Dad's older sister and his only natural sibling in all. I learned from the way my own older sister Marion often tries to mother me that big sisters have a deep seated and inbred, instinct to "protect" their younger brothers. I contend that it's even programmed into their DNA.'s.

These same feelings of displeasure played themselves out as well while I was working one Sunday afternoon at Bishop's when Saada - the owner's mother and the patriarch of the Beshara family and the restaurant as well as a close friend of my grandmother's, caught up with me at the cash register's booth that was located in the middle of the kitchen. Having known my father intimately since the very day he was born on Elm Street and who like just about everybody else in the Lebanese community had loved and adored him, she pulled no punches is letting me visually know of her utter disgust with what had recently taken place.

As I attempted to pay a customer's check to the cashier who was sharing the booth with Saada, "The Chief," as was her affectionate nickname in the restaurant, purposely caught my eye and glared at me with a deeply condescending look that clearly indicated to me anyway that she, who prior the Dad ordeal, held me in high regard and was one of my biggest fans in the restaurant, now thought of me as being lower than an adder. I can still vividly recall that the Chief's stare, so haunting at the time that it will remain etched forever in my personal infamy, literally stupefied and shocked the living hell out me.

I was so deeply shaken by it in fact, that after enduring it for several seconds, I immediately dropped the large, empty dinner plate that I was holding in my right hand that I was planning to deliver to one of my customers who was seated out in the dining room, to the tiled and hard, kitchen floor where it promptly shattered into pieces. Meanwhile, several waiters and waitresses who were standing nearby in the kitchen at the time and who were obviously alarmed at the loud noise that the broken dish had just made, quickly marched over to the cashier's booth and asked me what had happened. Still severely shell-shocked by Saada's penetrating "evil eye" however, I was totally incapable of providing them with any details and/or explanation whatsoever as to what had just happened.

What pains me even more than that horrible memory now is to think back on my own behavior in the aftermath of the incident. The shameful truth is that I failed to eat enough humble pie, as I now realize I should have, and seek out all my relatives - most especially my Aunt Elsie, and my equally appalled grandmother, and of course my deeply hurt brother and two sisters in as well and apologize to all of them and then beg their forgiveness.

Why didn't I ever do that? Well, with the benefit of 20-20 hindsight, I can now see that the main reason might very well have been my overweening pride - one of the seven deadly sins that I feel now looking back, that I as inflicted with at the time. As a young man, my fear of being rejected or belittled caused me to habitually project a sort of arrogance which bordered on cockiness that I hoped would mask my insecurity. That proud façade kicked in big time after the incident as a protective device. Shame on me for that. But life is about personal growth I guess.

Looking back now, I realize my failure to openly apologize to others could well have given people the mistaken impression that I was just a cold hearted and unfeeling punk who wasn't in any way remorseful for what I had done. All I can do now is assure any relatives who might still be alive and who might read this book. as well as you, dear reader that this was far from the case. The actual truth is that I was ripped apart by guilt and shame, which I've never fully resolved up until just recently. My bad though: I admit that I wasn't "fully man enough" to follow up on this matter and do the necessary repair work as I should have at the time.

Okay, enough of the negativity. As a silver lining to the above, I did learn that the buck stops with me. Dealing with the incident actually helped me become more a man. I've borne the hit all these years and I'll continue to bear it as long as I live. But at the same time and not intending to minimize my guilt in any way, I would like to state emphatically to all parents who might read this that it's harmful and unwise to drag your children into the middle of your marital disputes. Don't use them as ping-pong balls to whack at each other. Instead, leave the kids out of it and work out your issues by yourselves. Go see a marriage counselor or a professional therapist if you have to.

I'm thinking as I write this of a Lebanese - American man, - George A., a sweet, giving, and loveable guy and a good friend of our family, who became alienated from his five children for life after his wife poisoned their minds against him following their bitter divorce. The alienation eventually took its toll and tore the heart out of this lovely fellow. His unforgiving wife via a lifetime restraining order which she somehow managed to secure against him from the court, punitively prevented him from spending any time at all with his children.

The subsequent rupture that ensued from this callous hearted action between George and his five kids was so deep in fact that when he passed away about ten years ago, none of his kids even showed up at either his wake or his funeral.

According to a respected psychologist acquaintance of mine, this "mind-poisoning" nonsense takes place in parentally troubled homes more often than most people often realize.

I'm sorry to have to report that about a month after the hearing, Ma, now finding herself no longer either emotionally or financially sound enough to handle living on her own with me as her only support, abruptly returned to living with Dad and the rest of our family on Hampshire Street. Yes, my father and I had gone through this shameful and hurtful episode for nothing. Two weeks after Ma moved back home with the family, Dad phoned me with some bad news. He told me Ma was so distraught after her failed attempt at emancipation that he was forced to have her hospitalized for evaluation at the psych ward of the then named - Bon Secours Hospital.

Meanwhile, word got out among the Bishop's crowd that I couldn't swing the thousand-dollar-a-month living expenses on Berkeley Street by myself. My best friend at the time, fellow waiter - Mike Abodeely, who was one of the few people, along with Teddy George and Cliff Jourdì, who didn't judge or abandon me for what had taken place with Dad - paid me a visit after I returned to Berkeley Street from school one weekday afternoon.

He told me that on his own initiative, he had found what seemed to be an affordable place for me to live - as he described it - a single room with a bed, a desk, a bureau, and an adjacent toilet and shower, located in the furnished basement of the Staley Family's, single family in nearby Andover and just a stone's throw from Merrimack College where I was as I mentioned earlier, attending school. Another blessing from the universe I realized. Maybe God wasn't such a hard ass after all.

Abodeely further went on to detail that the rent at the house was only twenty - five dollars a week.

"Are you game, Chuck?" Mike asked.

"Yeah, I am Mike."

So, I promptly took down Mr. Staley's phone number from my good friend, immediately phoned the man, got his okay to move in, gathered all my belongings in a suitcase that night, and moved in the following day.

Chapter 8:
I Made It Through College and Now What?

Although the year following the incident with my father was as challenging as Teddy George warned me it would be, I was somehow able to focus my attention almost exclusively on earning my sheepskin - a cherished goal I had held deeply since my near expulsion from Salem State. Having my own apartment away from Lawrence and away from my dysfunctional family, and studying there four hours a night, allowed me not to dwell on what had happened with Dad. Also of help, was keeping myself busy during the day by attending all my classes, running, working out at the Y, and continuing to work as a waiter at Bishop's on weekends.

I think that it speaks volumes about the Beshara family, especially Abe, that they didn't terminate me after my ordeal with my father, since they were all life-long friends with Dad. If Abe had fired me, as I believe most employer friends in his situation would have, I never would have been able to fund the remaining two years of living alone, keeping my car on the road, paying my Y membership, and buying my daily food, as well as paying the $2500-a-year tuition at Merrimack. I owe the completion of my college education completely to Abe and the rest of his compassionate family.

Choosing to see the glass as half full, I came to believe the whole Dad ordeal could have been a lot worse and by buckling down on the books, as my uncle George Faris had earlier bade me to do, I toughed it out and earned my sheepskin exactly two years after I had transferred from Salem State to Merrimack. My

GPA? - a respectable 3.2, and I thought - good enough to get me into law school - I hoped, as that was my long - time goal for myself. And just as my good friend Teddy George had predicted, the social hostility around me, especially within my immediate family, greatly abated. I guess the old axiom is true: "Time heals all wounds," to some degree anyway.

Right after I completed my academic studies in late August of 1977, Dad told me he had set me up with an accounting job with Avco Missile Defense Systems (AVCO), in Wilmington, Mass., where he said I'd be working under the tutelage of his good friend and Accounting Manager there Pete Di Burro. Pete had been my Little League co-coach, along with Dad for one year when I was twelve, and he told Dad he had put my resume at the top of the pile, ahead of fifty other accounting graduates who were applying for the same position:

"The job's not for big money Chuckie," Dad said, "but money isn't everything son. Being happy at your work is more important than money, and I think you'll be very happy working under our good friend Pete."

Dad had worked as a cost analyst at AVCO during the mid-sixties, and he assured me that because the company was a well-funded government military contractor, the atmosphere there was relaxed, befitting a country club and that the job could be mine for life if I wanted it to be. Having just graduated a week earlier, and still drained from all the effort I had put into school and expecting to be admitted into Suffolk University Law School the following year, I turned down the job at AVCO.

Failing to fully understand my reasoning and believing I was "blowing a big opportunity," Dad was visibly disappointed in me, felt slighted, and later on told me so. Instead of getting up early in the morning and going to work at AVCO for the nine-to-five routine. Never being one to be afraid of going against the grain, I chose the easier route and contented myself with sleeping late every morning, working out in the afternoons, working weekends and three weeknights at Bishop's, and spending quality time with my then-girlfriend Denise L. at her Lawrence apartment.

Denise, an extremely outgoing, upbeat and highly spiritual young woman, always seemed to have a disarming smile on her face. She was the single mother of a four-year-old daughter - Melanie. Her previous boyfriend, who had fathered Melanie, took off right after Melanie was born and left Denise, just a mere 16 years old at the time high and dry. He never showed his face again, not even once, to see his young daughter.

To make matters worse, whenever Denise would take Melanie to her overly pious parents' house just three blocks away, they would belittle Denise for having had "sinful" premarital sex and conceiving a "bastard child" out of wedlock. They ignored young Melanie, as if she wasn't good enough for them, having emerged from their errant daughter's womb "illegitimately."

Ever since I can remember, I've had a soft spot for kids and I felt bad for the fatherless Melanie, so, I took the young girl to Canobie Lake Amusement Park two or three times by myself and would also let her tag along with me whenever I went to the grocery store or ran other errands. I could sense, as time passed, that She began viewing me as her adopted father. Reflecting back on my life, I think if fate had afforded me the opportunity, I could have been a very good and loving father like Dad was.

Denise very often seemed to be short on money. Due to her heavy financial obligations, she had to work two jobs in order to support herself and her daughter. She worked a nine-to-five job as a secretary in the probation department at the local district courthouse, then immediately after finishing work there, she would walk over to Bishop's, just a block from the courthouse, and moonlight for another five hours as a waitress. That's where the two of us met and eventually got hooked up. Being blessed with relatively low living expenses, I would slip her a fifty every now and then in order to help the struggling girl out.

Always positive in attitude, Denise brought out the best in me and showed up in my life at the exact time I was hurting and needed her to. As previously noted author Napoleon Hill put it:

"When one is truly ready for a thing, it puts in its appearance."

Sensing that I was still somewhat distraught over what had taken place with my father, Denise displayed wisdom well beyond her years, volunteering this timely and encouraging advice:

"Chuckie, you did a bad thing with your Dad. We all know about it. But you did some good things in your life too. Tell me; no matter how hard you try can you relive your error of yesterday and right it? I believe everything happens - good or bad, for a reason. It's all over now. So, stop beating up on yourself will Yah. I want to see you enjoying your life again."

A ministering angel perhaps, Denise proved to be a very good lover as well. Looking back, I can say with confidence that I learned how to make love from her. Moreover, our sexual interactions proved to be highly "therapeutic." As a result, I began to feel happier and more like my "pre - Dad-fiasco" self as the weeks passed.

On the nights I wasn't visiting Denise at her place, I'd make my way over to my older friend Joe Kattar's North Andover house and spend time with him, his always-welcoming wife Diane, and Joe's younger brother John (J.D.), who was my age, worked at the restaurant, and was even closer to me than his older brother was. Despite the unpleasantness that had taken place a few years earlier with Dad, which I'm sure Joe was aware of, he still thought the world of me and was proud of our mutual Arabic ancestry. He was especially enamored with the fact that I ran and worked out every day before work, and often told me he admired my self-discipline. He himself was extremely overweight, smoked heavily, and couldn't run even a quarter of a mile if you put a loaded revolver to his head. But more on our good friend Joe Kattar later.

Sometime in mid-February of the following year, 1978, Dad caught up with me at the Y while I was jogging around the indoor track there:

"Chuckie, yesterday I put a down payment on a single-family house in a nice neighborhood in South Lawrence. I thought it was time we moved out of Hampshire Street and into a safer and better area. Your mother and I and rest of the family want you to move in with us. It's a three-bedroom ranch, and I think it will be a lot more spacious and comfortable for you than where you're living now. We're planning to move in as soon as the papers go through. We're shooting for two weeks from today as being our move-in date. We could use your help moving in too. So, think about it son and let me know what you'd like to do."

91

I felt deeply conflicted about the offer. After all, I was out of the nest, independent, self-supporting, and answered to no one. Why would I want to take a step backwards in life and throw myself back into the middle of my parents' longstanding marital imbroglio? Hadn't I learned my lesson yet? Was I a glutton for punishment?

On the other hand, the thought of living in a modern, roomy house, as opposed to a cellar room, was very appealing. The decision was taken out of my hands when Mr. Staley told me shortly thereafter that he had just sold his house to a female horse trainer. When the new owner moved in only a weeks later, she asked me to leave ASAP. So, it was back home living with the family again. As a prominent psychologist once stated:

"We either go forward or backwards in life and going backwards is never a good thing."

As you will see later on, moving back home back then would prove to be the SECOND biggest mistake of my life.

Chapter 9:
Completing the Boston Marathon

One Wednesday afternoon in mid-April, just three months after I had moved back home, I ran into my good friend Bobbie Bourdelais and his buddy Dick Brane as they were walking into the Y just ahead of me.

"Chuckie, did you know Dick and I are going to run the Boston Marathon next Monday (Patriots Day)? We've been training together out of the Y here for six months for it. Ten miles in the morning before work and ten miles at night after work. We're hoping to run the whole race together and cross the finish line side by side. Wish us luck, will Yah?"

Almost immediately, the achievement wheels started turning in my head.

"Bobbie, I've only been running four miles a day around the Common, and I know I'm in nowhere near the running shape you and Dick are, but I'm going to run that race with you guys."

"Are you serious, Chuckie? Four miles a day isn't even remotely enough training for a twenty-six-mile run. You won't even make it halfway."

"Bobbie, please don't tell me what I can and can't do. Yes, I'm serious. I'll see you guy's Monday morning in Hopkinton (where the Marathon begins), at the starting line."

Somehow, the word quickly got out at the Y that I was going to try to run the race, and I heard that sizeable bets had been placed by a bunch of guys in the locker room as to whether I would be able to finish or not. My good friend and work out partner at the time - Marty Rubio, I later learned, booked all of the action.

On Sunday evening, the night before the Marathon, not wanting to drive the forty highway miles into Hopkinton by myself and then have to worry about retrieving my car later, I phoned Bourdelais and asked if I could hitch a ride to Hopkinton with him and Brane.

He responded, "You stubborn Lebanese. You're still going through with this? Okay, as you wish. Meet us in front of the Y tomorrow morning at ten o'clock."

The race was scheduled to start at noon. The three of us arrived together at the starting line at about eleven thirty. Because we were running in an unofficial capacity, we had to go to the back of the line, behind the registered runners. You see, the Boston Marathon Athletic Association had a policy back then whereby they wouldn't issue a male runner an official number unless he had run a previous marathon in three hours or less (I recall that the running requirement was three and a half hours for women), and both had to be documented.

There were well over ten thousand runners ahead of us. Most had been issued numbers, which they pinned to the front of their shirts. It was a chilly and damp day with the temperature hovering only around fifty degrees along with some accompanying, intermittent rainfall. Because of all the folks ahead of us, we stood in place for ten full minutes after the starting gun went off before we could even begin walking slowly, not running, to the starting line. Although the longest distance I had run before was an eleven-mile road race in nearby Methuen a year earlier, I was still holding up fairly well when we reached the 15-mile mark, much to Bourdelais' and Brane's amazement. To my two buddies' further surprise, I was still doing relatively okay thirty minutes later when we all reached the top of the infamous Heartbreak Hill, some nineteen miles into the race.

As the three of us arrived at the top of Heartbreak, we heard through radio intercepts from other runners in the race that Boston's proud son and previous four-time Boston Marathon winner - Bill Rogers ("Boston Billy"), had just crossed the finish in first place for win number five, in a time of two hours, nine minutes and twenty-nine seconds and in the process vested his co-favorite, Japanese rival for the that race - Tosh Seko. One afternoon about a year earlier, I had ventured into Boston's Cleveland Circle where Rogers operated his upscale running store and had the distinct honor of conversing with the great champion personally. Learning that "my man" had just won Boston again gave me the much-needed impetus to just gut it out, and "keep on keeping on."

Heartbreak Hill is not only one big hill as most folks are led to believe. It's actually a series of three long and steep hills, the last being the biggest and steepest. After reaching the summit of that final hill, I began to experience excruciating pain in my knees and shins - sure symptoms of undertraining. Bourdelais, looking over at me and assessing my condition, felt that it was time for him to speak up.

"Charlie, I can see the pain in your face. We're facing even tougher downhills now. Drop out now, before you hurt yourself. Dick and I will come back and pick you up right here after the race. You have nothing to be ashamed of. Everyone at the Y will understand. You've gone much farther than anyone thought you would. So, stop it NOW!"

I shot back: "I'm not stopping NOTHING Bobbie!"

The remainder of the race was run on downhills that snaked into downtown Boston. I knew from reading "Runner's World Magazine" that downhill running is much harder on the knees and shins than running on a flat or uphill surface and so, I knew I was in for a dogfight. I ran the remaining seven miles in agonizing pain. My shins in particular hurt so much in fact that every step forward was a separate act of will. As I struggled hard to just place one leg in front of another, I repeated over and over to myself an admonition that Dad - the ultimate competitor, had branded into my younger brother George's and my minds while we were growing up, that being:

"A QUITTER never wins, and a winner never QUITS!"

As we made our way down the hills and into the Hub, it seemed to me like we were never going to finish and I recall saying to myself over and over:

"This feels like an eternal stay in Hell."

I was hurting so bad that for a brief moment or two, at the time we entered the final, two-mile, downturn, home stretch. I was actually thinking of dropping out of the race. Somehow though, I managed to hang on to the very end and cross the finish line hand in hand along with Bourdelais and Brane. Our official time, as yelled out by the race clocker who stood at the finish line, was three hours and forty-five minutes. Upon later reflection the three of us all felt that this was a very respectable time and a much better one than anyone we had anticipated before the race began.

I can't even begin to explain to you the tremendous sense of personal victory I felt as the three of us sat down together, guzzled multiple bottles of water, wrapped our bodies in the aluminum blankets furnished by the Marathon Committee, and talked about the race in the runners' makeshift auditorium at the Prudential Center and I could tell Bourdelais' and Brane's newfound respect for me was mounting by the minute. "RESPECT." I was actually now "GETTING" a little respect for a change.

Needless to say, I was forced to take the following night off from work because my legs were so stiff and sore I could hardly walk. After congratulating me on my successful marathon finish, Dad remarked at home that I was parading around our Leeds Terrace house like a bowlegged man.

I'm sorry to have to report that Bobbie Bourdelais, whose mother - Doris worked side by side with me for years as a waitress at Bishops, died five years ago at the tender age of 60 from as best I know - a long bout with incurable cancer. Doris, meanwhile, passed away as well last year. Bobby's apparently self-prepared Lawrence Eagle Tribune obituary stated that he felt that successfully completing the Boston Marathon with Brane and me in 1978 was his "greatest personal achievement in life." He even went as far as to mention my name in his obituary along with Brane's.

"Thank you for thinking of me in that light after all these years and doing that Bobby. Good-by to you and to your wonderful mother. May God rest both of your souls in peace."

Interestingly, when I attended Bobby's wake to pay my respects to him, his wife and his still alive at the time mother, the latter was conspicuously absent. When I asked Bobby's wife why, she told me Bobby and his mom had had a major fallout some fifteen years earlier and hadn't spoken to each other since. Why do we inflict such pain on the people we love? I wondered upon hearing this sad news about these two very special people in my life, as I remembered my own mother's emotional "freeze out" of me and realized she and I could easily have gone down the same road poor Doris and Bobby did.

Chapter 10:
Finding A Place for Myself in Corporate America

Several weeks after the Marathon, I received a letter from the Suffolk University Law School Admissions Board stating that due to my poor grades during my second year of college at Salem State, they were denying me admission. I immediately phoned prominent local Lebanese - American attorney Clifford Elias, who was a part-time law professor at Suffolk and whom I had asked months earlier to intervene and help me get into his school.

He confirmed that the Admissions Board had given him the same reason for denying my admission. When I protested to Elias that I had done significantly better during my latter two college years at Merrimack and thought this should be factored into the decision, he said:

"Well, the Board doesn't see it that way. I've done everything I can for you, Chuckie. I'm sorry, but I can't help you anymore."

My lifelong dream of becoming a lawyer, which I had cultivated since my childhood days of hero - worshipping fictional lawyer Perry Mason on TV, was now shattered. Forced to look at other career avenues and having an interest in the stock market due to my frequent visits to the stockbroker's office in downtown Lawrence to check on my investments, I enrolled for the fall semester at Suffolk University's Business School which is located in downtown Boston.

I reasoned that securing an MBA degree would open up more doors for me than just a bachelor's degree in accounting could. I knew Suffolk wasn't top rung, like Harvard Business School, The Wharton School of Finance, or The Chicago Business School - (which my much brighter close friend - J.D. Kattar later attended). But given my poor grades at Salem, I knew couldn't have gotten into those great schools even if I had applied to them. Suffolk was a second tier, but well-respected, working man's school and I reminded myself that's what I was a "working man" and Suffolk was the best I was going to be able to do. At least for the time being.

Living at home and still working as a waiter on weekends, I embraced the new opportunity. Because some of the business courses I'd taken in college were waived from my Suffolk curriculum, I earned my MBA by having to take only ten courses, which I successfully completed in only fourteen months' time. MBA programs typically run for two, full years.

A week after I graduated in early September of 1979, Dad proudly threw a multiple graduation party in honor of three of us who had simultaneously graduated that year - me from Business School, my brother George from college, and my sister Pamela from high school. Some sixty folks showed up at the family cookout in the back yard of our suburban Leeds Terrace house - relatives on both sides of the family, including my Aunt Elsie and her family, multiple friends, and even Lawrence Mayor John Buckley, whom my family knew very well. Dad, as usual, did all the cooking on a huge, red-brick grill built into the ground in our back yard. What a much needed and festive day that turned out to be!

In early December, several months after the backyard festivities, I felt it was time to set my waiter's vest aside and enter the "real work world." Accordingly, I put together a resume and sent it out to the Human Resources Departments of a dozen or so successful companies in the area. These firms included - Wang Labs, Digital Equipment, and Fidelity Investments.

I had learned from a counselor at Suffolk's Job Placement Office that my earlier dream of working on Wall Street wasn't a realistic one since those firms typically hired only Ivy League MBA graduates - the cream of the crop. So, I didn't even bother to apply there. And besides, I liked the idea of being a big fish in a little pond and had no desire to throw myself into the hectic, large pond, rat-race of Manhattan.

I surmised that sending out cold resumes was the wrong way to find a job. Your CV ends up being thrown into a pile on some non-decision-maker's desk, along with hundreds of others, and eventually tossed into the "circular file." What you really need is a personal contact within the company or else a headhunter who can plow through the red tape and speak directly to the person doing the hiring.

With that in mind, I contacted the supposedly well-respected headhunting firm of Winter - Wyman and Associates located just off Route 128 in Natick where corporations were plentiful and all the action was. According to their half-page ad in the Boston Sunday Globe, they specialized in finding employment for accounting and finance folks.

The receptionist I spoke with over the phone suggested I come into their office and interview with their "top business headhunter," a man by the name of Mark Gleckman. The woman assured me Gleckman was a decent and highly qualified man who would do right by me. I scheduled an appointment with him for the following week. Years later, I alarmingly read a Boston Globe investigative article, the heading of which warned:

"Watch Out For Headhunters: If You're Not Careful, They Can Ruin Your Life."

Unarmed with this knowledge at the time, I went in and met with Gleckman. After quickly perusing my resume and sizing me up correctly as a highly ambitious sort who, perhaps misguidedly, intended to climb the corporate ladder too quickly, the well-dressed thirty-year-old said to me in a voice oozing with charm:

"I have a great job sitting right here for you Charles. One that will really showcase your many talents. I think it's the perfect fit for an over achiever like you."

Gleckman now had my undivided attention.

"I'm intrigued Mark. Tell me more,"

"Charlie, Frank Digirolomo - a former financial star at Singer Corporation in San Francisco, is now the head financial officer of Epicure Corporation, (EPI) a well-known speaker manufacturer in Newburyport, not too far down the road from you in Lawrence. Maybe you've heard of the EPI line of speakers? That's them. Well, Frank is along in years now and desires to retire soon. He's looking to leave Epicure in three years. He told me that his plan is to hire a young go-getter like yourself and 'groom him' personally to take over his position when he retires. ...

Gleckman went on: "Taking this job will save you years of clawing your way to the top, which I can tell is where you want to end up. What do you say, Charles? Are you up to the challenge? Shall I call Frank today and set up an interview?"

"OK, let's do it Mark."

So, the following week, I met with Digirolomo at his company's factory. Bewilderingly, the EPI financial head never really looked at me in the eye during our fairly short discussion. Instead, he just told me a little bit about his company, said he was looking to hire a Cost Accountant at the salary of twenty thousand a year, and asked me if I would be interested in taking the job. A relative un-savvy, neophyte at the time, I failed to ask Digirolomo about the grooming - his-own-replacement scenario that Gleckman had detailed to me.

Without securing any real promises from Digirolomo as to what my future with his company would look like but with an offer of twenty - K a year in hand, which was considerably more than I was making as a waiter at Bishops, I told the EPI guy that I would take the job and start as soon as he wanted me to. Sporting an oddly sheepish, half smile, Digirolomo then said, without further discussion:

"In that case, let's shoot for your start date for a week from today. It's good to have you on board, Chuck."

We then both stood up, shook hands and then promptly parted company. I remember being struck by the weak clasp of the financial head's right hand to mine.

Roughly two months into my employment, I found out that Gleckman's claims of rapid advancement at EPI were pure crap. Digirolomo wasn't planning to "groom me" to take over the financial reins because he wanted to retire from Epicure soon. On the contrary, he had his eye on the President's job because the head of the company wanted to retire and Digirolomo was next in line. In short, the man had no desire at all to leave EPI as Gleckman had told me before.

I found out too that the only reason Digirolomo had hired me as a cost accountant was because EPI's parent company - Penril Corporation, out of Baltimore Maryland, had been on his back for ages to hire one so that they could get a better handle on Epicure's true manufacturing costs. In other words, I'd been hired into an essentially "hostile" situation. Armed with these new and highly disturbing revelations, I angrily phoned headhunter Gleckman:

"Mark, why the Hell did you con me into taking this dead - end job? There's no future for me here at this company. Was the meager commission you earned worth derailing my career for?" He answered:

"Charles, trust me. I related the specifics of the job to you exactly as Frank Digirolomo related them to me. If you will even believe it, he even chiseled me down to accepting half my normal commission. I'm out 2000 bucks. So, you work it all out with HIM." Click!

The job at EPI turned out to be a nightmare as upon reflection, I soon realized that I had without question, committed the terrible crime of "aiming to low," (a mere cost accountant being an MBA?) And even worse, none of the other folks in the office would even talk to me. Mostly white racist, Yankee rednecks from up north, they all childishly viewed me I was later told by one of them as a possible Arab terrorist. Perhaps for this very reason, none of them would even return my hellos when I arrived at work in the morning.

Digirolomo ignored and shunned me as well. With no job direction from him whatsoever, I was left to my own devices and had nothing productive to do all day. I spent most of my time perusing thru the Boston Globe Newspaper, checking my stock investments over the phone, and playing solitaire and chess on my laptop. Needless to say, an overachiever by nature, I found this dynamic to be extremely discouraging and isolating.

During about my fifth month at the job in a vain attempt to get more involved in the company and "make the best of the situation," I approached the Head of Manufacturing in his crampt, make - shift office inside the manufacturing plant and asked for his help in creating a much - needed cost accounting system. A mustached, elderly man with white hair and nauseatingly bad breath, he shockingly responded with:

"Accountants like you produce nothing. You're just glorified bean counters. NO, I won't work with you on that. Get lost fella!"

By my seventh month, this whole "nowhere" scenario had taken an enormous psychological toll on me and, although I had never been a quitter in my life, I started thinking seriously of giving up and resigning. Before doing so though, I arranged a two-week vacation for myself to California in order to clear my head and gain some additional perspective on the situation.

First, though, I sought out Dad's advice, and as is usually the case, he gave it to me:

"Son, I don't like the way you've been looking lately," he said. "Talk to me. What's going on with you?"

"Dad, I can't stand my job. It's making me miserable. The people there are bigots and won't even talk to me, and my boss is treating me just as badly. In fact, I actually consider him to be an even bigger asshole than the others are."

105

"I know exactly where you're coming from Chuckie. I was forced to endure some of that racist crap with some of the prejudiced, Irish folk myself who worked along with me in City Hall when I first went to work there. And, I've had some bad bosses too. Given all that, maybe the best thing for you to do is to just leave your job. Don't make a hasty decision though. Go out to L.A. as you've planned and meditate seriously about it before you finally act."

Two weeks later I returned from the West Coast and handed in my letter of resignation. Digitolomo accepted it without a word of discussion and seemed like he didn't even give a care. Several weeks after having left EPI, I began sending out resumes again. ... Crickets.

A Human Resource administrator at Fidelity Investments, who at least had the guts to be up front with me, finally told me he couldn't hire me because he'd been given a "bad reference" from Digitolomo. When I pressed him to be more specific, he said that Digitolomo's chief complaint to him was that I had failed to show up for work twice during winter snowstorms. After three months of unsuccessful job hunting, I finally came to the stark realization that due exclusively to my former bosses' unjustified blackballing of me, it was going to be impossible for me to land another financial/accounting job.

About six months after leaving Epicure, still out of work and now desperately low on money, I was forced to take what was available - a microcomputer sales position at Computer Town located in nearby Salem N.H. The job was way out of my field and well below my academic qualifications, but it didn't require a past employment check. As my ever - positive-minded Dad liked to say:

106

"Everything always works out for the best." We would have to see about that.

I settled into my new job, at least the other employees said hello to me in the morning and soon began to realize I was more of a "people person" than a "numbers guy." I quickly learned how to work and program the "user-friendly." Apple computer (our main-selling product), along with its equally user-friendly software, and sold my share of computers.

To my pleasant surprise, I found that I thoroughly enjoyed going to work every morning, loved what I was doing, and made enough money to at least pay all of my bills. (I was still living at home at the time, and Dad refused to take room and board money from me until I got back on my feet, so, my living expenses were very low.) I soon began to feel happy and contented again. Even better, as the months passed, I began to think I had finally found my "niche in life" - Computer Sales.

Looking ahead, I reasoned that if I spent a couple of years at Computer Town honing my sales skills, I could then apply for a more financially rewarding and prestigious computer sales position at one of the much larger, higher flying computer companies based in the area (ie. Digital Equipment, Wang Labs, and Prime Computer, among others).

Shortly after starting at Computer Town, I became close friends with a fellow salesman, Chris L., whose desk was right next to mine. We jointly purchased an audiotape by famed sales trainer Tom Hopkins entitled: "The Art of Selling" and faithfully listened to the tapes that the super salesman had recorded while driving to lunch together in his late-model Saab each noontime. These tapes helped us hone our selling skills, and we both became quite confident interfacing with prospective clients.

107

Further fueling my confidence that I could eventually make the transition to a higher-level computer sales job (when I was fully ready to of course), was the knowledge that I had a "personal in" at Digital Equipment (DEC), the multi-billion dollar and fast-growing computer company located just ten miles down the road from our South Lawrence residence.

My contact at DEC was a former high school classmate who still remained a good friend - Jack M. He had been a successful salesman at the tech giant for a good number of years and I was sure that I if I ever approached him in the future to help me get a computer sales job at his firm, that with his close contacts that I'm sure that he had developed at his company over the years, he could have gladly made that happen.

ACT II: NOW THE REAL NIGHTMARE BEGINS TO UNFOLD

Chapter 11:
A Failed Persian Gulf Work Experience

Several weeks before Christmas in 1981, my Lebanese-born second cousin - Fatek Hashem, approached Dad and me at home about the possibility of my working for a company called Universal Industrial Marketing Company (UNIMAC) in the United Arab Emirates (UAE). Fatek told us he had worked as a salesman for UNIMAC in the past (I later found out this wasn't true). He was in the States at the time, getting married to an American-born woman he'd met during a previous visit to America from Lebanon and was trying to set up an import-export business with my father, whom he loved and admired deeply.

Fatek spoke to Dad and me about his many business contacts in the U.A.E. and the money that could be made if these contacts could be put in touch with sellers of in-demand American technological products. This piqued Dad's interest and he expressed a strong desire to be cut in on the action.

About a week before Christmas, at Fatek's request, I spoke, long-distance, with the owner of UNIMAC, Sami El Malik. El Malik detailed his professional background to me, which included nine years as a top salesman for NCR Computer Company in the Middle East and five years as president and sole owner of UNIMAC, then explained his business plans in thickly accented and broken English:

"Market for microcomputers and business software exploding here in Gulf, Mr. Charles Ead. I have huge potential market base of Emirate businessmen who purchase minicomputers from me while I at NCR. So, I must take on sales associate. I look for someone young, ambitious, speak both English and Arabic and have workable knowledge of computers and business software. Do you know anyone, Mr. Charles Ead, who fits description and would be interested in working with me in Gulf?

At the time I was more than open to new opportunities, and the mental wheels began to spin:

"My own background actually ties in quite well with what you're looking for." I cautiously offered. "Depending on what the earning potential is, I might consider taking on the job myself."

El Malik made an "Ahh" of pleasure and surprise. He asked me to fill him in on my background:

"I'm twenty-five years old and speak Arabic fairly well. My background -"

El Malik cut me off and fired a question at me in Arabic. After I correctly answered it, he laughed approvingly and asked me to go on.

"I earned a B.S. degree in accounting and an MBA degree," I continued, then took him through my experience at Epicure and Computer Town. "I'm well-acquainted with three microcomputer systems - the Apple, the IBM, and the Hewlett Packard (HP) - as well as with a wide range of business and word processing software programs."

"Any interesting products on horizon?" he asked.

"In addition to the Apple, which is selling like hotcakes, one of the most promising new product lines at our store is the Logical machine," I told him. "Much pricier than the Apple, it has a revolutionary 'English programmable' operating system that allows the average user to write his own software programs in English." I explained some of the product's other notable features to him.

"Hey, that sound fantastic," he said and announced without further ado, "I like to get Middle East distributorship for Logical computer."

I told him that was a distinct possibility. The UNIMAC owner went on to say:

"From way you describe your sales experience light. But I can tell you well-educated, articulate, and smart fellow and I confident I could teach you ropes of selling and make you good salesperson within a short time. I pay you a fifteen-hundred-dollar month salary, plus sizeable commissions on computers and business software you sell. I also provide free lodging and free use of company car. With you and I as only sales reps calling on former NCR customers, you earn $200,000 first year. I very confident of that." I liked what I was hearing. ... A lot.

"If things go well first few years," he continued, "I hire additional salespeople and make you sales manager. As head of sales staff, you have opportunity to double, even triple, initial income."

That was all had to hear. Elated, and feeling strongly that my ship had finally come in, I accepted the job right there on the phone. My Dad and cousin Fatek were standing right next to me during the phone exchange, anxiously waiting to hear its outcome.

"Welcome aboard, Charles," Malik concluded. "Please contact Logical Machine Corporation and tell them I wish secure exclusive distribution rights to their computer in Middle

East. I will wire $10,000 letter of credit. I want you purchase Logical Computer from distributor and bring with you to Emirates as demo model. I reimburse you for your plane fare when you arrive in Abu Dhabi. I wish you and family Merry Christmas and safe trip to Gulf."

And that was that!

Owing to my Arabic roots, I was excited about the opportunity to work and travel in the history-rich land of my ancestors. I was equally enthused about the opportunity to work closely with the apparently highly seasoned El Malik. A nice side bonus was that under the U.S. tax code at the time the first $75,000 of foreign income was fully tax-free.

Making and saving money was important to me at that time, not only for myself and my then-fiancée - a Lebanese-born senior-year college student at the time - but also for my parents who were in severe financial difficulty and whom I badly wanted to help out.

And so, on a frigid January 11th morning, I hugged my parents and a few well-wishing relatives goodbye on our black-ice-encrusted front steps, and Fatek and I drove off for Boston's Logan Airport in his rented car, dressed like Eskimos against the fifteen-degree temperatures.

"We won't be needing these where we're going, Chuckie," Fatek said, pointing to our fur-lined hats that Dad had given us.

I had no idea how very true my cousin's words would turn out to be.

We arrived at Logan in time to enjoy a warming cup of coffee before departure, then sailed off into a cloudless New England sky. I watched my snow-covered homeland disappear beneath us with a sense of dawning adventure and just a twitch of anxiety. A new and exciting chapter in my life had just begun. Perhaps, I even thought, my ship had finally come in.

Before traveling to Abu Dhabi in the UAE, we made a two week stop in Lebanon to visit with Fatek's parents and my mother's brothers and sisters, all of whom lived in Byblos during the winter months -Ahoura during the summer. Byblos was a relatively peaceful Christian town twenty miles north of the civil-war-torn capital, Beirut. Several of my relatives there claimed Byblos was the oldest city in the world (although some scholars say the Syrian capital of Damascus is older). Lebanon is a stunningly beautiful country - mountains, ocean, orange trees, and has a mild, Mediterranean climate similar to that of California as well.

If this is what the Middle East is like, I thought, I've made a very good decision. A person could get used to this. Fatek unsuspectingly proved himself to be a highly outgoing fellow. He took me to see all my relatives, most of whom I'd never even known about before. As I mentioned earlier, my mother was born in Lebanon and emigrated to the states when she was 18 years old.

It turned out I had a seemingly endless supply of aunts, uncles, and cousins in Byblos. Everyone was elated to see me - Rose's son, and I got invited to a new house every night for dinner. It was a great time. I loved the food, the attention, the goodwill, and the connection to my newly discovered family. Fatek and I are kibbee, stuffed grape leaves, and hummus until we were ready to explode.

Most of my relatives asked with fascination about life in America. It seemed they were mentally recording everything I said for some important future use. They all wanted to talk politics too and were not afraid to express strong and unpopular opinions (i.e., Why is America sticking its nose in the Middle East where it doesn't belong and causing mayhem for us here in the Arab world?) Being very parochial and politically unsophisticated at the time, I usually kept my mouth shut, as I had no viable answer for them.

Twice during our visit, Fatek and I drove into Beirut (the erstwhile "Paris of the Middle East"), where I witnessed firsthand the devastation that eight years of civil war and factional fighting had brought to the once thriving banking and tourism capital. Conspicuous when we entered downtown area were the many bullet-ridden office buildings.

We also observed long lines of disenfranchised souls begging for handouts at intersections. Hamra Street, the highly upscale, main shopping drag that I was told once rivaled Rodeo Drive in Beverly Hills, was almost completely deserted - the apparent aftershock of a car bomb explosion that had killed a half dozen people during the crowded lunch hour two days earlier.

I was still faithfully maintaining a five-mile-a-day running regimen during this period of my life, and I saw no reason to vary it while in Lebanon. I would break up my days by taking noonday runs through Byblos and its adjacent valleys. My cousin Miziad, who was about my age and whose parents - Nemer and Nuhad, (Nemer was Ma's older brother), I was staying with, would often jog along with me. The Lebanese weren't a sports-minded folk, and so our runs created quite a spectacle. Many of my teenage cousins, in fact, were so taken by our daily jogging, they often followed us with their cars and bicycles. Folks driving by would often slow down and stare at us out their windows as if to say,

"What the Hell are those two clowns doing?"

In response, Miziad and I just waved and smiled innocently, amused at the attention.

One about my fifth night in Lebanon, I had a fun night out with my cousin Fatek at the casino, which was located in the neighboring, sea-side town of Junee. Shooting craps, it was all my night as a very attractive, middle-aged woman standing next to me at the overcrowded dice table got hot and threw ten passes in a row. Backing every one of her throws, I ended up netting myself a cool $1200 profit on an initial, $200 investment.

At or around midnight, just as we were heading out of the casino, cousin Fatek, aware of my success that night, walked over to a pay telephone in the main lobby and phoned three of his close friends and invited them to join the two of us at a popular, Byblos, night club. Once the five of us were seated at the night spot, right up close to the stage where the belly dancer and the Arabic music playing musicians were doing their thing, Fatek's friends introduced themselves to me then thanked Fatek for inviting them.

When the waiter finally arrived at our table, Fatek took control of the situation and without even asking me if it was OK, promptly ordered a $300 bottle of scotch and a Mazza platter (by far the most expensive item on the menu), which the waiter informed us would be loaded with a wide assortment of Lebanese food and delicacies, all of which Fatek insisted to be paid for with MY winnings that night at the casino. So, there wasn't a huge amount left in my wallet when the five of us finally left the establishment at or around four o'clock the next morning.

Being basically a good sport most of the time though, I didn't really mind Fatek's presumptuous actions all that much, really I didn't. After all, my cousin had gotten me a highly lucrative job in the Gulf. Wasn't the man deserving of at least a token payback for that? So, with this in mind, instead of getting angry or making a scene that might have very well embarrassed all of us, I just let it slide and contented myself with knowing that we all had an enjoyable time for ourselves that evening and shared some fun together, although I must admit, it did prove to be a bit tiring for me.

Needless to say, I cherished my time in Byblos, and after our two full weeks there felt nourished, loved, optimistic, and ready to take on the world.

Just before leaving Lebanon, though, a hard dose of Middle Eastern reality struck me in the face. It occurred in Byblos while cousin Miziad and I were taking an innocent stroll through the famed city after one of our daily runs. As we approached the Mediterranean waterfront, we met up with three Syrian soldiers who were dressed in neat, bright-green uniforms and who were apparently patrolling the beach.

I cordially greeted them in Arabic with a cheerful "Murhaba Shabab" (Hello, guys) - much as I would have politely greeted a group of police officers walking a beat in the States. To my surprise, the tallest of the three, apparently interpreting my greeting as some sort of facetious insult, got in my face and shouted in angry English:

"Go to Hell, you rich, spoiled American."

Now highly angered myself, I reacted instinctively, in an un-Christian, tooth-for-tooth manner, and gave it right back to the guy in kind, again in Arabic:

"Idee-feek, ya-kulb - (Screw YOU, you dog)."

As one of the other soldiers then pointed his rifle at my cousin and me, Miziad grabbed me tightly around the neck with his right arm and dragged me away. As he did so, he shouted in English:

"Shut up, Chuckie! Just shut up. These guys will kill us. Let's just get the Hell away from here."

Potential disaster averted. I guess I still had not fully comprehended that Lebanon was in the midst of a full-blown civil war and was being policed by the self-serving Syrians.

On the morning of January 22nd, Fatek and I bid our relatives a thankful farewell, hitched ourselves a ride to the Beirut Airport from Fatek's older brother - Maween, then an active colonel in the Lebanese Army, and took off for Abu Dhabi. The moment we stepped off the plane onto the heat-softened tarmac, it was obvious we were not in Lebanon anymore. The temperature in the Arab Emirates was pushing 85 degrees, but at least there was a hint of a sea breeze. El Malik meanwhile, was awaiting our arrival in the airport terminal.

He was a middle-aged man of medium build and height with a pot belly that hung unbecomingly over his belt, and he seemed like an amiable chap. He told me I was going to be staying with him at his apartment. This was a bit of a shock, I must admit. I am a fairly private person and had been under the distinct impression from our telephone conversation that I would be awarded my own apartment. I'm not sure I would have agreed to the job at all had I known I'd be sharing my quarters with my new boss and business partner. But I surrendered to the arrangements graciously. Life was going to be an adventure for a while, so I might as well roll with it - right? We then promptly headed off through Abu Dhabi in El Malik's black, late-model, four door, air-conditioned Mercedes.

Abu Dhabi is port city on the Persian Gulf, artificially built on desert. Where the climate in Lebanon was Mediterranean and pleasant, the Emirates was much hotter and more humid. I'm not a great lover of intense heat, so this was shock number two. I wondered why neither of my hosts (Fatek or El Malik) had forewarned me about the extreme climate. It certainly seemed a point of interest, but there was nothing I could do about it now except try to adapt.

I moved into El Malik's apartment with my one suitcase full of clothes. He had a decent-sized living space and, thankfully, I was given my own room.

The apartment was decorated tastefully by local standards but would not have made the cover of Interior Living in the US. There was a "confectionary" feeling about everything - imitation gold trim everywhere, baroque crystal, and sugary-looking oil paintings that nearly gave me a toothache. Also, oud music and loud Arabic singing poured from the stereo night and day, invading my "personal space."

Although I wanted to flex my muscles by exploring my new city, the heat really confined me to the A/C'd apartment most of the time. I knew I would need to find my own place as soon as possible, but for the time being I simply had to adjust to the conditions and learn how to perform well in my new career. That would need to be my sole focus.

On or about my third day at El Malik's, I awoke about six a.m. to very loud music coming through my bedroom window. At first, I thought that it was from a tasteless teenager blasting his car radio, but when it continued for fifteen-minutes I knew this wasn't the case. When El Malik awoke about an hour later, I asked him about the noise. He told me it was coming from an Islamic Minaret in the park directly across the street from his apartment; it was the call to morning prayers for the local Muslim faithful. He went on to explain that all Muslims, when called to prayer five times a day, immediately stop whatever they are doing, kneel down in the direction of Mecca - Islam's holy city, and chant their prescribed prayers to their God - Allah.

Wow, I thought to myself, these Muslim folks are much more faithful and disciplined in practicing their faith than the majority of Christians I knew back home. Their daily devotion greatly elevated my view of the Muslim faith and made a lasting impression on me, even to this day and seemed to directly contradict the closed minded, western notion that Islam is somehow a sham religion.

Moreover, in my many daily interactions with the Muslim folk of the Emirates, I found them to be the most self-effacing, kind, helpful, welcoming, and genuinely humble and authentic people you could ever want to meet. It was always a pleasure for me whenever I got the opportunity to interface with them. Not surprisingly, I would later on in life develop a strong interest in the study of comparative religions, most especially in Islam. Cousin Fatek, meanwhile, his introductory mission now accomplished, left Abu Dhabi and returned to America to be with his new American-born, bride-to-be, Donna.

Much to El Malik's surprise, I remained faithful to my daily running regimen during the entire first three months of my stay. Somewhat bewildered by this, he didn't try to dissuade me but rather adopted an attitude of bemused tolerance. Perhaps there was a good reason the locals didn't do much running; I perspired greatly and lost a great deal of body fluid each day. A weight-check, in fact, indicated I had dropped about fifteen pounds over the course of those first few months.

As the weeks passed, dehydration became a serious issue for me. But I didn't worry about it much because I was young and healthy and, like most young people, immortal in my own mind. And there was a further reason I kept up my exercise routine despite the heat: I had actually become addicted to running (ask any runner; this can happen), and if I didn't run each day, I would feel physically sick and found that I couldn't even sleep at night. So, it became complicated, feel sick from running or feel sick from not running.

Compounding the climate problem was the fact that the tap water had a very high bacteria count, and so bottled water was recommended by the health authorities for all consumption. Because it wasn't always readily available, however, I was sometimes forced to drink from the faucet, just to avoid vomiting. This practice caused occasional diarrhea, but I did not realize just how dangerous it was. Drinking bad water is a major regret for me, looking back.

As spring approached, the humid conditions in Abu Dhabi, coupled with the five-mile-a-day running regimen I faithfully (and somewhat inexplicably) maintained, really began to wear me down. By early April, I felt anemic and stressed out. I needed a break or something was going to give.

In mid-April, feeling homesick, and *just plain* sick, I flew home, with El Malik's blessing, in order to spend the Easter holiday with my family and my fiancée. Still not fully accustomed to international travel however, and mistakenly believing the UNIMAC owner wanted me back in Abu Dhabi ASAP, I stayed only three days at my parents' house before jumping back on a plane and returning to the UAE.

I was in such a rush to get back to the Gulf, in fact, that I didn't even bother to unpack at home and barely had a chance to say hello to everyone. I did converse with Fatek for about ten minutes however on Easter Sunday where he was a dinner guest at my parent's home. Not wanting to appear to be a wimp though, I assured him everything was OK with me and El Malik back in the Gulf. Everything wasn't okay, of course.

Three days was a woefully insufficient time to readjust my bodily clock and try to get some much-needed rest. I spent much of my time in the U.S. saying hello to old friends at the Y and dashing around visiting relatives. I even managed to bang out a five-mile run on Easter Monday. And just the next day - (Tuesday), I jumped back on a plane and returned to the Gulf, another draining, fourteen-hour, international flight.

Thus, as you might imagine, when I arrived back in Abu Dhabi, I was physically spent. Far from replenishing me, the trip home had further worn me down. As the even hotter month of May approached, the Gulf climate grew ever more stifling, with temperatures now hitting the hundred-degree mark nearly every day, along with exceedingly high, 80-percent humidity. I was discovering that the Persian Gulf makes Houston in the dog days of August seem like Boston in January.

In response to the heat, on or around May first all governmental agencies in the UAE and most private businesses, including ours, began shutting down from noon until three in the afternoon every day in order to let employees go home and take a "siesta" in their air-conditioned apartments. It was so hot outdoors that, although I somehow managed to kick my addiction and stop running completely, I still became drenched with sweat just walking the quarter mile from the UNIMAC office to my apartment building each noontime.

The unrelenting heat and humidity, coupled with my travel-induced exhaustion, made me feel like a fish out of water. As May proceeded, I was no longer adjusting at all. The fact that neither cousin Fatek nor El Malik had informed me about the oppressive Gulf climate, which was only worsening as summer approached, haunted my thoughts daily and added to my irritation.

I was equally disenchanted with the fact that El Malik seemed to have reneged on his promises to provide me with either an apartment of my own and/or a car to drive. Adding further to my frustration, the UNIMAC owner and I still hadn't called on even one of his former NCR sales clients as he had told me we would, and I was nearly five months into my stay.

At least he was at least making good on his promise to pay me a modest 1500-dollar-a-month base salary. But had I traveled halfway around the world and left my fiancée and my social support system for that; to earn 1500 bucks a month? Hell, I could have earned that amount back in the States just shining shoes.

Now instead of calling on potential clients and earning some healthy commission money - as El Malik had said I would, I found myself spending my whole workday drinking cup after cup of American coffee, and just killing time by playing video games on the Logical Computer I had brought along with me from the U.S. and bullshitting with the four English-speaking expatriates El Malik had shipped in from nearby India to man our office.

Those poor souls were lucky to earn salaries of even three hundred dollars a month, half of which they felt compelled to send back home to their poverty-stricken families in India. I recall that the most talkative and charismatic of these Indian fellows was an overweight, dark skinned, middle-aged man named Abdullah. He and I hit it off well and conversing with him often greatly helped to pass the time. When El Malik did pop into the office from time to time, I had a hard time getting his attention. He would arrive like a phantom and, with an overly serious look on his face, wave a cursory hello to me and/or the expatriates and then exit as quickly as he came in, without so much as a good-bye.

Even worse, El Malik never once gave daily work direction to any of us. I tried many times to initiate conversations with and get closer to him, but these efforts proved fruitless. There seemed to be some sort of mysterious and impenetrable wall between the two of us. Does this dynamic sound familiar? Was this an Epicure - Digirolomo style, "Deja-vu all over again"?

On or around May 10th, with my frustration and uncertainty reaching a climax, I sat down and talked with my boss one night at his apartment and let it all out.

"Mr. Sami, I am truly grateful for this opportunity you've given me, but I'm having a terrible trouble with the climate conditions here and you've reneged on three major promises you made to me" (which I proceeded to outline). After getting Dad's support during a long-distance telephone conversation, I told El Malik I had decided to resign from my job and return home.

Without hesitation, Mr. Sami punched back:

"I apologize about weather, Charles. I thought cousin Fatek warn you about it before you coming here. I not lie, I disappointed that you having hard time. I hoped better for both of us. And as for not calling on clients, you might have found already, time viewed differently here than in States. We take our time getting things done in Middle East. What we can't do today, we just do next day."

By when - Christmas Sami?

He then phrased his sentiment in Arabic for me, "Bukra, Inchallah (God willing, tomorrow)," and continued, "I sorry you impatient man. I plan get things rolling soon. But if you feel things so bad here, I no objection release you from employment contract and you return home where pace of life much faster, and weather more to your liking too."

Not fully satisfied that El Malik was being totally authentic in his response, I handed my resignation letter to him the following day, booked a flight home to Boston for May 15th, one week later - some sort of work-contract visa problem, which wasn't fully explained to me, forced me to have to hang around Abu Dhabi for an additional week, which given the fastly intensifying heat, was definitely not to my liking.

One night during the middle of the week that followed, and right after finishing dinner with El Malik in his apartment (which occurred rarely), the UNIMAC owner shocked me with these revelations, seemingly out of nowhere:

"Before you leave, Charles, I want be up front with you and get few things off chest."

"Sure. What do you want to tell me Mr. Sami?"

"First, I want you know I never like you from first minute I meet you. And second, I find out by calling owner of computer store you work at in States that you charge me extra

200 dollars for Logical Computer you and Fatek bring with you to Gulf. I your employer. You should not make money off me like this. This really piss me off Mr. Charles:

"Whooh, hold on here Sami!

"Couldn't you have told me all this a lot sooner?" I fired back. "And you're quibbling about a 200-dollar markup on a ten-thousand-dollar, forty-pound machine that I was forced to lug through three airports? I was still working at Computer Town when you asked me to buy that machine for you! Shame on you, Mr. Sami. And what exactly is it about me that you don't like?"

It should also be noted that because El Malik, (for some unexplained reason), wouldn't allow me back into his air conditioned, UNIMAC office after I handed in my resignation letter, I was forced to spend the entire following week aimlessly walking the streets for hours on end in the intensely, humid outside heat just waiting for my booked flight back home to come to fruition. (Spending my days in El Malik's apartment wasn't a practical option for me either because it wasn't air-conditioned, due to the fact that El Malik wanted to save money on his air-conditioning bill.) The end result, I lost a good four pounds alone during this extended, seven-day, time lag.

The ensuing trip home required me to remain awake for forty-eight straight hours - twelve hours before boarding the 8:00 p.m. flight out of Abu Dhabi, then, because of lengthy stopovers in London and New York, a twenty-eight-hour flight. The transatlantic flight from Heathrow in London to Kennedy in New York was filled to capacity so there were no empty seats on which I could lie down and sleep, which I desperately wanted to do. As soon as I arrived at Boston's

Logan Airport, I struggled to get to a pay phone and called my best friend at the time, J.D., who luckily was at home, and asked him to pick me up.

Not expecting my arrival, J.D. took a full hour to get himself together and then an hour after that to show up at the airport. It then took another hour for J.D., and his older brother Joe, who had come along for the ride to drive me home. While driving me to my parent's Leeds Terrace house, the elder Joey, noting how quiet I was in the back seat, said:

"Chuckie, something happened to you out there in the Gulf. Do you want to talk about it with us?"

"No, Joey. Just Leave me alone, will Yah? I'm exhausted. I just want to go home and crash."

When the Kattar brothers dropped me off at my parents' house, my mother immediately greeted me at the front door with an expression of alarm at my gaunt and dehydrated appearance.

"Chuckie, you look terrible! You've got to see the doctor."

I took a look at my watch and saw that it was now well after two in the morning. I hadn't slept for almost two full days:

"Ma, please. I'm totally exhausted. When I finish unpacking, I'm going to bed. Then I am going to sleep and sleep and sleep for as long as it takes. Talk to me about doctors when I get up, whenever that will be."

Oddly enough, although I slept for the next twenty straight hours, I found I was still quite fatigued when I finally awoke from bed late the following evening.

Chapter 12:
The Good Doctor Denapoli

"Who is that man standing behind the curtain?"

Shortly after I awoke late in the morning of the following day - May 17th, my second full day at home, my mother told me she had scheduled an appointment for me at 4 o'clock that afternoon with her physician, Dr. Jorge Denapoli of Andover.

"In case you haven't noticed, Ma, I'm all grown up now. Thank you for your concern, but I'll see a doctor of my own choosing, if and when I feel it necessary."

"Oh, Chuck, please. Look in the mirror - you look terrible! So gaunt, so thin, so sallow. Please, let a doctor take a peek at you. I have already made the appointment. What will it hurt to talk to him? Please, Chuckie, you *need* to see him! Please. Please."

The pleading went on unabated for fifteen minutes. Everyone has his limit. I finally agreed.

We arrived via my mother's car at the physician's address in the stately old town of Andover, Massachusetts. Denapoli's office was in a nineteenth-century brick building a stone's throw from Phillips Academy, where several of our nation's presidents and famed actor Humphrey Bogart received their secondary school educations. The doctor was doing well for himself. I hoped that meant that he was competent. And that I wouldn't have to wait long. I headed inside.

"I'm coming in too, Chuck." said my mother. It was not phrased as a question.

"I will go in alone and *you* will wait here," I responded firmly. "Thank you again for your motherly concern, Ma, but I think I can handle this myself."

"No, I'm coming in," she repeated, avoiding eye contact with me, but with a determination in her voice I had rarely heard before. I didn't argue. She followed me up the old brick steps and inside to Denapoli's waiting room. Ten minutes later, the lanky, fifty-year-old or so Denapoli emerged from his office, greeted my mother, introduced himself to me, and asked me, in a quiet, Latin-accented voice, to follow him into his consultation room:

"I think I should be there too," my mother said, exchanging an anxious and cryptic look with Denapoli:

"Why don't you wait here for now?"

the doctor said, seeming to choose his words with unusual care. Something was being communicated in the looks I saw in both of their eyes, but I wasn't sure what it was:

"I'll call you in after I finish my evaluation."

Even this small degree of involvement on my mother's part - joining the doctor and me after the exam, struck me as odd and inappropriate, given my age. But I wrote it off as a mother's prerogative and followed Denapoli out of the waiting room. Denapoli and I then sat down in his consultation room, decorated in hunting club motif and I gave him my recent history:

"I came back two days ago from a five-month work experience in the Persian Gulf, Doctor. It didn't go well. I was running five miles a day in the oppressive Gulf climate and steadily losing weight and getting dehydrated. On top of that, the flight home caused me to remain awake for over forty

129

straight hours. I still feel hugely jetlagged. I weighed 160 pounds when I left for the Emirates in early January and 135 pounds when I got home. The relocation, the bad water, and the international travel has definitely left me feeling anemic, stressed out, and irritable."

I recall being struck by the fact that Denapoli wasn't writing anything down. He just stared intently at me from beneath his wiry, overgrown eyebrows, his fingers laced together in a TV-doctorly manner. After I finished outlining my complaints, Denapoli asked his secretary to call my mother into his consultation room. My mother sat beside me. She said nothing at first, just stared abstractedly at an oil painting of spaniels chasing a fox.

"He had a blood test before he left for the Gulf," she finally blurted out, flashing a worried glance in my direction. "It came back with a very low potassium level. Look at him. Look at that awful, jaundiced skin!"

Denapoli however, didn't seem to hear her. Instead, he turned to me, paused for effect, and said:

"I am a psychiatrist, Charles, and I have been treating your mother for many years."

I was stunned, to put it mildly. Why was my mother still seeing a psychiatrist? I knew she'd had that brief psychiatric hospitalization after reuniting with Dad in the mid-70's, but I thought she'd long since recovered from that. Maybe she was still struggling with the tragic loss of my brother Mark. As previously mentioned, my eight-year-old younger brother had been struck down and killed by a drunk driver many years earlier while crossing a street near our house.

Mark had been the apple of my mother's eye, and his death tore the guts out of her. Maybe she still needed help coping with that loss. Or maybe it was her ongoing self-described marital problems with Dad or even her troubles with her oldest daughter Marion who seemed at her envious aunt Elsie's tutelage to despise her and was always undermining everything she did, or maybe a little bit of all three? The bigger question, of course, was *What was I doing here?* I'd had no history whatsoever of mental or emotional problems.

I'd like to state at this time in case the reader might suspect that our family has a history of organic or genetic mental illness, it does not. The most significant aspect of my exam with Dr. Denapoli was that he did not conduct one. He neglected to check my vital signs, blood pressure, heart rate, temperature, and weight. He failed to order a blood test. He didn't take a past medical history. Moreover, the good doctor failed to make any attempt whatsoever to address the possible causes of my skin jaundice.

Instead, without even administering a routine psychological exam or asking me any probing questions, the psychiatrist made a "snap diagnosis," claiming that I was suffering from manic depressive psychiatric illness (better known today as bipolar disorder) and that I needed Lithium medication immediately to treat it or else. Surely, I thought to myself, this guy's elevator doesn't go to the top floor.

Dumbstruck to the point of amusement, with a huge grin on my face, I asked the misfit if this was some sort of joke although it didn't appear that he was joking. I further said to myself how in Hell could this weasel possibly have formulated such a diagnosis in twenty minutes without having conducted a physical or psychological exam or ordering any lab tests? So, a moment later, I further shot back:

131

"I'm impressed, Doctor, at how easily you formalized your opinion of my mental health. Am I to also assume you are so gifted like the prophets of old that you have the ability to predict the future too?" Before he had a chance to answer me, my mother lashed out:

"Don't you talk like that to the doctor, Chuckie! He knows what he's talking about." My mood quickly dissolved from amusement to irritation.

"I'm sorry, Doctor, I don't place any credence in your shoot-from-the-hip diagnosis. My complaints are physical and organic in nature, not psychiatric. I'll be finding another doctor. Thank you for your time. Have a nice day!"

Denapoli appeared angered by my words. That wasn't my problem, though. I then rose from my chair, left the room, and went out to my mother's car and waited for her. My mother, meanwhile, remained behind and conversed further with Denapoli for what seemed to be another twenty minutes or so.

The following excerpt from the College of Legal Medicine textbook, Legal Dynamics of Medical Encounters, states that Denapoli was obligated to have done significantly more investigating before formulating his diagnosis:

… "After the establishment of the physician-patient relationship, a careful record of the patient's history will ordinarily precede diagnosis and treatment. As with other tasks, physicians must exercise due care in eliciting relevant matters of past medical history from patients; the failure to do so can form the basis of a malpractice allegation.

On the way home, my mother repeatedly pleaded with me to return to her shrink's office:

"Chuck, you need the lithium medication. The doctor knows what's best for you. Please, please, Chuckie, let's go back!"

"Ma, I'm not going back there! The guy's a psychiatrist! What the Hell did you bring me to him for? The monkey didn't even bother to examine me."

She resisted giving me a straight answer, but it was clear from the look in her eye and the quiver in her chin that her psychiatrist, whom she apparently idolized, had thrown a major scare into her about me.

During the ensuing summer, I lived at my parents' house. It proved to be a difficult and stressful time for two reasons. First of all, in late June, I was wiped out of most of the $7,000 I had saved while working in the Gulf when Dome Petroleum stock, of which I had purchased two thousand shares at the price of eight dollars a share on margin plummeted to a dollar a share. With the rapid loss of my equity, I felt pressured to find a job and replenish my savings in a hurry.

Secondly, I was confined all day to my parents' suburban home without the use of a car. This put me in the constant company of my mother, who nagged me like a broken record to go back and see her hero, Denapoli.

On the plus side, a two-month hiatus from daily exercising had positive effects on my health. By mid-July, I had put back a lot of the weight I had lost in the Persian Gulf and my energy level had increased markedly. For this reason, I neglected to undergo a comprehensive medical exam.

That was a big mistake. Looking back, I should have gone right into Mass. General in Boston the day after meeting with Denapoli and had a thorough medical workup by a physician who specialized in illnesses folks typically contract during extended stays overseas. Had I done so, I know could have properly pinpointed my health problem and could have avoided the horrors that followed. But, of course, hindsight is always twenty - twenty.

Feeling better, I wanted to give the Persian Gulf another tries. There were genuine opportunities to be found there for someone with my skills and background, and at that in my life I still subscribed to secular values like "Whoever dies with most toys wins." I focused my job-search on U.S. companies that did business in Saudi Arabia and the other Gulf states. I was driven then by a harmful desire to get rich by snagging what I felt was my share of all that oil money that flowed like water in the Gulf.

Reflecting on my first ill-fated Gulf experience, I concluded that if I did a better job of planning my travel schedule, cut back on my heavy running regimen, and drank only bottled water, I could function successfully in the Gulf. As you will soon see, this proved to be a pipe dream. I couldn't return to my old job with UNIMAC and El Malik because of an Emirates law that prevented re-entry into the country for one full year after terminating an employment contract.

After a month of aggressive job-hunting, I landed a computer sales job with Al Moamar Company, Prime Computer's Middle East distributor, based in Dhahran, Saudi Arabia. Upon hearing news of this, Joe Kattar, who was always up front with me, phoned me with some advice I wasn't ready to hear:

"Chuckie, I don't want to see you get hurt any more than you already are. Why the Hell do you want to go back to the fucked up Middle East again? You had a terrible experience over there. Are you a glutton for punishment? If computer sales is your thing, why not ask Prime Computer to find you a job with them here in the states?"

134

Of course, Joe was right, but I just couldn't see it at the time. Highly 'money-driven' (which I'm happy to say I no longer am), opinionated, and headstrong, I went ahead and accepted the job. Several weeks later, I underwent a two-week sales training course at Prime Computer's headquarters in Natick Mass. Opting to give the oppressive summer heat of the Gulf a chance to subside, I asked Prime if I could wait until mid-September to report to work in the Gulf port city of Dhahran, where Prime's Middle East subsidiary was located. They checked with the Dhahran office and said this plan was fine with them.

Around eleven o'clock in the morning on August 18th, while I was peacefully drinking a cup of coffee in the kitchen of my parents' home, four Lawrence police officers knocked at the front door. My expectant mother let them in:

"We're here for Charles, mam," one of the cops said.

"I'm Charles, officer," I said. "Is there a problem here?"

Without a word of response or explanation, the cops then quickly grabbed hold of me, dragged me out of the house, and shoved me into the back seat of their cruiser:

"What the Hell is going on here? Is someone going to give me an explanation? What the Hell is going on here?" I shouted.

My only answer was the slam of the cruiser door. The police drove me to Holy Family Hospital (formerly Bon Secours) in Methuen. My mother meanwhile immediately followed us in her car.

I was greeted at the hospital emergency room by three large male orderlies - goons would be a more accurate word, who were clearly awaiting my arrival. Judging from their biceps, I knew where these guys spent their off-hours: Gold's Gym:

"Now is someone going to explain to me what is happening here?" I demanded.

Perhaps I didn't phrase the question correctly. The three muscular gentlemen carried me up three flights of stairs, my feet dragging behind me, to St. Dymphna's psychiatric ward, where Dr. Denapoli, head nurse Eleanor Lennon, and my mother were waiting to sign me in.

Yes, even though I hadn't seen or spoken with Denapoli since our initial encounter *three months earlier*, the doctor had evidently convinced my parents to have me "pink papered" for ten days in order to forcefully administer the lithium I wouldn't take voluntarily. I realized right then I had stepped on a landmine.

I later learned that my father's attorney - Iggy Piscitello, had been the one to process Denapoli's Section 12 commitment paperwork through the court system. I learned much later on that Denapoli had overcome my mother's initial objection to having me involuntarily hospitalized by convincing her that once I was in "treatment" for a few days, I would 'realize' I needed the lithium and go along with the program. I was subsequently confined against my will in the locked St. Dymphna's psychiatric ward for the next eight days.

The ward was a warren of small patients' rooms - all painted in the most baffling and nauseating shade of orange pink I've ever seen - surrounding a large open area that contained a nurse's station and a gathering area for patients. I can still recall that there were chains and padlocks covering the heavy screened windows.

During the day, patients attended various "groups," conducted in the open central area or in one of the smaller conference rooms. During the evening, they read books, watched TV, hung out, or paced the floor. The issues that were discussed in the group sessions had little or no bearing on my life. It was clear that my main purpose for being here was to be administered psychiatric medications in a "controlled setting" and to provide the hospital and Dr. Denapoli with a revenue source.

Incredibly, Dr. Denapoli refused to meet with me during my entire forced hospitalization. He simply ordered the staff to administer lithium three times a day. On the two or three occasions that I stood up for myself and refused the medication, a trio of orderlies grabbed me, held my mouth open, and physically forced the lithium down my throat like a dog being given antibiotics. In my opinion, this constitutes battery. Massachusetts mental health laws also hold this practice as expressly illegal. It occurs, however, with alarming regularity in psychiatric institutions.

Throughout the late morning and early afternoon of my first day of confinement at Holy Family, I frantically phoned at least a dozen relatives and close friends, using the ward's pay phone, and asked them to contact my father and get me released:

"Please try to reason with him. I need to get out of here."

These efforts proved fruitless, however. Dad's mind was closed on the matter. He refused to budge an inch. Clearly, Dr. Denapoli had gotten to him as well, brainwashing him into believing my health would seriously deteriorate without the prized lithium. As detailed earlier, my Dad, eight years now deceased, was an American - born, first generation, Lebanese American. He was an intelligent, energetic, outgoing, likeable, and happy-go-lucky guy. He was considered by all who knew him to be a good man, a trustworthy man. At the time, he worked as a City of Lawrence tax assessor.

On my second day of confinement, concluding that my father wasn't going to budge, I phoned a half-dozen local attorneys. Because they were all professionally acquainted with my father in his capacity as a city official, however, and respected him greatly, none were willing to "get involved."

A review of the Section 12 involuntary commitment document Denapoli drew up shows that he openly lied on it. He stated I was "suicidal" and "a danger to myself and others." Both of these claims were utterly baseless. On the ward, I was quite vocal about my displeasure at being there. I wasn't threatening or intensely agitated, but neither was I shy about expressing my resentment about my involuntary confinement to any staff member I happened to see.

About nine o'clock on the fourth night, the head nurse on duty, Denise Zappala, finally got tired of hearing me complain. Accordingly, she apprised me of the fact that I had a legal right to sign myself out of the hospital under a "three-day notice" provision. In other words, if I gave the hospital three days' advanced written warning, I could simply walk out on my own. That was my legal right. In a bizarre twist worthy of a Douglas Adams or Lewis Carroll novel, however, the three-day notice carried with it she further said the stipulation that I must first sign what is called a "conditional voluntary admission document."

"Let me get this straight," I said, "In order to leave the hospital because I was placed here involuntarily, I first have to claim that I came here voluntarily?"

"Essentially, that's correct," the nurse replied.

"Don't you see the humor in that?"

"It's the LAW Charles."

"But I didn't enter this place voluntarily, unless you consider being dragged out of your home by police and muscled into a locked ward by three goons a voluntary option"

"Listen, Charles, that's the way it is. The only way you're walking out of here in three days is if you sign the paper."

"You know where you can put that paper," I told her. "But it might not be of much use by the time you dig it out again."

In my mind, there was no way I was going to play along with such a farcical scenario. I hadn't entered the hospital voluntarily. To state in writing that I had would have been an outrage. One I thought might come back to haunt me in unexpected ways. Nurse Zappala finally got through to me, however; there was simply no way - none, that the hospital was going to permit me to sign myself out until I signed the conditional voluntary. With a sickening sense of moral surrender, I signed the paper. She, in turn, handed me the three-day notice. After I signed it, she told me that I was free to leave three days later.

I experienced dreadful humiliation when, on my fifth day of admission, my ex-college girlfriend, Lisa, who worked as a nurse in another department, walked into the psych ward to deliver some papers to the charge nurse and saw me there. This young gal who once held me in high regard now looked down on me with alarm and pity in her eyes.

"Chuckie, what the Hell are *you* doing in here?"

"Good question; ask the staff; they don't tell *me* anything."

We exchanged small talk, but it was clear we were not on equal footing. I could see it in her eyes and hear it in the way she carefully couched her questions. She had a respectable position at a respectable hospital, after all, and I had just been psychiatrically committed. She politely excused herself and wished me the best, backing out of the room with a look of awkward disdain in her eyes that I will never forget. It was a look I would soon be getting used to, however. Much to my dismay, and through no intention of my own, I haven't seen or heard from my ex-flame since.

On the afternoon of that same day, a representative from the Greater Lawrence Psychiatric Associates clinic, of which Denapoli was a co-owner, showed up and asked me to take a psychological test. Still reeling from being dragged from my home and locked up against my will, I told him to get lost. The gentleman refused to take no for an answer, however. I had to admire his tenacity. He hung around, pressuring and cajoling me, for over an hour. He eventually wore me down, and, just to get him the hell off my back, I finally gave in and agreed to take the damn test.

Because I approached the test in a rather refractory manner, however, I left many of the questions unanswered. In his notes, the tester cautions against placing too much credence on the results:

TESTER: ... "Mr. Ead was agitated throughout testing and at several points he insisted that he did not wish to continue. However, the examiner was able with persistent and mild pressure to get Mr. Ead to resume. ... Because of his agitation all throughout testing and his resistance to the very idea of being tested, test results should be viewed with care as they may not represent his optimal effort.

I later had the opportunity to review the background profile that accompanied the test report and was compiled and written by Denapoli. As With his Section 12, I found in it many glaring untruths. False reporting, I have discovered, is a massive and widespread problem within the mental health system. "Facts" are collected via hearsay, rumor, or second-hand information and entered in the patient's record. Then, if the client is transferred to another hospital, new records are derived from the original set and further distorted. Every subsequent stay at another hospital produces further distortions and exaggerations, on and on the down line.

Like photocopies made from photocopies made from photocopies, each iteration of the patient's records strays further from the original "truth." Falsehoods and speculations take on the weight of fact by being repeated and distorted multiple times in writing.

In my case, Denapoli wrote that I had been stopped by police on multiple occasions for excessive speeding. The truth is that I'd been stopped only once, and it was for going 80 miles an hour on a highway. Big Deal; not exactly a capital offense. Later records from other hospitals, building upon this initial falsehood, implied that I was a habitual offender on the road.

Denapoli also wrote that I was "fired from my job in Saudi Arabia." This was also untrue. I resigned, and I didn't work in Saudi, I worked in the UAE. His report stated that I was an only child. I have a brother and two sisters, as you know. If he had talked to me, I could have told him that.

And finally, here's where the falsehoods stop being mere annoyances and become truly libelous, Denapoli's report stated that while flying home from 'Saudi Arabia' (It was actually Abu Dhabi) in mid-May, my "manic-like behavior" caused the plane to make an "emergency landing" in Washington, D.C. The vastly less dramatic truth was that on a

141

return trip from Washington in late July to pick up my Prime Computer work visa from the Saudi Embassy, I vomited and the flight attendant escorted me to the back of the aircraft to help me clean up.

No manic-like behavior. No emergency landings. Lies and exaggerations in one's psych record can create the false illusion of a history of psychiatric disturbance, which affects the way you are treated down the line.

On the morning of the fourth day of my hospitalization, head nurse Lennon entered my room and fixed me with a stare. Uh-oh, I thought.

"Dr. Denapoli just called me. You're not going to like it." I groaned and awaited the details. "He found out that you signed the three-day note. He said to tell you that if you don't tear it up right now, guess where you're going."

"My guesses haven't been paying off too well lately. Enlighten me please."

She answered, "The Big House." I stared at her blankly. "Danvers State Hospital."

The words hung in the air like a death sentence. Everyone who'd grown up in northeastern Massachusetts knew that Danvers State Hospital was a psychiatric institution straight out of the pages of a gothic horror novel. Mere mention of the name triggered images of tall, barred windows, castle-like towers, medieval corridors, lobotomized patients, and screaming, drooling madmen - images which would later turn out to be pretty accurate. The Danvers threat was extortion, plain and simple, in order to just get me to go along with the program. The rules of the game were laid out plainly for me:

"If you don't want to go the Big House, you need to rescind your three-day notice immediately. So, it's either withdrawn the notice or go to a lock-up facility from which you can't sign out. Your choice. Either way, you're not going to walk."

It's funny but, thinking back, I remember that the doctor's ultimatum actually shocked me. At that time, I still believed the system to be essentially fair: if the law says a patient can sign out in three days, then the hospital must uphold that law. Period! Nope.

I have since learned that power plays aimed at defeating the spirit, if not the actual letter, of the law are as rampant in the mental health system as in any sleazy business enterprise. Maybe even more so. At least in business they don't smile and tell you it's for your own good. Unable to get in touch with Denapoli to verify his threat, I refused to know to either him or the charge nurse.

"Tell the good doctor he can send me to Hell if he wants. I'm not tearing up my three-day note!"

Denapoli's Danvers State threat proved, just as I suspected it was, to be a cheap bluff by an inept poker player.

On August 26th, the eighth day of my confinement, the three-day notice I had signed matured, and I was finally released from the hospital. I returned, shell-shocked and humiliated, to my parents' house.

A review of Denapoli's June 1988 affidavit to the court (I'll explain how I ended up in court later) indicates that the psychiatrist lied about the whole affair. As one example, Denapoli claimed that prior to his hospitalizing me at Holy Family, he saw me on two separate occasions at his office (May 17th and May

143

19th). An outright fabrication. I saw Denapoli only once at his office, on May 17th. There was no second visit. As a second example, Denapoli sheepishly tried to shift the responsibility for my hospitalization from himself onto to my parents:

DENAPOLI: ... "On August 18, 1982, the plaintiff's family arranged for him to be admitted to the psychiatric unit of the Holy Family Hospital."

If, as Denapoli claimed, my parents had arranged for me to be admitted to the hospital, why then did he have to prepare the Section 12 involuntary commitment papers? And come on, did my parents really think up the idea of putting me in the hospital all by themselves, or did Denapoli sell them on the

... "Patient had requested to leave A.M.A. (against medical advice) from the psychiatric unit. He had completed a three-day notice which expired on 8/26/82. Dr. Denapoli had a meeting with patient, Rose Ead, himself and social worker on 8/26/82. Dr. Denapoli explained to Charles and his mother his diagnosis of manic- depressive illness, his need for medication and further psychotherapy and his need for blood tests to evaluate his lithium level. Dr. Denapoli recommended that patient remain in the psychiatric unit for further therapy. Patient's mother Rose Ead refused to sign patient out against medical advice and went along with the doctor's recommendations. It was further explained by Dr. Denapoli to patient and his mother that the decision was Charles' as he is not committable." ...

Denapoli repeatedly misrepresented the truth in his medical records as well. In the Holy Family Discharge Summary, he claimed he had performed a "physical examination" of me while

144

I was in the hospital. Although I do recall the nurses drawing blood from my arm three or four times, most probably to check my lithium level, neither Denapoli himself nor anyone else at the hospital ever physically examined me. In fact, as mentioned earlier, he refused to even meet with me during the eight-day hospitalization. He refused to even look at me, never mind touch me.

The reason I'm so clear on this fact is that on three separate occasions I approached Denapoli on the ward as he was exiting his morning staff meetings with the nurses in the hope that he might explain to me why he had put me in the hospital. Each time I approached him however, he simply turned and walked away, shutting me out. I did not get a single second of the man's direct attention.

Another instance in which Denapoli's written statements don't jibe with the truth concerns the issue of how I was admitted to the hospital. He claimed in his September 15, 1982 Narrative Summary that I willingly entered the hospital, then gave my approval to being locked up:

DENAPOLI: ... "He was most reluctant to undergo psychiatric therapy but eventually agreed to be hospitalized at the Psychiatric Unit of the Holy Family Hospital."

Again, I was literally dragged from my home by policemen, then, a few days after my lock-up, coerced into signing a "conditional voluntary" agreement so that I could sign myself out of the hospital as expediently as possible.

Returning to Denapoli's Section 12 document, further lies are found there. He stated that he "personally examined me" just prior to forcibly hospitalizing me at Holy Family. As the records

145

corroborate, three full months went by between the one time I saw Denapoli at his office (May 17) and his pink-papering me (August 18). I did not see him prior to my hospitalization.

And finally, there is an alarming lack of specificity and substantiation in the psychiatrist's answer to the very important question on the Section 12 commitment papers:

"Evidence supporting my opinion as to why the involuntary hospitalization is necessary." Denapoli nebulously penned in: "Hypomanic behavior, resistive and argumentative (I didn't realize argumentativeness was a crime!), flight of ideas, delusions of grandiosity, depressed moods with suicidal preoccupations, severe impairment of judgment." Severe impairment of judgment about what doctor?

Nowhere in any of my hospital records does it ever state that I was suicidal. Because I wasn't. Not at all. There's no way that Denapoli can pin the report of "suicidal preoccupations" on my parents either. Here's an excerpt from my mother's April, 1987 affidavit:

ROSE EAD: … "Because I was concerned about his health, I took him with me to be examined by my psychiatrist, Jorge Denapoli of Andover, Mass. Charles had never been seen by Dr. Denapoli or any other psychiatrist before this. I did not feel that he was a danger to himself or anyone else. He was just sick."

There were simply no facts to support Denapoli's claim of "suicidal preoccupations." And what facts did he have to substantiate his "flight of ideas," "delusions of grandiosity," and "severe impairment of judgment" claims? None. The reason I am harping on this is that the hospital records that

146

originated with Dr. Denapoli became my active nemesis for a full decade of my life. Had these records been accurate, it is entirely likely that my life would have taken a different course.

The problem is *no one oversees the veracity of psychiatrists' records.* Anything a psychiatrist, nurse, or staff person chooses to say can and often does appear in your records as fact. These manufactured truths are later accepted as facts by other treatment teams and can have a snowballing effect on your credibility and perceived state of mind. My lifelong battles with the psychiatric profession began with Dr. Denapoli and the false impression he created by fabricating information in my records. To this day, I still deal with the fallout of that *one failed visit* with this man.

I cannot state this too forcefully: psychiatric records cannot be trusted. If you have ever had so much as one short stay in a psychiatric institution, my advice to you is this: obtain a copy of your medical records, as is your full legal right. What you find in there might very well surprise you. I can almost guarantee you will find falsehoods and/or unsubstantiated assumptions stated as fact. These falsehoods may be affecting your life in ways you don't understand.

Chapter 13:
My Second Hospitalization – Baldpate

Although I wasn't required to report to work in Saudi until mid-September, Denapoli's forced hospitalization prompted me to get away as soon as I could. On September 6th, about two weeks after my release from Holy Family I had my younger brother George drive me to Logan Airport. Right there on the spot, armed with the half-inch stack of paperwork I needed in order to get into the tourism-unfriendly Kingdom, I found and caught a flight to Dhahran, the port city on Saudi Arabia's northern coast where I'd be working.

About all I knew about Saudi Arabia back then was that it was hot, - very hot, and that public beheadings over minor crimes still took place there. Oh well, that didn't deter me. It couldn't be much worse than what I'd just been through. At least not in my mind at the time.

As the plane pushed through the dense cloud cover blanketing Boston and burst out into clear blue, open sky, my face and shoulder muscles un-knotted and my blood pressure dropped. I felt as if I was escaping the States with my life and sanity. My breathing became easy for the first time in weeks. Not many people leave the United States in search of freedom in Saudi Arabia. But I did.

After some hours of peaceful movie watching and magazine reading, I nodded off and slept like a contented cat. The rough landing awoke me from sleep, and I had to shake my head to remember where I was. Saudi Arabia. Yikes. Okay, time to get on with *your life, Chuck.* This time I knew what to expect with the climate and with my own physical limitations, and I was determined to make this situation work.

148

The cab ride through Dhahran to my apartment was not auspicious. Though I spoke some Arabic, the driver evidently did not. I found this very strange, since Saudi Arabia does not encourage visitors and certainly does not have an open-door policy with regard to immigration. To this day I don't know what language he was speaking.

If it was Arabic, it was a dialect I did not know existed. What I did know was that the car's air conditioner was broken and that the driver was sorely in need of a bath. And in a country that possessed a quarter of the world's oil reserves, the car ironically seemed to be down a quart; the pistons in the engine rattled and banged. The cab noisily wound its way through the well-maintained and highly presentable main streets, and then through more questionable backstreet neighborhoods, where dark alleys yawned and suspicious female eyes glared from under hooded, black cloaks and hijabs.

As I stated earlier, Prime Computer had promised me suitable living quarters when I accepted the job, I was careful to insist on that point. But my third-floor, two-room, walk-up apartment turned out to be a tiny, stuffy, ill-smelling shithole, complete with cockroaches and filth flies. The term "deferred maintenance" jumped instantly to mind. The miniscule kitchen was practically unusable, the air conditioner was on its last gasps, the water in both the sink and the rattletrap toilet was brown, and the bedroom had no windows but that didn't seem to prevent swarms of mosquitoes from finding their way in.

But Hell, the place was my own and I would not complain. I supposed with time, attention, and a good deal of spending, I could make it livable. It certainly was not a very cheerful Start Space for the new game of Life I was about to begin playing. My first few nights in Dhahran were marked by grave misgivings, intense perspiration, and military-level insect attacks. After a few mornings, I looked like the "didn't use product" picture in a Cutter's Deep Forest Insect Repellent commercial.

I gave myself a week to become acclimated to my new "home" and then sought out my new employer. Happily, the offices of Prime Computer's Middle East subsidiary - Al Moammar Company, were more promising-looking than my apartment. They were clean, fully air conditioned, and fairly modern and spacious. I was welcomed warmly enough upon my arrival by my new boss, an Englishman, and by my fellow salespeople, a couple of whom were British as well. Perhaps I would make a few friends here and soon be on my way to making good money as I had planned. Things were looking up.

I had barely begun work, though, when the climate conditions once again began to affect my physical health. Because of my busy work schedule, I was constantly forced to shuffle back and forth between the humid outside weather and my air-conditioned car and office - in-out, in -out; hot - cold, hot - cold. The Saudi desert climate was oppressively clammy, just as had the UAE climate had been. I had thought that by staying hydrated and avoiding strenuous exercise, I could avoid the worst of its effects. I was distressed to learn that I had gravely miscalculated. I earnestly hoped my bad reaction was an adjustment phase that would soon pass.

To my great dismay, just three weeks after my arrival in Dhahran, my health condition began to unravel quickly. Specifically, I began experiencing aching joints and muscles; shooting pains in my arms, lower back, and chest; and throbbing headaches - real whoppers. Also, my head felt as if it was filled with thick fluid that was clouding my thinking process to the extent that I couldn't process and absorb the new information my job required me to learn. Moreover, my skin and head became unbearably itchy, and my energy level began to wane again.

On or about September 22nd, I phoned Dad and told him I was in trouble and needed his immediate help to get back home. At his recommendation, I phoned Mr. Louis Zraket - a close friend of his who was then general manager of a Saudi electronics company in the west-coast, Red Sea port city of Jeddah - across the desert and some 1,500 miles away from where I was residing:

"Mr. Zraket, I'm sorry to impose on you like this but I feel quite terrible," I told him. I proceeded to catalog my ailments. Zraket didn't even wait for me to finish:

"Charlie, I just talked to my good friend - your father, over the phone. He's very worried about you and asked me to check you out. So, I want you to fly here to Jeddah right away and spend the upcoming three-day Muslim Haag holiday at my house with me and my family."

Realizing I was in trouble and feeling quite desperate, I agreed to do so. I didn't know what good such a visit would do, but at least it was a plan. And so, the following day, I flew across the Saudi desert to Jeddah on a flight Zraket had booked for me. When Zraket greeted me upon my arrival at the expansive and modern Jeddah Airport, I was so sick I could barely hold my head up.

Zraket lived in a lovely condo on the Red Sea waterfront and was gracious and welcoming, as were his wife and adopted teen age son. Sadly, they were all forced to watch me pace around their house like a shooting gallery target and scratch myself raw during the remainder of my arrival day. By the third day of this, their graciousness had begun to wear thin:

"Chuckie, I can see there is something seriously wrong with you," said Zraket. "Your father and I spoke over the phone just a few minutes ago. He's even more worried about you now than he was before. We both feel it's best for you to return to the U.S. and get medically evaluated as soon as possible."

I hated the idea of admitting defeat, but I realized Zraket was right; there was something seriously wrong with my health. After being assured by my father in a phone conversation from Zraket's home that I'd be allowed to stay at his house and seek a proper medical workup without his or Denapoli's interference, I decided to return home.

Zraket graciously lobbied his Saudi superior, who, coincidentally, was a cousin of the owner of the company I was working for, to intervene on my behalf and have my two-year work contract terminated. Zraket then got me on a plane back to Dhahran and the next day instructed his nephew, Issa K., whom I knew and who worked at the Dhahran Airport, to pick me up at my apartment and make sure I got on a plane headed for home. I was so ill, I don't think I could have pulled it off without Zraket and Issa's angel-like assistance.

After an exhausting and seemingly endless eighteen-hour flight, I arrived back in the U.S. Dad was waiting for me at Logan and drove me home. During the ride, he told me that after I had phoned him for help during my final week in Saudi, he had done some checking around with his golf friends at the Indian Ridge course in Andover.

"Chuck," my Dad said, "I hit upon this guy, a Dr. Kenneth Emonds. He's a highly regarded physician in Lawrence. One of the guys even called him a miracle worker. I think Emonds can be a major help to you with your medical problems."

152

Still reeling from the Denapoli fiasco a month earlier, while repeatedly assured by Dad that Emonds wasn't involved with psychiatry in any way, I agreed to give the guy a shot.

During the first week of October, I met with Emonds in his modest office, located on the fourth floor of a six-story medical building in Lawrence - a far cry from Denapoli's plush Andover office. Framed degrees from some sort of institute hung on the wood-paneled wall. I wanted to get a better look at them, but politeness prevented me from walking up close and staring at them. They might have been from McDonald's Hamburger University for all I knew.

Emonds was an impressive figure - tall and well-dressed, with wild, curly black hair and a polite but serious demeanor. Right after he shook my hand and introduced himself to me, I asked him if he was in any way involved with psychiatry. He assured me he wasn't. Satisfied, I proceeded to detail the health complaints I had experienced in Abu Dhabi and then later in Saudi.

I also detailed, reluctantly, my dealings with psychiatrist Denapoli as well as my forced sojourn at his hands at the Holy Family psych ward. I went on to make it clear that I didn't agree with Denapoli's manic depressive diagnosis and subsequent forced treatment. Emonds responded by saying:

"Oh, I'm in total agreement with you, Charles. I hope that ordeal hasn't left a 'bad taste' in your mouth."

Following our discussion, Emonds gave me allergy tests, drew blood, and took a urine specimen. Next, after telling me my skin was jaundiced and that I might have a liver problem, he instructed me to undress from the waist up and lie on his examination table. I promptly obliged. He methodically worked

153

his hands over my abdomen, feeling to see if my liver was swollen. He told me it was. After finishing up his exam, Emonds instructed me to return to his office in a week to discuss the results of the workup.

One week later, I met with the new doctor for the second time. "The blood test you took, Charles, evidenced a very high *kryptopyrrole* level, which confirms my suspicion that you indeed have a liver infection. Your skin jaundice is caused by a liver problem. Your liver is so infected right now, in fact, that it can't break down wheat, sugar, and yeast. Whenever you eat these foods, you toxify and poison your body."

He paused to let me digest this information, then continued:

"Adding to this, the heavy running you were doing in the high-heat/high- humidity climate of the Persian Gulf caused dehydration and a depletion of your vital body minerals. This has stressed out your body. That's why you've been feeling so weak. To remedy this, I'm placing you on a "wheat-, milk-, and sugar-elimination diet. I also want you to take a regimen of 'megavitamins' to replenish your body chemistry."

The vitamins he listed for me included B-6, super B, zinc, insurance formula, folic acid, calcium-magnesium complex, vitamin C, lecithin, and L-tryptophan. His nutritional approach made more sense to me than Denapoli's snap bipolar diagnosis had, so I decided to give Emonds' treatment program a shot.

Although my father had told me Emonds was a top-notch physician, I found out during my third or fourth office visit in late November that he wasn't even a licensed M.D. I became concerned about Emond's medical background when I found out, to my outrage, that he had instructed my father, without my knowledge, to mix lithium tablets (prescribed by his associate, Dr. O'Shea, a pediatrician) with the megavitamins I was taking. Lithium was the anti-bipolar drug Denapoli had forced me to take.

When I confronted Emonds about both the lithium and his background, he told me he was a dissatisfied former police officer who, by going to school nights, had earned his Doctor of Psychology degree just two years earlier. Psychology? This after denying that he was in any way associated with psychiatry? Technically, psychiatry and psychology are different, but it sure seemed like hair-splitting to me. Emonds went on to detail that taking additional courses in orthomolecular medicine and nutrition had gotten him, in his words, a "great job" treating hyperactive and behaviorally troubled children nutritionally in the office of his associate, pediatrician Dr. James O'Shea.

After my traumatizing experience with Denapoli, the discovery that Emonds had been dishonest as well, greatly unnerved me and shook my confidence in both the psychologist and my father. Shaking it even further was the fact that four weeks of this diet/megavitamin treatments hadn't gotten me feeling any better. I had faithfully stayed on the diet and taken all of the megavitamins as prescribed, but I actually felt significantly worse than when I had begun this experimental treatment plan a month earlier:

"Doctor, this business of giving me lithium behind my back is demeaning and way out of line. And you're not even a licensed M.D. I'm sorry, but I won't be coming back here anymore."

His reaction shocked me. The polite and even-tempered "doctor" morphed instantly into the tough and grizzled street cop:

155

"Hey, look it kid, if you don't want to continue with our program here you're going to have to go back in the psych hospital. Got that buddy boy?"

Wow, where did Dennis Franz come from?

That same day, Emonds followed up by phoning my father and blasting me out behind my back. This really ticked me off. What right did he have to violate the confidence of our doctor-patient relationship and discuss my health condition with my father? Was he my doctor or my father's doctor? This was turning out to be a sad replay of the Denapoli fiasco. My father, still believing the policeman-turned-night-school-shrink knew what he was doing, tried desperately to get me to reverse my decision:

"Chuckie, you haven't done what the doctor told you to. You've been off your diet, and your health isn't getting any better. Your mother and I want you to keep seeing Dr. Emonds. We want you to stay on the diet and to keep taking the lithium and the vitamins."

Dad was trying to contain his irritation, but it was leaking out of him. Two weeks later, Emonds showed that his threat of re-hospitalizing me was no bluff. Around three o'clock in the afternoon on or around December 21st, my father and Iggy Piscitello, the lawyer, drove up to my parents' house together in the esquire's beach wagon. After entering quietly through the front door, the two men converged on me. Then, with the help of my misdirected Lebanese-born first cousin - Nadim, who was visiting my mother at our house, the three men muscled me (still very weak), outside and shoved me into the back seat of Piscitello's late model station wagon. As if to justify his actions, as we exited the front door, Nadim, who was about my age, uttered in a loud voice,

156

"What's this, an MBA sitting at home?"

"What's going on here, Dad?" I then asked in horror. "Where are you taking me?"

"We're headed to Baldpate Hospital, son. Dr. Emonds ordered this."

I'd had heard of Baldpate but didn't know much about it. For one thing, I did not know it was a private psychiatric hospital. As soon as we arrived there some thirty minutes later, Iggy got out of his car and walked up to a well-dressed, middle-aged man who was standing outside and seemed to be awaiting our arrival. After conversing briefly with Piscitello, the man marched inside. Ten minutes later, he came back out, accompanied by three huge male orderlies. I guess large male orderlies come in threes. They approached Iggy's car, yanked me out of the back seat and dragged me into the hospital. My father and his attorney immediately followed us inside.

Baldpate consisted of a handful of modest-sized red clapboard buildings situated on a rustic hundred-acre lot in upscale, rural Georgetown, Mass. With its rolling hills and stately pines, it housed about sixty patients, most of whom were free to roam the grounds. If you had to get your head shrunk, there were worse places to end up, I supposed. But still, the stubborn fact remained that there was nothing at all wrong with my mind! After my father and Piscitello signed me in, I was placed in a locked, windowless room with two other male patients. I asked the younger of the two why he had been put in the hospital.

"Oh friend! I just shot a state trooper dead "because he tried to write me a ticket on 495 north," he said with a twinkle in his eye. "Why are YOU in here?"

I answered him in kind, "I shot the judge to death who committed me here - along with his whole family."

"Oh! I think this is going to be the beginning of a great friendship." He said.

The other patient in the room, meanwhile, kept confidently asserting he was Napoleon Bonaparte. I thought that only happened in 1960s sitzoms. After what seemed like hours of waiting in the room with these two gentlemen, I was taken by an orderly to the small residential room that I was to share with a gaunt, seemingly saner fellow whose name I never learned.

Late the following morning, after I asked about a half-dozen times, the head nurse on duty finally granted me permission to make a telephone call. As soon as she handed me the phone, I called Emonds to find out why he had put me in the hospital. The ex-cop told me that because I didn't make myself "amenable" to his treatment program he had "no choice" but to re-hospitalize me. When I voiced displeasure with this answer, the psychologist quickly hung up on me.

Was this America, with our guaranteed Bill of Rights, or was I still in Saudi Arabia?

A review of Emonds' Section 12 commitment paper indicates that in response to the question asking for evidence supporting the commitment opinion, he listed: "Hod tests, Manve Factor Analysis, Absolute Basophil Count." Many years ago I asked a couple of top internists at world-renowned Mass. General Hospital about the tests Emonds performed on me. Both internists emphatically told me they'd never heard of the tests and called them "bogus."

On the third day of my confinement at Baldgate, I met for about twenty minutes with staff psychiatrist Patrick Quirke, who was in charge of my care. Quirke was a bald, flabby, well-dressed man of about fifty:

"I don't belong in here, Doctor. I'm physiologically, not psychiatrically, ill."

"You're gravely mistaken, son," he replied, his arms folded over his ample belly. "Your previous bipolar diagnosis is both correct and final."

When I told Quirke I didn't agree, he retorted that my repeated "denial" of being psychiatrically ill actually indicated a lack of insight into my condition. And because "lack of insight" was one of the symptoms of bipolar disorder, my denial of having the illness "evidenced" that I was, in fact, suffering from it.

During the course of my intensive research into psychiatry, I have learned that such circular logic has been rampant in the mental health business for centuries. It is the exact same logic that was used by the Catholic Church for punishing heretics during the Spanish Inquisition: Refuse to admit you're a heretic and we'll you torture you to death on the rack; admit you're a heretic and hey, guess what, you get the rack too.

Quirke's repeated ignoring of my legitimate organic complaints and discharge requests left me feeling frustrated and helpless. He refused to let me sign myself out of the hospital because it was the middle of winter and I had no place to stay. My father, you see, had made it clear to me that he would refuse to allow me back into his house if I signed myself out of all of my relatives and friends to refuse me shelter as well.

It became crystal clear to me that both my parents had bought into the false psychiatric narrative a hundred percent, and in so doing had become *part of the problem*, not *part of the solution*. Don't get me wrong. Mom and Dad are basically wonderful people. They've been nothing but loving and supportive throughout my life. I couldn't have asked for better parents. And I knew even then that they were acting out of love and had my best interests in mind. But they were simply wrong.

Their mistake was holding psychiatrists in too high esteem and believing all members of the medical profession to be divinely ordained, incapable of making even the slightest mistake. In my parents' world view, there was no real option but to go along with "the experts."

What I learned from my ordeal is that doctors put their pants on one leg at a time, just like the rest of us and that they bleed red like we do too. No human being is infallible. As my older sister Marion - a registered nurse who works for the Massachusetts Board of Medicine, a state agency that disciplines errant physicians - repeatedly tells me, doctors, nurses, and, especially, psychiatrists do in fact make mistakes and make them more often than you would think.

On the morning of January 7, 1983, my cousin Nadim broke protocol with Dad and phoned me at the hospital and generously offered to let me stay with him, his new wife Houda his brother Assad, and his sister Christine in their first floor, Warren Street, Lawrence apartment. Immediately upon learning of this positive development, I walked over to the nurse's station, told the head nurse I had secured a place to live, and signed a three-day notice requesting my release from the hospital. Three days later, immediately following my official discharge. Nadim and his younger brother Assad picked me up in Nadim's car and brought me to their apartment.

During the first few months I lived with Nadim and his family, I was sick as a dog and never could get myself well. I was so tired, I usually slept till mid-afternoon. To their credit,

160

my cousins never bothered me and let me sleep as much as I wanted to. I still had the skin-rich problem, too, and experienced recurring pain in my muscles and joints, along with frequent vertigo and headaches. My arms and legs were so weak, I couldn't even lift a shovel to help my cousins clear their driveway following an early February snowstorm.

In late March, when the weather broke, I was eager to contribute financially to the household, so I reached out to a contact at city hall and got a job with the City of Lawrence Parks and Property Department. Because Bill Foley, the Superintendent of Parks and a good friend of mine who I worked out with at the Y, knew I was in poor health, he assigned me the token job of sweeping up and cleaning the city barn. An MBA graduate, I swallowed my pride and gratefully accepted it. At the end of my first week, though, seeing I was too debilitated to handle even this easy menial job, Foley confronted me:

"Charlie, you're sick kid. You're going to get yourself hurt around here. Take some time off and get yourself well, okay? I hate to do this, but I'm going to have to let you go."

It's one thing to *accept* a garage-sweeping job when you have an MBA degree; it's another to lose that job because you can't handle it. Cousin Nadim, seeing that I was too sick to work and earn any money, didn't ask any room and board money from me. He did make it a condition of my staying with him however, (per the strong-arming of my father who was providing him with part-time work in his tax preparation business), that I begin seeing psychologist Emonds again.

I initially refused to go along with this, but Nadim refused to budge. And he held all the cards. Needing to keep a roof over my head in the middle of winter, I ate crow, did as Nadim insisted, and reluctantly placed myself under the ex-policeman's care again.

Emonds once again treated me with megavitamins. My cousin Christine - Nadim's older sister, and a senior college student at the time, as was Nadim, and who was living with us, oversaw my medications and dutifully gave me the assortment of vitamins at the appropriate time every day. Emonds also mixed in lithium carbonate (with my knowledge this time; I couldn't do anything about it) in order to "control my bipolar disorder."

Because Emonds was only a psychologist and wasn't medically licensed to prescribe medication, he went ahead and forged his associate Dr. O'Shea's name on the lithium prescriptions he gave me. Was this legal? I seriously suspected not. But at that point psychiatry had taken control over my life, like a third world dictator. I could only march to its commands. Emonds also arranged for me to get periodic blood tests at Lawrence General Hospital so he could monitor my 'lithium level.'

On the plus side, because I didn't have to work, I was able to stay home and get a lot of sleep. As the spring arrived, I began to feel stronger by the day. By the first of May, my jaundice had cleared up and I felt strong enough to start swimming at the Y. Maybe, I started to think, this megavitamin thing was working and wasn't a snake oil remedy after all?

Nadim, seeing that my health was rapidly improving, approached me one afternoon in the kitchen, pulled a C-note out of his pocket and handed it to me.

"Cousin, I know you've been feeling better and getting out of the house a little more lately. Take this for some spending money while you're out and don't worry about paying me back."

Nadim was known by the family as a person who "played every angle." In fact, he once told Dad,

"Uncle Fred, what you consider to be "illegal" America, we consider to be "smart" in Lebanon."

But say what you will about Nadim, he had a heart of gold and he came up big for me that winter.

My mother would occasionally come over to Nadim's house and visit my cousins and me. It seemed that nearly every time she did so, she would say the same thing:

"Chuckie, Dr. Denapoli told me again that you still belong in the hospital!"

And my feelings of safety and peace of mind would melt away like snow in April.

Then in late May, Nadim, who was the only one in the household working (and only part-time at that), got laid off from his contract job. This came at a bad time as his wife Houda was just about to give birth to their first child. My first cousin, seeing that my health had markedly improved, asked me if I would be willing to help him out by returning home and living with my parents again.

Because of the deep animosity I had built up toward my parents due to their role in my two previous hospitalizations and their zeal to see me iv long-term psychiatric treatment, the last thing I wanted to do was move back in with them. But what other choice did I have? Nadim wouldn't budge. It was either that or live on the streets. My back was to the wall again.

After some heated debate with Nadim, I received the blessing of my father and very reluctantly moved back in with my parents. Unlike other mistakes that I had made in the past, this one was forced upon me. I made the move knowing full well that I was walking right into a live hornet's nest.

Chapter 14:
My Third Hospitalization

Danver State- The Holy Family Again

Late in the afternoon on May 26th, about two weeks after I had moved back home, I predictably became embroiled in an argument with my mother about whether or not I needed to be hospitalized. My physical symptoms - the scratching, the tiredness, and the irritability that went along with them - were still somewhat of a problem. Needless to say, this was affecting my highly confused mother negatively.

Shortly after the argument, I passed out on the kitchen floor. Yes, my knees went out from under me like a tired boxer's and my cheek smacked into the linoleum. My mother then put in a frantic call to my father at his city hall office. Dad immediately called Dr. Emonds.

Fifteen minutes later, *four* Lawrence police officers burst through the front door like a band of Navy Seals, and made their way in. *Jeez, why didn't they call in the SWAT team, too?* After checking in with Emonds via the kitchen phone, the officers converged on me and without explanation, muscled me to the ground, then cuffed my hands behind my back.

The quartet, apparently had been given their marching orders by Emonds. The cops then dragged me, handcuffed, and out the front door and then without a word of explanation shoved me into the back seat of one of their two cruisers which were parked in front of our house. I was then driven to the Lawrence General Hospital emergency room, where Emonds and my father were anxiously awaiting our arrival. After taking

164

a cursory look at me, the ex-cop excused himself, leaving my father and me alone in a treatment cubicle. I complained to Dad that the handcuffs were severely hurting my wrists but he took no action to have them removed.

After about an hour, Emonds returned and informed us that the only psych hospital that had a bed available was the dreaded, medieval Danvers State Hospital. After mulling this fact over for a few seconds, my father, if you can even believe it, gave the psychologist the green light to go ahead and commit me there.

Just as Emonds had forged pediatrician O'Shea's name on the lithium prescriptions, he also penned O'Shea's name on the Sectional 12 commitment papers. Not only is this unethical, but I am certain it is illegal too, and possibly criminal as I was never evaluated by Dr. O'Shea. In fact, to this day, I've never even met the man. After signing the commitment order, Emonds finally agreed to have the painful handcuffs, which were causing my wrists to bleed, removed. About thirty minutes later, I was strapped down with thick leather bindings by a pair of hospital orderlies and transported in a van directly to the state facility.

Danvers State was a setting right out of a horror movie. (In fact, after the main building closed in the mid-1980s, at least one horror movie, *Session 9*, was shot there.) It was a sprawling, gothic, red-brick affair, complete with towering spires and tall, barred windows with ornate cornices. Known alternately as The Castle, The Castle on the Hill, The Big House, and The Witch's Castle, Danvers was a place of lore and legend. It was reputed to have served as the inspiration for some of influential horror writer H.P. Lovecraft's fictional asylum references. Unruly local children, at least in my childhood anyway, were commonly threatened by parents and teachers with a trip to The Witch's Castle to keep them in line.

Built in the late 19th century, Danvers had been in business from the days of "moral treatment," through the degrading "snake pit" era and the days of hydrotherapy, electric shock therapy (still in use when I was there), insulin shock therapy, and psychosurgery, right up to the modern, more "humane," medication-driven 1980s.

The locked ward on which I was placed was situated on the third floor of a five-story building. Bleak, gloomy, and dungeon-like, it housed about sixty beds. These were lined up in rows of ten on either side of a long corridor that split the ward in two. At the front end of the ward was the staff room and nurse's station. Adjacent to that was a cold, prison-like toilet and shower room and a padded solitary confinement room into which the staff threw patients who gave them any trouble. I saw this practice played out within twenty minutes of my arrival. A strong stench of body odor permeated the ward. No one seemed to notice though.

The ward was inhabited largely by the most "hopelessly hopeless" of the mentally ill. As an example, immediately upon arrival, I saw a male patient openly masturbating in the middle of the room. No one on staff made any attempt to deal with this. An elderly female patient licked the floor while muttering a prayer. An old gentleman cruised up and down the ward acting like a tractor with a bad piston, while a middle-aged woman cried out to Jesus for forgiveness, then cut loose with a chain of obscenities that are still etched in my memory.

Many of these poor souls were long-term veterans of the mental health system and had been institutionalized most of their lives. Several of the older patients later confided to me that they had undergone lobotomies in the late Fifties/early Sixties. How, I asked myself, was anyone supposed to become mentally and emotionally healthy in such a fucking place? The concept was ludicrous.

After spending three days at Danvers State, I was transferred to the psych ward of Holy Family Hospital - St. Dymphna's, the place where Dr. Denapoli had first hospitalized me. I was grateful and elated to be out of Danvers, but still craved my freedom. Immediately upon arrival at St. D's, I signed a three-day notice to initiate my discharge. Because Dr. Denapoli, citing a lack of compliance on my part, refused to treat me there again, staff psychiatrist Ibrahim Bahrawy was delegated by the hospital to oversee my care.

Late in the morning of the following day, Dr. Bahrawy - a short, well-built, middle-aged man with a graying mustache and thick glasses, came into my room and introduced himself. This act of professionalism was at least more than Denapoli had displayed on the same ward a year earlier:

"Hello, Charles. I'm your treating clinician."

I immediately noticed his Arabic accent. Vaguely hoping we might share a bond, I asked him where he was from, and he told me he was originally from Egypt:

"Well, I'm Arabic, doctor, just like you."

Seemingly unimpressed, Bahrawy performed a cursory eyes-ears-and-throat exam, sat down beside me, and gave me a half-wince, half-smile. He then pulled my three-day notice from his yellow notepad. "Why did you sign this, Charles?"

"Doctor, I earned an accounting degree from college and an MBA from Business School," I said, trying to give him some essential background on myself. "And nothing was handed to me. My parents didn't have much money so, I had to work my way through school. I've had a job since I was fourteen years old. I think I have done well in life. I've been responsible and come up the hard way. (At the time, I viewed the need for mental health treatment as a form of moral failure; my views on this have since evolved). I don't feel I belong in this place. I need a different brand of medical care than what you're providing and so I'm leaving the day after tomorrow to find some."

I then detailed to the psychiatrist the snowballing treatment mistakes that had begun when Dr. Denapoli had misdiagnosed my organic ills as manic depression a year earlier. (Bahrawy failed to reveal to me that Denapoli was his business partner in a private psychiatric clinic. I didn't learn of this until years later when I obtained and reviewed my medical records.)

Bahrawy interjected sharply:

"What would you do, Charlie, if I was to release you from the hospital?"

"I'm glad you asked, Doctor. I'll tell you exactly what I would do. A week before my hospitalization, I had an interview with the Martin Marietta Corporation. They were impressed with my background and want to fly me down to their Orlando, Florida headquarters in mid-June for a second interview. They have me in mind for a marketing analyst position there. Accepting the job would require me to relocate to Florida. I view this as a welcome opportunity to get away from the Lawrence area where, thanks to my recent psychiatric experiences, I just don't feel happy or comfortable living anymore." Bahrawy cut me short:

"I was told you have been in conflict with your parents and disruptive in your behavior while living at their house."

"Yes, Doctor, I have been in conflict with my mother and father. I was not aware this was illegal or anyone else's business."

168

I felt anger boiling up inside and took a deep breath:

"The reason for the conflict is that they have allowed this psychiatric thing to be shoved down my throat. They have unwittingly been party to a transgression of my rights and to my humiliation in front of all my relatives and friends. Our relationship was always a good and healthy one, Doctor, but it's been ruptured by the fact that they refuse to listen to how I feel. When I complain about my forced treatment, my father responds by such saying things like:

"Don't be ashamed of being a manic depressive, son, Winston Churchill was one too."

"He doesn't get it. No one does. Manic depression is a faulty diagnosis that was made prematurely by a third-rate psychiatrist who didn't even medically examine me. Now my psychiatric history has snowballed and taken on a life of its own."

Bahrawy stared at me with a practiced mask of patience under which his irritation was clearly visible. I went on. "I couldn't relax around my parents, Doc. Every time the doorbell rang, I was afraid it would be the police coming to haul me away again." I further informed the doctor that the high level of tension in the house due to my parents' longstanding financial and marital difficulties was only adding to the problem and told him that at the time of my third "incarceration" a week earlier, they were not even speaking to each other.

"Please don't judge a book by its cover Doctor. There's much more here than meets the eye."

The staff psychiatrist quickly shot back:

"I don't care about your parents' problems. They don't have anything to do with your being in the hospital. You have a 'chemical imbalance' in your brain. That's your problem, not them."

169

When I began to disagree, Bahrawy cut me short:

"Look, I don't want to talk about this crap anymore, OK?"

Still believing I could get Bahrawy to see the complexities of the situation, I explained to him that my parents' focus on my health issues was their way of imposing some structure on their chaotic lives. I told him my predicament was worsened by the fact that the physical symptoms I was suffering prevented me from being able to work or exercise on a regular basis. Running had always served as a great way for me to vent my frustrations and maintain a healthy frame of mind.

With regard to the work issue, psychologists have long recognized the unhealthy effects on a person's frame of mind when he's sick and out of work for a long time. Dr. McLaughlin - the head of the psychology department at Merrimack College, my alma mater, explained it to me this way when I yearn later talked to him about it:

"Typically," McLaughlin said, "The individual caught in this situation gets frustrated, disgruntled and resentful because he feels that through no fault of his own, he's lost control of both his identity and his destiny in life. Furthermore," the professor explained, "not working and being productive deprives the unemployed person of experiencing a sense of self-respect, self-esteem and self-worth, which he needs to feel good about himself.

"And because the individual caught in this snare often has idle time on his hands to think, he tends to overly focus on his predicament. This devil's brew of negative psychological variables often causes the out-of-work person to become over-anxious, on edge, and anxiety prone." Along these same lines, the American Psychologist magazine essay, "The Psychological and Social Effects of Unemployment" notes:

... "Work in America is the means whereby a person is tested as well as identified. It's the way a youngster becomes an adult. Work shapes the thoughts and the life of the worker. For most of us in adult life, being out of work is not living. ... Unemployed workers typically experience considerable tension, anxiety about the future, and feelings of resentment. ... And there is good evidence that losing one's job can increase health risks, exacerbate chronic and latent disorders, alter usual patterns of health seeking, and exact numerous other social and interpersonal costs."

I told Bahrawy that given the present conditions of my life - the chronic illness, the unemployment, the constant fear of being re-hospitalized, the lack of having my own space, the financial and emotional turmoil of my parents, and the feeling of suffocation and insecurity - it was only human that I'd be on edge and prone to occasionally flaring up. It wasn't as if I'd assaulted or threatened my parents. I had simply expressed verbal anger and frustration.

Proof that it was my living situation - not a mental condition that was causing my occasional flare-ups was the fact that my behavior had been completely calm during the five months I had lived with my cousin Nadim and his family. Getting the stiff-necked psychiatrist to see my side of the story, however, was like trying to teach an elephant to do the chicken dance. No matter what I said, it just went in one ear and out the other:

"The resentment you exhibited towards your parents is not a justified reaction to their allowing you to be hospitalized, but instead a *symptom of your illness*."

"What illness are you talking about, Doctor?"

171

"Manic depressive illness (bi-polar disorder, a chemical imbalance in your brain); that's what you have."

Bahrawy then said that because my condition required the administration of mood-stabilizing and brain-altering medication, he was placing me on lithium and Thorazine, a powerful antipsychotic. He concluded by telling me that because this medication had to be administered in a controlled environment (why I couldn't take this medication as an out-patient, however, was never explained), I needed to remain hospitalized"

"I don't agree that I have manic depressive illness or a fucking chemical imbalance in my brain doctor; that's all bullshit. So, I am going to leave the hospital as soon as my three-day notice matures."

Bahrawy fixed me with a "don't screw with me" stare and firmly stated:

"I'm letting you know now that I'm going to do everything in my power young man, to prevent that from happening!"

Chapter 15:
My Sham Guardianship Hearing

"Don't worry son. You'll get your trial, and then you're going to hang"

– A judge to a young client of attorney Abraham Lincoln's.

I soon found out that Bahrawy meant what he said. The following morning, Holy Family attorney Clifford Elias marched into Lawrence District Court and filed a petition for civil commitment. He also requested, and was granted, an *ex-parte* order making my father my emergency temporary guardian. This prevented me from signing myself out of the hospital until a formal commitment hearing could be conducted.

That same day, my father's attorney, Iggy Piscitello, filed a petition in probate court requesting that my father be appointed my temporary legal guardian for ninety days. As legal guardian, Dad would be given full authority to govern my medical treatment. This conferred a wide range of powers on him. He could confine me to a psychiatric facility involuntarily as well as approve the administration of antipsychotic medication against my wishes. I learned all of this indirectly, of course, via phone calls and staff communications. Clearly, this thing was taking on a life of its own and heating up fast.

The day after Piscitello filed the petition, Lawrence attorney Philip Byers, another close friend of my father's, was appointed by the probate court to serve as *guardian ad litem*. His duty in this capacity was to conduct an investigation of the whole process and detail his findings to the probate judge on

173

the day of the hearing. Byers' Guardian-Ad-Litem report states that he interviewed me, my parents, Dr. Emonds, Dr. O'Shea, Dr. Bahrawy, head nurse Debra Lennon, hospital attorney Elias, and friend Joseph Kattar, who adamantly believed, as the psychiatrists did, that I was suffering from manic depression.

Did he really need to interview all these folks, especially Dr. O'Shea, who had never laid eyes on me? Hell, why didn't he interview the four Lawrence police officers who had handcuffed me and dragged me out of my parent's house a month earlier too?

On June 4th, Byers did come to the Holy Family Hospital to interview me, as was his legal duty. Unfortunately, because I was so heavily medicated, I couldn't communicate effectively with him. I barely remember the interview at all. Byers acknowledged this fact in his Ad Litem Report:

REPORT: "At my meeting with him at the Holy Family Hospital, he was highly medicated with lithium and thorazine, according to his nurse, and as he spoke to me, he had difficulty remaining awake."

I believe Dr. Bahrawy deliberately overmedicated me so as to impair my ability to effectively communicate with Byers. The following excerpt from the manual, *Your Rights as a Mental Patient in Massachusetts*, indicates that over-drugging patients prior to legal proceedings is a known ploy by unprincipled psychiatrists:

"Watch out for medication changes. It is not uncommon for doctors to begin, discontinue, or change your medication shortly before a hearing, making you appear your worst before a judge. Ask your lawyer to help you in getting the right medication (or no medication), whatever is proper for you, so that you can appear in good shape before the judge."

On the morning of June 8th, the guardianship commitment hearing was conducted before Judge Albert Pettoruto in Lawrence Probate Court. Like the trial portrayed in the movie classic *To Kill a Mockingbird*, the proceedings proved to be a Kangaroo Court from soup to nuts. The transcript of the testimony indicates that Dr. Bahrawy, Dr. Emonds, both my parents, and family friend Joe Kattar testified. Also present at the hearing was Holy Family attorney Clifford Elias, who, as I stated earlier, thought so well of me that he had lobbied hard to get me into law school just three years prior to the hearing.

Because guardian *ad litem* Byers had reservations about my being present in the courtroom while my parents were testifying (hmm, I wonder why), I wasn't allowed to leave the hospital and attend the hearing, which was held just down the road. This directly violated my constitutional rights under Massachusetts Law of Civil Commitment Chapter 123, which provides for due-process safeguards. The Mental Health Legal Advisors Committee publication specifically spells out:

"When initially hospitalized, patients must be notified of their rights and given the opportunity to obtain legal advice. They are entitled to notice, legal representation, the opportunity to be heard and the right to cross examine witnesses against them if their commitment is sought. The law further guarantees that the respondent has the right to call witnesses in his own defense. The rules of evidence, including the rules of hearsay evidence, apply, and statements made by the respondent to his psychotherapist cannot be used against him at trial."

Since I was completely broke and couldn't afford to hire an attorney of my own choosing, the Probate Court had appointed, *pro-bono*, North Andover attorney Donald Smith to represent me. This development unnerved me because I learned through the hospital grapevine that Smith had interacted professionally with my father for many years in his capacity as a city tax assessor.

However, I assumed the man was a professional and that once we met, I could persuade him regarding my sound state of mind and the misguided stance of my parents. Unfortunately, Smith failed to come to the hospital and meet with me prior to the hearing, as was his legal duty. Obviously, we weren't dealing with Atticus Finch here.

The Mental Health Legal Advisors Committee (MHLAC) publication, *Representing the Ward - The Lawyers Role*, specifically outlines the responsibilities of an attorney representing a ward at a guardianship hearing:

"Representation of a proposed ward in these kinds of proceedings will require considerable time and effort by the attorney. The very reason the Supreme Judicial Court has required that decisions about the invasions of privacy of a person's liberty that are part and parcel of forced medication and involuntary admission are to be made in the court room rather than the nurse's station, is to insure that the applicable law is applied after a full presentation of the relevant facts - that is, only upon due process of law. Counsel's assistance in the presentation of facts is, of course, an important element of a process the accuracy of which depends on an aggressive presentation of competing views. *Consequently, the attorney should take his/her direction from the client. The attorney must obtain as much assistance from his client as the latter is capable of giving.*"

Since I was not present at the hearing, I know only what I learned from the court transcript. Dr. Bahrawy was the first witness to take the stand. He told judge Pettoruto, as expected:

"Mr. Ead is suffering from bipolar disorder (or manic depression) and a 'chemical imbalance' of his brain and in turn needs prolonged inpatient treatment. He also suffers from severe insomnia and has been abusing other patients on the ward." The latter part of Bahrawy's claim was an outright falsehood and is directly refuted in the June 28th Discharge Summary, which was written by Bahrawy ten days after the hearing:

"So far his anger has been directed towards his guardian, not towards the staff of the hospital or any other patients."

After Dr. Bahrawy finished testifying, my father took the stand. Dad had always been a magnificent storyteller who was known to rival George Lucas in his creativity. True to form, his testimony was characterized by gross exaggerations, false innuendos, and outright error. As an example, he claimed that I was observably unstable during the two months prior to being hospitalized. But the fact is I hadn't even been living with him for the two months before I was hospitalized. Most of that time I had been living with my cousin Nadim and his family. And take note of what Dr. Emonds wrote in his May 31st medical report to the probate court:

"On 4-26-83 (one month before my hospitalization), he was doing as well as could have been expected. ... His cousin (Nadim) stated that he was behaving well and taking his medication and vitamins as prescribed."

177

My father also claimed that I summoned the police myself to take me to the Holy Family Hospital in August of 1982 (when Denapoli first hospitalized me); that I consented voluntarily to go to Baldpate Hospital in December of 1982 (when Emonds forcibly hospitalized me for the first time); that I had been seen driving on the wrong side of the road; and that I had agreed to seek immediate psychiatric treatment from Dr. O'Shea, (a pediatrician mind you) upon my return from Saudi Arabia in October of 1982.

None of these statements were true. If you'll recall, I never even met Dr. O'Shea and I entered treatment with Emonds only under assurances from both him and my Dad that he was not in any way connected with psychiatry. Dad concluded his testimony by passionately telling Judge Pettoruto, in what seemed to be a telling revelation of his true motive in over-protecting me throughout this ordeal:

"I lost one son, Your Honor, (referring to my younger brother Mark). I'm not going to lose another!"

Following my father's testimony, my mother took the stand. As previously noted, her treating psychiatrist Denapoli had frightened her into believing serious harm would come to me if I didn't receive inpatient psychiatric treatment. This scare theme was later reiterated by Dr. Quirke at Baldpate and then again by Dr. Bahrawy - Denapoli's business partner. My mother, still in a state of fear and still a great believer in the infallibility of doctors, was prepared to do whatever it took to ensure I receive this "life-saving" treatment. No doubt, her desire to see me get well drove her mysterious false testimony.

She swore I had been breaking dishes and kicking furniture at home. The fact was, raising my voice was as far as my anger has ever gone.

"Both I and Dr. Denapoli," she said, "want Chuckie in the hospital, and we both want him to stay in the hospital until his current treating doctors see fit to release him."

Dr. Denapoli wasn't even my treating psychiatrist anymore. What the Hell was he still doing in the treatment mix?

After my mother finished testifying, my old one-time friend Joe Kattar took the stand and mercilessly drove the nails into coffin. Right after he swore on the Holy Bible to tell the truth, he gave totally fabricated and damaging testimony: Here it is:

Fabrication #1: "Your honor, I personally witnessed him (me) talk to himself in a self-deprecating manner on a regular basis since 1968." When my court-appointed attorney Smith interjected that I was only in the seventh grade in 1968, Kattar conveniently moved the date ahead:

"Oh, that was 1972, I'm sorry."

The truth was, I didn't even meet Kattar until 1976, four years after that.

Fabrication #2: "I once observed him punch the brick wall of a local Burger King with his fist."

I don't know where this one came from. It never happened. Is it possible that I struck a wall with my hand one time in an expression of anger? I suppose so. Do 75 percent of adult males in America do something stupid like this at one time or another? Is it an early symptom of a deteriorating state of mind? In any event it never happened anyway.

Fabrication #3: "During the period just prior to his May 26th hospitalization, he had been spending three evenings a week at my house, and on the last night there, he trampled on my neighbor's lawn, ate three bowls of fruit salad in a minute and a half, gesticulated uncontrollably in front of me and my wife, then beat himself in a Tarzan-like manner."

Nope, sorry. That didn't happen either.

Fabrication #4: "I saw him jogging in the high snow during the height of the infamous blizzard of 1978."

The true facts are that I spent the entire first two days of the blizzard snowing in at my then-girlfriend Denise Lefebvre's Lawrence apartment, shoveling out snow with mutual friend Bob Bourdelais - the guy I ran the Boston Marathon with later in the spring of that same year. Anyone who lived through that historic snowstorm will know that jogging through its deep snow would have been physically impossible.

Fabrication #5: "I recently saw him running on the track at the local YMCA, with a 103-degree temperature and bleeding feet, until he passed out."

I wonder how he could tell my temperature by looking at me. I have never passed out at the Y, and Kattar never once went there. If you saw him, you would know that.

Fabrication #6: "While I was recently over his parent's house, I observed him threaten his father's life, break glass, and destroy furniture."

No broken glass, no broken furniture, no death threats. Verbalized anger perhaps; yes, maybe I'll agree to that!

As I mentioned, to this day, I am still not totally sure as to what Joe Kattar's true motivation in lying about me before the court was. He and I had initially met in 1976 while we were both working the night shift at Bishop's. I was working my way then through Merrimack College. He was a probation officer moonlighting as a french-fry cook. Joe's uncles, the Beshara brothers together, owned Bishop's.

Not long after meeting at the restaurant, Joe - who, I'm sad to report, died a painful death a few years ago at the age of 66 from lung cancer, and I became good friends. A stoutly built, passionate, and college educated guy with a great sense of humor, he was, as I mentioned earlier, deeply proud of our mutual Arabic ancestry. He was the big brother that I never had. What drew us together even more was our intellectual kinship in the midst of the mundane, blue-collar working environment of the restaurant. For example: when the restaurant was slow, Joe and I would entertain each other in the kitchen by playing Latin word games and discussing the ups and downs of the stock market, in which we both had a strong interest.

Shortly before I befriended Joe, I also befriended his younger brother John (J.D.), who was closer to my age and was working his way through college like me as well. Because J.D. was athletically inclined and worked out with me at the Y, I had more in common with him than I did with Joe, who didn't play sports, wasn't in shape, and smoked heavily.

Besides our both being diehard Boston Celtics and New York Yankees fans, J.D. and I played racquetball and basketball together at the Y, and backgammon and chess together at our respective homes. In addition, the two of us would often break away on weekends and drive down to Atlantic City and play blackjack and/or shoot dice in the casinos there. We also went

181

to the broker's office together two or three times a week to monitor our stock investments. In fact, our mutual fascination with Wall Street eventually led both of us to pursue and earn our MBAs.

Again, as for Joe Kattar's motivation for his false testimony, I can only speculate, but here are two fairly plausible explanations that come to mind. I admit though, that it is only 'speculation' on my part and may not be correct and I will be more than willing to offer my apology to anyone, including close former associates and/or family members of Joe's, who most likely knew him even better than I did, and who can convince me it is off base:

The First Explanation: Kattar had become extremely pissed off at me just prior to my embarking for the Persian Gulf and could very well been still nursing a grudge leading all the way up until the time of the hearing. Why? Just for not coming to visit him when he was sick with a serious disease and confined in a hospital. In my defense, I didn't even know he was sick at the time.

And the Second Explanation: Kattar had suffered most of his adult life from what psychologists have termed a "helper's complex" which caused him to always deliberately throw himself full force into every difficulty in a "savior-like mode".

But one thing Joe Kattar did know from his lengthy experience as a court officer was how the 'system' worked. Whatever his darker motivations might have been, it's clear that his immediate purpose in providing such vivid and damaging testimony was to make me appear to be a nut and an immediate danger to myself and others, thereby satisfying the legal requirement for forcible commitment in the State of Massachusetts.

Kattar, like my parents, was doing "whatever it took" to get me the help he seemed to believe I needed. But couldn't he have gone a more truthful and less damaging route? If he really believed I needed psychiatric help, and wanted to be up front with the court, he could have simply said to the probate judge something akin to the following:

"Your Honor, I have known Chuck Ead for some six or seven years now. Although he's a wonderful kid and a great friend, he's presently in the worse shape I've ever seen him in. Like the doctors and his parents who just testified, I am highly concerned about his well-being. And like them, I believe his problem is psychiatrically rooted. So, for his own good, I ask this court to grant guardianship to his father so that he can commit him forthwith to a psychiatric facility and get him the help he needs."

I wouldn't have agreed with Kattar, but at least I would have respected him. I hope the picture is clear to you. In summary, the future course of my medical treatment was now driven by a punitive ex-cop, an envious and/or an obvious emotionally disturbed probation officer, two well-meaning but fear-driven and misguided parents, a legal stiff who had dropped the ball and was way in over his head, and a non-medically trained judge.

Following the morning hearing in probate court, Judge Pettoruto, guardian *ad litem* Byers, and attorneys - Smith, Elias, and Piscitello came to the Holy Family to take testimony from me. The session took place in one of the hospital's conference rooms and lasted about two hours. In further violation of my due process safeguards, none of the five legal people in attendance, not even my own court-appointed attorney - Smith if you can even believe it, made any attempt whatsoever to inform me that witnesses had testified against me earlier that day in probate court.

Thus, I had no knowledge of the false and/or grossly exaggerated testimony that had been given, especially by my friend Joe Kattar, and therefore had no opportunity to rebut any of it. I believe my attorney Smith should have taken an adversarial role toward his legal opponents during this hospital session, but he failed to do so. Such was the camaraderie amongst the lawyers, in fact, that I felt like I was interrupting their tee times. The previously quoted manual, *Your Rights as a Mental Patient in Massachusetts*, states:

> "You have a right to be present at your court hearing. The hearing usually takes place in a conference room at the hospital. The judge sits at a table with the hospital doctor, the hospital's lawyer, you, your lawyer and any witnesses. Witnesses (clergyman, employer, teacher, friend, hospital social worker, hospital volunteer) are given a chance to speak in your behalf. You have the opportunity to speak for yourself."

During the questioning, guardian *ad litem* - Byers asked me what I thought was wrong with me. I told him I had been suffering from an organic, not a psychiatric, illness during the previous year. In support of this, I cited Emond's depleted body chemistry diagnosis because it was the only reasonable explanation I had at the time for my organic complaints.

My attorney - Smith, not having met with me before the hearing, remained impotent and failed to offer any defense. He just sat there like a log with his eyes glued to his blank, yellow, legal pad and said absolutely nothing during the entire hospital hearing. Left to my own devices, I tried my best to answer the seemingly endless questions that were put to me by Byers and Judge Pettoruto. By the condescending and dismissive way Judge Pettoruto was questioning me, it seemed clear to me that he had fully accepted the manic depression diagnosis beforehand, as well as my need for immediate inpatient psychiatric treatment.

On June 21st, two weeks after the hearing, Pettoruto (surprise, surprise), issued a written decree granting my father's ninety-day legal guardianship and civil commitment requests. Meanwhile, third-string, court-appointed attorney - Smith, in harmony with his other failures, neglected to inform me that I had a legal right to appeal the probate judge's decision.

Allow me to stand on a soapbox for a moment here. It has always been my strong belief that our legal system is skewed in favor of the wealthy. If I hadn't been penniless at the time of the hearing but rather had an extra ten grand laying around to hire a more competent lawyer, I'm positive he could have had this guardianship nonsense put to bed in my favor in a half an hour. I guess it's true what the legal community has been saying to poor and marginalized folks since time immemorial:

"How much justice can you afford Sir?"

It is my contrary belief that justice and access to our court system should be the right of every American citizen, rich or poor. Forgive me but I just had to get that out!

Chapter 16:
A Crucifixion at McLean's Hospital

Although Dr. Bahrawy strongly believed he could treat me adequately at Holy Family Hospital, Joe Kattar had a far different agenda. Not satisfied with the damage he had done by falsely testifying against me at the guardianship hearing, he pushed the envelope even further ahead by zealously lobbying Dad to have me transferred, against both Dr. Bahrawy's and my own wishes, to McLean's psychiatric hospital in Belmont Massachusetts - supposedly the top-rated psychiatric treatment facility in the country. According to what Kattar told Dad, celebrities like James Taylor, Joan Kennedy, and numerous others stars and politicians and their family members had been successfully treated there; a designer mental hospital, if you will.

"I'm confident that they'll finally get Chuckie well there Fred," Kattar repeatedly claimed to Dad.

And so much to Bahraway's and my displeasure, away I went.

During the ensuing four months that I was forcefully confined at McLean's, I died a thousand deaths. A consortium of a dozen or so attractive and well-maintained red brick buildings set on a plush 100-acre lot in the plush, well-to-do Boston suburb, of Belmont, McLean's is an institution that has hosted a great deal of cutting-edge psychiatric research. The quality of its "lodgings" was a bit higher than what I had previously experienced - the rooms were clean and sunny, the lettuce was fresh, and the water was Poland Springs - but involuntary commitment is involuntary commitment, no matter how crisp the romaine. I settled in with a less-than-chipper attitude.

The day after my admission, staff psychiatrist - Robert Linden, a 35-year-old, yuppie looking academic sort, complete with leather elbow patches, longish hair and red-rimmed Ivy League glasses, came into my room and told me he was assigned by the hospital to oversee my treatment. I could tell that unlike Denapoli, Emonds, Quirke, and Bahrawy before him, who I felt were mere Single - A players, this guy was a major leaguer, and I quickly sensed that I was in for a formidable challenge. A self-described, Harvard Medical School graduate, Linden appeared to be shrewd, street smart, gregarious, and more importantly, capable of being totally ruthless if he had to be. I took the liberty of starting our conversation off:

"Let's spare each other the formalities doctor and just cut to the chase. I am a well-educated, intelligent and highly accomplished man. I'M A SOMEBODY. I don't believe that I belong in this place. So, I want you to release me from this hospital and out into free society right now."

"Charles, Charles, Charles my boy," he said very calmly and facetiously, "You're a sharp kid. Don't you get what's happening here? What this is all about? I'm NOT going to release you. We got you now. We own you! Did you know that this hospital is being paid fifteen hundred dollars a day by your father's Blue Cross - Blue Shield insurance company just to house you here? It doesn't cost us even a fraction of that to feed you three meals a day and provide you with heat and hot water. Maybe what? A hundred dollars a day in total, if even that much. ...

"You're a numbers guy. Do the arithmetic. The rest of what we get paid here is gravy for us. Cash cows like you keep hospitals like ours financially afloat. And how much do you think I myself get paid just for paying you a brief, ten-minute visit with you twice a week? Two hundred and fifty dollars a visit, Charles. You're a winning megabucks ticket to us, just waiting to be cashed." …

"I can see that you're potentially going to be a 'hard case' for us. You seem to have a bit of the rebel spirit in you, my boy; an agitator if you will. Although we like a challenge, we don't like hard cases or agitators here. We value conformity and order instead. We like patients who go along with the program and do what they're told. Capeesh?" I wasted no time in responding:

"You mean to tell me that all this crap I'm being subjected to all boils down to money? I find that totally obscene and hard to believe."

"Charles, didn't they teach you in Business School that the profit motive drives everything in this world? Maybe you weren't paying attention or staring out the window when your professor tried to explain this to you." …

"Let me be a little more blunt with you," he went on. "I'm not going to fuck around anymore here. If you fight us, "boy" we'll make it very tough for you here, and let me assure you, we know exactly how to. (That was the third time Linden called me "boy," - a derogatory term given to unlucky, black teenagers by Klu Klux Clan members in the Jim Crow south just before they lynched them and very often set them on fire and burn them to death simply for having the audacity to smile at a white girl who happened to pass by them on the sidewalk.). On the other hand, if you view your stay here positively, as well just a well-earned, extended vacation, and give us no trouble, I promise we'll go easy on you."

I couldn't believe he was actually laying things out in such bald terms. I responded:

"Doctor, I can see that you're very twisted. You strike me as a man who has a cash register for a brain and a bank vault for a heart."

The psychiatrist was quick to respond:

"Charles, I'm going to be the bigger man in the room here and overlook those childish insults. Come on now; a guy with your education should have come up with better comebacks than those, don't you think? But at the same time, I want you to know that I'm five steps ahead of you in here."

"Is that so Doctor Mengel? You may be five steps ahead of me, but I want you to know too that I ran the marathon, so I'm twenty-six-miles ahead of you.

Linden's victorious smile was now replaced with an enraged sneer. He rose from his chair and, after placing his brown, soft-leather yuppie briefcase-bag around his shoulder, angrily shot back:

"You two-bit, little, smart ass! Where do you get the fucking nerve to talk to a man like ME that way? You're going to find out very soon buddy boy who's boss around here."

Did you catch it? He said "boy" again.

And so there I was, back on the psychiatric treadmill again. During the ensuing four seemingly endless months that I was confined to Belknap 5, - the locked, manic-depressive ward, Linden gave me plenty of earnest nods and concerned *harrumphs* but, like the treating psychiatrists before him, wouldn't listen to a word of my claim that I had been misdiagnosed by Dr. Denapoli. To do so would be to back down and also to break some unwritten "fraternal code" among shrinks, No, he was out to "teach me a lesson," and he had his own punitive agenda in mind that had nothing whatsoever to do with good psychiatry.

Several days after my admission, Linden placed me on heavy dosages of Lithium as well as other psychotropic medications. Welcome to the Machine. I curled up on my Crate & Barrel bed with its nice Bed & Bath bedspread and immediately went unconscious for about twenty hours straight. This was to be the story of my four-month stay- physically reeling from the body blows of one forced medication after another.

The medical records show that every two weeks or so, Linden and his drug therapy research partner, Jeffrey Jonas MD, changed my medication, using me as a literal guinea pig for the drug companies that I later learned paid McLean's and the psychiatrist huge fees and kickbacks for testing their drugs on the hospital's often-unwitting patients.

Psychiatrist Jonas would repeatedly mix up various cocktails of psychotropic drugs for me to take with the lithium. This practice is called polypharmacy. The drugs they gave me included: haldol, thorazine, mellarii, prolixin, ativan, lithium litrate, and desipramine. Research indicates that all of these drugs can have very harmful side effects.

Of course, because I was under legal guardianship, the good doctors weren't required to inform anyone except my accommodating father as to what they were doing to me. Thus, they seemed to view me as a very large, very surly lab rat. When I told Dad what was taking place with the drugs, hoping he would confront Dr. Linden and stop the practice, he responded in a macho manner:

"Oh, stop acting like a little baby Chuckie."

Drs. Linden and Jonas used me as a lab rat for the Food and Drug Administration (FDA) as well as for the drug companies, without my knowledge or consent. I never volunteered for any of their drugs to be administered to me. These FDA drugs included acetaminophen, Inderal, and Tegretol. The previously quoted College of Legal Medicine textbook, Legal Dynamics of Medical Encounters, states that this was not only immoral but also illegal:

"The Food, Drug and Cosmetic Act authorizes the Department of Health and Human Services to regulate the use of investigational drugs. The regulations issued by the department require the investigator to certify that: ...he will inform any patients, or their representatives, that drugs are being used for investigational purposes, and will obtain the consent of the subjects, or their representatives, except where this is not feasible or in the investigator's professional judgment or is contrary to the best interest of the subjects." ...

The regulations define consent to mean:

"That the person involved has legal capacity to give consent, is so situated as to be able to exercise free power of choice and is provided with a fair explanation of pertinent information concerning the investigational drug, and/or possible use of a control, as to enable him to make a decision on his willingness to receive said investigational drug. The latter element means that before the acceptance of an affirmative decision by such person, the investigator should carefully consider and make known to him, the nature, expected duration, and purpose of the administration of said investigational drug; the method and means by which it is to be administered; the hazards involved; the existence of alternative forms of therapy, if any; and the beneficial effects upon his health or person that may possibly come from administration of the investigational drug."

Although he never told me why, I believe it was for punitive reasons, Linden gave written orders to the nursing staff not to allow me to leave the locked ward ever - not even to go outside on the back porch and get some fresh air for a few minutes. You would have thought I had tried to assassinate a sitting president. In addition, the staff refused to allow me to turn the TV I had in my room on and/or to keep with me and play the radio my parents had brought me from home.

Most of the time I sat in forced "groups," talking about mind-expanding issues such as why Walkman time had to be limited to two 30-minute periods a day and which TV shows should be played in the rec room after dinner.

Or I paced around the circular ward like a grouper fish in the New England Aquarium's central tank.

Unless, of course, the staff had me on "room schedule," which they quite often did. Under this prison-like policy, I had to remain in my room without explanation for forty-five minutes out of every hour. Not surprisingly, my incarceration and the subsequent lack of exercise, coupled with heavy dosages of water-retaining psychoactive medication (particularly the lithium, which is a salt), soon fueled a forty-pound weight gain.

The nursing staff watched us all as if we were specimens in a nature show, and in the spirit of George Orwell's '1984,' painstakingly logged everything we said and did in their daily notes. The doctors greatly valued these notes. They religiously reviewed them every morning at their staff meetings, which they held with the nursing staff each morning before starting their rounds.

It seemed to me that for every minute of time the staff spent actually interacting with patients, they spent five minutes taking notes on the encounter. None of the staff seemed to want to interact with me very much at all unless it was to draw blood to monitor my lithium levels. Every time I turned around it seemed a different nurse was jamming a needle in me. I felt like a pin cushion.

A standard staff practice was to engage in the game of "privileges." The game was played like this: When a patient behaved the way the staff wanted him to, he or she was awarded a gold star on the "privileges bulletin board" that hung next to his name on the ward wall. "Minor privileges" earned you "minor benefits" like being able to leave the locked ward for thirty minutes to go for a walk. As you moved up the privilege ladder, you earned higher rewards like the right to talk on the ward phone for twenty minutes without the staff listening in as they typically did or being allowed to leave the locked ward for a full hour or more and go to the hospital cafeteria alone.

You had to be careful, though, because if you screwed up even just once, the staff would punish you by taking away all the privileges you had earned and making you start all over again at the bottom of the totem pole. I refused to buy in; I told the nurses from day one to forget any potential privileges for me - I didn't want them.

One afternoon, when it was my turn to use the ward pay telephone, I called a prominent, Boston attorney in order to gain his help in securing my release from the hospital. Unfortunately, in the middle of our discussion, I heard a loud click. When I then tried to re-dial the attorney's number again, there was no longer any dial tone. I realized then that the nurse's station had been listening in on my call, (a common practice on psyche wards), didn't like what was being communicated, and in turn, and had terminated my initial call and prevented a second one. Upon reflection, I clearly got the message being impressed upon me by the staff:

"Don't you dare let anybody on the outside know what's going on in here."

The queen of nurses on Belknap 5 (B5) was Paula. If you're familiar with Nurse Rached from One Flew Over the Cuckoo's Nest, you have some idea of the ardor with which Paula ruled her roost. The only difference between the two of them was that this Mclean's chick was violent. Unit B5 was her little empire during all the hours when the psychiatrists were not present. Paula was a muscled type, with tight, drawn-back brown hair and a perpetual sneer. She looked as if she might have been a member of the East German swim team before they made steroids illegal. Paula liked control. Paula liked obedience. Paula liked conformity. Paula did not like me.

In the middle of the ward was a locked solitary confinement room, which the staff referred to euphemistically as the "quiet room." Completely barren, with plain white walls, and windowless, it held no bedding, toilet, or wash basin. Whenever a patient would raise their voice too loudly or otherwise disrupt the smooth functioning of the evening shift rituals, Paula would "sentence" them to solitary confinement for a day or two to teach them a lesson. Not an hour or an afternoon, mind you, but a day or two.

This Paula played it so rough that she made the notorious Baca - the brutal, chief Egyptian taskmaster of Goshen, look like a boy scout. It's interesting to note that the ward nurse engaged in this practice exclusively during the evening shift. During the daytime hours, in front of the doctors, she was the quintessence of reasonableness, and her attitude was all about:

"Do you want to talk about why you don't want to take your meds, Timmy?"

At night, when the doctors weren't present, it was:

"Take your meds, buddy boy, or else. You got a problem with that?"

Being in control of the ward seemed to be all that mattered to Paula. She openly despised me because I would regularly point out to her that she and other staff had no right to lay their hands on and physically abuse the other patients a common practice on B-5.

A little dose of reality: I have since learned from several mental health professionals who had the courage to speak out that it's widely known by insiders that mental hospitals employ a significant number of emotionally disturbed orderlies, both male and female. These people actually apply for jobs on psych wards in order to be able to beat up patients without fear of detection or retribution.

In their honest moments, these sickos admit to getting some sort of high, akin to a runner's endorphin high, by converging on patients (often in teams of two or more), tackling them to the ground, and then walloping the living daylights out of them. They proudly refer to this behavior in wrestling terms, calling it a "takedown." Present-day psychiatry may claim these practices are exclusively a thing of the past, but trust me, they are not, and are in fact more rampant now than they ever were.

Case in point: One night Paula and two other staffers dragged Emily - a fellow patient and my closest friend on the ward, kicking and screaming, into the solitary confinement room and left her in there for a two-day stint. A painfully thin, college graduate, who, like me, had been forcibly hospitalized with the help of her parents, Emily was a sweet and harmless soul. When I unsuccessfully tried to stop the assault on her (verbally, not physically), Paula told me in no uncertain terms:

"I'm going to get you for that pal! Watch your backside."

One thing you could say about Paula was she always kept her promises. About six o'clock on a quiet Friday night, just one week after the Emily incident, she marched into my room unprovoked and without warning and said:

"Dr. Linden told me to say hello and to tell you your telephone privileges are being indefinitely suspended."

"Why?" I inquired warily.

"Because I told him you violated your room schedule twice yesterday."

A cheap and manufactured excuse I thought. The ward telephone was my only contact with family, friends, and the outside world, so this purely vindictive action upset me tremendously. I in turn, banged the top of my dresser with my fist and shouted:

"You haven't screwed with me enough yet?"

Glaring triumphantly, Paula pointed her finger at me and replied:

"Payback time, Charlie."

She then charged out of my room. Moments later, she returned with four staff members at her side. Under the ward nurse's direction, the quartet then seized me without warning and took me to the ground. Paula then kicked me, quite hard and deliberately, in the chest, stomach, and testicles. Each of the staffers then proceeded to kick the living daylights out of me.

Following this, again under Paula's orders, each of the four grabbed one of my limbs and dragged me out of my room and into the main corridor. Who knew that drawing and quartering was one of the innovative therapeutic techniques being pioneered at McLean's? With a victorious smile on her face, the head nurse paused for a moment to land a square kick to my groin then yelled to her cohorts with clenched teeth:

"Now, let's take the little, fucking, black Arab to the quiet room!"

Next, in full view of about a dozen fellow patients who were lined up in the main hall viewing the spectacle as one would a highway accident or a parade, the four staffers dragged me, limb by limb, some forty feet down the corridor to the solitary chamber.

"In there," the ward boss bellowed.

The four thugs then *threw* me into the chamber head-first. My face and right shoulder collided with the hard chamber floor. Paula and company then kicked me a few more times for good measure, left the room, and slammed the heavy door behind them. After I cleared my head, I slowly staggered to my feet. I could see I was bleeding from somewhere. The only sound that reached me in the soundproof room was the turning of a very loud lock.

That evening, as I lay there alone and despondent on the frigid floor of the barren solitary chamber, licking my wounds, my mind mysteriously began to harken back to happier times.

197

Among the thoughts that came to mind, I recalled the tremendous sense of security that I felt as a kid as I sat at the picnic table under the apple tree with my Jidoo and him seated next to me and with his right arm wrapped around my neck and couldn't help asking myself:

"How did it all come to THIS?"

During the late morning of my third day in solitary (Sunday), I realized I couldn't handle any more punishment. Not a spiritual believer at the time and having drifted away from God since my St. Rita grammar school and Central Catholic high school days I cried out:

"God, if you exist and are real, I'm at the edge of the cliff. I need your help right now! I feel like I'm about to crack up all alone in here."

I followed up this cry for help by blurting out a string of Hail Mary's, one after another and several Our Fathers. I was surprised that I still remembered the words from Catholic grammar school. This spontaneous outburst of prayer proved to be the first step in a deep spiritual journey that would sustain me through thick and thin, as you will see - not just for that day but through the rest of my life - right up until the present. Nothing major seemed to happen after this, but a strange and quiet feeling came over me telling me I was going to be okay.

Although I was forced to remain in solitary for the remainder of that Sunday, staring aimlessly at the four empty white walls with nothing to either eat or drink, I somehow made it through until I finally was let out by a staff nurse at around 8 o'clock the next morning. The previously quoted *Your Rights as a Mental Patient in Massachusetts* spells out the law on solitary confinement:

"Solitary confinement: A patient is placed in a room alone. Seclusion may be either closed door or open door. Like restraint, seclusion by law can be used only in emergency situations where there is the occurrence of a serious threat of extreme violence, personal injury or attempted suicide. (Seclusion may not be used punitively.)

Seclusion may be used only on written authorization of the superintendent, facility director or designated doctor, and can be ordered for no longer than three hours (not days).

"No adult may be kept in seclusion without a staff person in attendance who is specially trained to understand, assist and afford therapy to the person in seclusion. (No one remained in attendance with me.)"

"Any space used for seclusion must provide for complete visual observation of the secluded resident in every area of space. The space must provide appropriate and safe ventilation, heating, light and access to bathroom equipment, and must provide appropriate attention to the physical and mental comforts of the resident." (No bathroom access, little visibility, and no comforts were afforded me.).

As the weeks turned into months, my life at McLean's brought on feelings of loneliness, monotony, and sensory deprivation, with every day seeming worse than the day before. My confinement was so agonizing in fact, that I recall that the first thing that I did each morning after awakening from sleep was to curse the very day of my birth. As you might imagine, these negative feelings began to fuel high levels of agitation.

The previously quoted Case Report (August 28, 1983), written by Dr. Linden, acknowledges all this:

"His hospital course here was characterized by little change, his behavior varying from quiet and resentful to pacing, agitative and belligerent. He has shown no assaultive behavior. His conversation has focused almost exclusively on discharge, and he has shown no insight into his illness."

"There is no history of paranoia, ideas of reference, thought insertion or withdrawal, somatic delusions, auditory or visual hallucinations, or any other frankly psychotic thoughts beyond grandiosity (be specific here, doctor), throughout the course of his illness. He has shown no assaultive behavior.

"He has received numerous speeding tickets, (not true) but there was no history of alcohol or other substance abuse. There was no history of depression. The patient completed an MBA at Suffolk University."

The McLean's nurses' notes repeatedly state that I did a great deal of "restless pacing" in the halls, which the staff, of course, attributed to being a symptom of my "illness." Deeper inspection, however, indicates that this pacing was due to an akathisia reaction to the plethora of powerful neurologic medications Drs. Linden and Jonas were pumping into me. The medical records indicate that the hospital doctors knew about and suspected this:

"Dr. Jonas (weekly Progress Note, 7-12): "Possibility of akathisia should be considered. Perhaps a propranolol would be of use."

"Dr. Linden (Case Report, 8-23): "After examination by Dr. Lavinsky (another staff psychiatrist who treated me at McLean) for a question of akathisia playing a possible role in his agitated behavior, he was begun on propranolol."

The medical records further indicate that, just as they had done with my akathisia -induced pacing, the nursing staff categorized my having "no insight into my "illness" and my preoccupation with being discharged as symptoms of my illness too. Let me ask this: If a person knows he is not suffering a psychiatric illness, is angry about being confined against his will, and is consequently highly motivated to ask to be released, what is the appropriate way to behave? Pretend he's happy to be incarcerated? Thank the staff for a much-needed gonad kicking and solitary confinement lock-up? Pretend to have insight into a nonexistent illness? It's the old "confess you're a heretic" syndrome again.

One afternoon, my now deceased first cousin and Godfather showed up at the hospital to pay me a rare visit. Just before he left and right after I had just made clear to him the horrors that the hospital doctors and staff were subjecting me to, with the hope that he'd take some action and do something about it, he instead, shrugged off my complaints by saying:

"Well Chuckie, you'll just have to try and make the best of it."

In early September, the ninety-day temporary guardianship that Judge Pettoruto awarded my father three months earlier in Lawrence Probate Court was about to expire. Wishing to keep me hospitalized however, Dr. Linden instructed my father's attorney to request another hearing to extend it. The hearing took place at Salem Probate Court in Salem,

Massachusetts on September 12th. Just as with the first temporary guardianship hearing on June 8th, I wasn't allowed to attend the proceedings. The Finding of Fact document indicates that Dr. Linden showed up and testified:

"Your honor, Mr. Ead is suffering from bipolar disorder, is mentally incompetent and unable to care for himself."

Without any evidence to the contrary being presented, the probate judge readily accepted Linden's claims and extended the guardianship for another thirty days. Another hearing was scheduled for October 13th, one month later, at the same Salem Probate Court for the purpose of ending the temporary guardianship and making it permanent. Unlike with the June 8th and September 12th hearings, I was allowed to attend these proceedings. This time, my court-appointed attorney Donald Smith at least took the trouble to come and see me at the hospital prior to the proceedings. From what transpired during his brief visit, though, I almost wished that he hadn't.

First of all, my *father's* attorney - Piscitello strolled into the hospital right alongside Smith. When I later asked Smith what Iggy was doing there with him, he told me they had *driven up to the hospital together* and Piscitello had just "come along for the ride," primarily because he knew the way. Our judicial system uses an adversarial model; these guys were supposed to be on opposing sides, not ride-sharing and chit-chatting! When Smith and I sat down together to talk privately in my room, the words from his mouth disheartened me further:

"Look, Charlie, I've been talking quite a bit with your father and legs. Why don't you stop fighting this thing, huh? Put in your time here, do what the doctors tell you and get yourself well. We all love you, kid, and we're all rooting for you too. We all want the best for you."

Given this; consider the following excerpt from the previously quoted MHLAC essay, "Representing the Ward; The Lawyer's Role":

"The attorney for the proposed ward in a guardianship petition which seeks the authority to medicate and/or to admit to a mental facility should adopt an adversary posture. It is important, though not always easy, to resist the temptation to slip into a best interest or paternalistic type of representation which is no more appropriate in these cases than in any other legal matter."

When the court day arrived, McLean's transported me to the Salem courthouse strapped down like Hannibal Lecter. At the hearing, Linden again testified that I was suffering from bipolar disorder and was mentally ill and incompetent. The probate judge extended the guardianship for another sixty days. Again, my court-appointed attorney who was at least now present at the hearing, remained completely silent again in my defense. A week later, without my knowledge and absent even a hearing this time, the Court officially made the guardianship permanent (for the entire remainder of my life).

At about this time I phoned my fiancée. It was the third or fourth time I had tried to reach her by phone during my McLean's hospitalization. She failed to answer each time I called, so, I was forced to leave short messages on her answering machine. She didn't return any of my calls, and I understandably became concerned as to what was up.

We had talked of getting married and raising a family together right before I left for work in the Persian Gulf. She had assured me before my departure that she loved me so much she would even be willing to relocate to the Gulf with me if things worked out that way. She also told me that she had "loved me" from only the second time she saw me.

Apparently, the word love means different things to different people. She answered the phone this time and informed me she wasn't happy I had called. Lacking any sense of humanity, she then proceeded to drive the nails into my hands and feet:

"Chuckie, get this straight. The game has changed. I don't want to be involved with you anymore. Your treating doctor told me you're mentally ill. What employer in his right mind is going to hire an ex-mental patient? You'll never be able to get and hold down a good job and support me and a family now. I and your future kids will have a terrible life with you. No, I won't bear your offspring into the world to suffer along with you. So, stop calling here. If you call again, I'll call the police." Click!

Not exactly until death do us part: I must say. My future fiance's response really stung me at the time and although I struggled my best during the weeks ahead to remind myself that: "it is what is, and that life goes on." I just found it very hard accepting it and letting it go.

But I quickly realized at the same time, that my suddenly ex-fiancée was the least of my troubles at the time though. I needed instead to try to figure out how and why I had been psychiatrically railroaded and what could be done to get my freedom back.

As I noted earlier, at the time of my McLean's hospitalization, my parents were having major financial troubles. Already burnt out emotionally because of their longstanding marital problems, the added financial pressure on them of this was almost too much for them to handle. Against this backdrop, they were also being forced to cope with my ill health and medical treatment situation. Understandably, it all proved too much for these two, poor banged-up people to deal with, especially my mother, who was just holding herself together emotionally by the skin of her teeth.

McLean's head social worker Susan Phelps was familiar with the dynamics of my parents' marital and financial problems, thanks to a dozen or so meetings she had with them during the course of my hospitalization. Ma and Dad would come together to the hospital together every Wednesday afternoon and talk things over with Phelps, after which they would pay me a visit. Some illuminating excerpts from those Phelps meetings:

MEETING 7-29-83: "Met with Mr. and Mrs. Ead. The meeting unveiled a tumultuous marital situation. Mrs. Ead accused Mr. Ead of causing burdensome financial problems. Parents stated that this has created stress and tension in the home for many years. Communication between the parents has broken down and with their son's illness, they are experiencing tremendous stress."

MEETING 8-5-83: ... "Mrs. Ead then raised the issues that had come up in mtg. last week. The Eads each acknowledge longstanding marital problems w/a separation taking place about 10 years ago. The marital issues were raised in the context of discussing present financial difficulties w/some outstanding bills. Mrs. Ead believes her husband is careless managing money and is angry at her husband's current wish to re-mortgage their home to pay debts. The lack of trust between Mr. and Mrs. Ead was masked and communication was characterized by resentment, anger and fear. Mrs. Ead feels vulnerable financially and the house represents much security to her.

MEETING, 8-12-83: ... "Mr. and Mrs. Ead are in the midst of a marital struggle focused on financial concerns. For many years their marital relationship has been alternatingly indifferent and tension ridden. ... She reports tension in the marriage from the beginning with her husband. She describes him as impulsive in financial matters. There were several marital separations, with Mrs. Ead and the children returning after a couple of wks. Mrs. Ead was hospitalized for depression in 1976. She lost weight and was anxious regarding her sister's safety. She responded to unknown medication treatment and was discharged in 2 wks. Mrs. Ead has had periodic contact w/ her psychiatrist (Denapoli) from this hospitalization. Mrs. Ead also became (unreadable) at discussing her 8-year-old son Mark who was killed by an automobile in 1968."

MEETING 6-16-83: … "At the end of the mtg. Mrs. Ead showed her husband a recent discontinuance of their house insurance that she had just received. Marital tensions have been longstanding and currently Mr. and Mrs. Ead are at a major impasse in resolving these financial stresses and display little capacity to negotiate. It is a major control struggle."

MEETING 8-25-83: … "Mr. and Mrs. Ead remain at a point of marital tension and mtsg. to continue.

MEETING 9-1-83: … "Mrs. Ead is prone to linking son's illness to the behavior of her husband (Hmm, is it possible that her need to bolster her anger at my father was a reason she had to view me as "crazy"?) and the sessions continue to require much structure. Mr. Ead meanwhile, has difficulty discussing his fears frequently assuming a defensive stance"

MEETING 9-16-83: … "Mr. and Mrs. Ead are in the process of negotiating a marital separation with Mrs. Ead focusing constantly on financial issues. Mr. Ead stated that

206

he was leaning towards separating and buying the family house from his wife. Mrs. Ead expressed a wish to avoid court lawyers and work it out as 'people.'"

MEETING 9-23-83: ... "Parents' marital status remains difficult and they are having trouble communicating."

MEETING 9-30-83: ... "Mr. and Mrs. Ead continue to have marital issues that they are unable to negotiate effectively."

The reason I bring up my parents' intense, well-documented struggles is that the top brass at McLeans, pseudo staff psychologist Miss Phelps in particular, failed to even consider my simple, "common sense" assertion that my parents were overplaying my ill health situation because of an overload of stress and tension in their own lives.

I have learned from reliable people in the mental health field that this is a fairly common dynamic. When things break down in a marriage, there's a tendency for the partners to focus excessively on their offspring, to seize on a child's illness and turn it into a crusade. It takes the attention off the marriage and gives the parents a false feeling that they are behaving purposefully, something they have lost the ability to do within their own relationship. This isn't rocket science folks. It's Psychology 101.

McLean's failure to consider these factors is baffling and inexcusable when you take into account the fact that I repeatedly advanced this explanation to Dr. Linden, Dr. Jonas, social worker Phelps, and the rest of the hospital staff. But of course, I had tried the same tack at Holy Family with Dr. Bahramy and where had it gotten me?

207

It should also significant to note that several, telephone discussions that I had my younger brother and two sisters in which I pleaded with them to intervene and lobby my parents to have them take their feet of the gas-peddle, proved totally fruitless as all three remained mysteriously awol from the beginning to the end of my entire ordeal.

A few days after the guardianship hearing, Dr. Linden strolled into my room with a huge, self-satisfied grin on his face. I knew trouble was brewing:

"I'm sorry to be the bearer of negative news Charles, but the neuroleptic medication we've been giving you for the last four months hasn't worked, so, I'm now forced to try something more aggressive."

"Something more aggressive - like what doctor?"

"I'm going to start administering ECT (electroconvulsive therapy, i.e. shock treatments) on you next Wednesday."

Was this part of the good doctor's therapeutic plan or was he just making good on his *we'll get tough on you if you rebel* policy?

"No doctor, you're not going to fry my brain like an egg; I'm not going to let you."

Linden, realizing my wishes didn't really matter, went ahead and phoned my legal guardian father and asked his permission to perform the ECT on me. Dad, now fully brainwashed to the psychiatric narrative, granted the psychiatrist's request without hesitation. As psychiatrist and activist Peter Breggin confirms in his landmark book, "Toxic Psychiatry," shock treatment often causes permanent memory loss and irreparable brain damage:

"Electroshock or electroconvulsive therapy involves the passage of an electrical current through the brain of the patient to produce a grand mal or epileptic seizure.

The shock induces an electrical storm that obliterates the normal electrical patterns of the brain, driving the recording needle on the EEG up and down in violent, jagged swings. The brain waves become temporarily flat, exactly as in brain death, and it may be that cell death takes place during this time."

"To the extent that it works at all, shock has its impact by disabling the brain. It does so by causing an organic brain syndrome with memory loss, confusion, and disorientation, and by producing lobotomy effects. The shock works by damaging the brain and making patients more simpleminded, less self-aware, and more docile. Several shock doctors have found that a large percentage of ECT patients report significant memory blanks and continuing memory dysfunction years after shock treatment."

In a frenzied panic, I called about a half-dozen relatives and asked them to get in touch with my father and have him call Linden and stop the treatments. All, however, refused to "get involved." One of them - my much older first cousin Joe Habib and the older brother of my godfather, even had the audacity to sheepishly say to me:

"Well, Chuckie, why don't you go ahead and try it. It might help you. What have you got to lose?"

Well, how about a big chunk of my brain cells, Joe?

209

As soon as our good friend, head nurse Paula got wind of the happy news, she charged into my room like a satisfied lioness after a hunt:

"Linden is going to start the ECT next week. How do you like that, smart guy?"

As the days crept closer to D-day (Wednesday), I grew more and more apprehensive. Eventually, I couldn't eat or sleep. On Sunday morning, realizing I had no legal, mental or emotional recourse, I hit my knees with my still-weak faith and began praying feverishly:

"Old Man upstairs, I'm at the end of my rope again. Help me, please! Please get me out of this horrifying thing!"

I continued to pray for the remainder of the morning, not packaged church prayers like the Hail Mary or the Our Father, just "man-to-man" talk straight from the gut. As fate would have it, that same Sunday afternoon, I received two spiritual cards and a third card of "well wishing" from my Aunt Elma, - Dad's older, half-sister. Appropriately enough, the three read as follows:

The Prayer to Saint Jude

"Good St. Jude, cousin of our Savior, glorious Apostle, and faithful servant of Christ Jesus! Although the name of the traitor has caused many to forget you, I honor you and call upon you for help, especially when things seem most hopeless. Come to my assistance, Good St. Jude. Strengthen me and protect me in my anguish, my tribulations and my sufferings, especially the ones I present to you now (They're about to fry my brain, man.). Intercede for me, that I may praise the Lord with you and the Saints forever and ever. Amen."

210

The Prayer of Saint Padre Pio

"I want to be only a poor Friar who prays. Pray, hope and don't worry. Worry is useless. God is merciful and will hear your prayer Prayer is the best weapon we have; it is the key to God's heart. You must speak to God not only with your lips but with your heart. In fact, on certain occasions, you should speak to Him only with your heart"

Aunt Elma's Wishing You Well Card

"We are not what happens to us. No matter what the circumstances are that might make you feel otherwise. You're still the same wonderful person everyone knows and loves, and we're all rooting for you."

- Be Well Chuckie, Love Aunt Elma

And although I'm not a Muslim, I for some reason remembered from my days in the Persian Gulf, that the preface of the Koran - the Muslim Holy Book, opens with the words,

"In the name of God, the Merciful, and the Compassionate."

On Tuesday morning, just twenty-four hours before shock treatments were to begin, a flood of new patients on the ward caused a highly unusual shortage of beds. At the same time, I was informed by Dr. Linden that my father's medical insurance coverage was going to run out on me that same day. The latter meant that McLeans, not being paid anymore, wouldn't be able to treat me for even a day longer.

And so, for these two seemingly coincidental reasons, Dr. Linden signed papers that afternoon authorizing me to be transferred pronto out of McLeans and back to the psych ward at Holy Family, from which I had initially come - ECT thank God averted! Unlike Maclean's, Holy Family had agreed to treat me at their facility there this time free of charge. When I say it's all about the money with these people, I'm not kidding even a little.

Yes, the Lord lives! Thank you, Saint Jude. Thank you, Padre Pio, I repeated in my mind, over and over, after Linden gave me the great news. That evening I was shipped out. I never thought I'd be glad to see the Holy Family psych ward again, but I was, at least for a short while.

My treatment there was supervised this time by staff psychiatrist Lawrence Levine. He was about forty years old, heavy set, dark skinned, and mustachioed. He had a stoic sort of persona -even-keeled and steady; a no-nonsense, dispassionate sort. I hoped he had some semblance of an open mind and would listen to reason. Nope! *Bipolar Disorder, Chemical Imbalance* again. My records were once again diagnosing me.

Based solely on my previous psychiatric history, psychiatrist Levine placed me, once again, on heavy dosages of lithium and prolixin. Bristol Myers Squibb, the manufacturer of prolixin, has published the following information about the drug:

"Warnings: Neuro Malignant Syndrome; Tardive Dyskinesia (TD): Tardive dyskinesia, a syndrome consisting of potentially irreversible, involuntary, dyskinetic movements may develop in patients with neuroleptic drugs."

A potentially fatal symptom complex sometimes referred to as Neuroleptic Malignant Syndrome (NMS) has been reported in association with antipsychotic drugs. Clinical manifestations of NMS are hyperpyrexia, muscle rigidity, altered mental status and evidence of autonomic instability."

"The risk of developing the syndrome and the likelihood that it will become irreversible are believed to increase as the duration of treatment and a cumulative dose of neuroleptic drugs administered to the patient increase. There is no known treatment for established cases of tardive dyskinesia, although the syndrome may remit, partially or completely if neuroleptic treatment is withdrawn. Given these considerations, neuroleptics should be prescribed in a manner that is most likely *to minimize the occurrence of tardive dyskinesia.*"

I remained confined against my will at Holy Family under Levine's care for exactly two months. I remember one particularly painful visit that occurred during that stay. My close friends, the four Najjar brothers, Simon, Elie, Maurice, and Joe, showed up together on the ward to pay me a visit. All of the Najjars, including their older sister - Marie, their "salt of the earth" parents, and their never-married, wonderful aunt - Melia, had thought the world of me. The family had fled the early years of the civil war in Lebanon and come to settle in Lawrence right after the oldest sister was shot to death when a renegade, masked gunmen burst into their home while the family was eating dinner in their home located in the town of Zahle.

Upon arriving in Lawrence, Simon, the oldest of the four boys, opened a Lebanese family restaurant called Bashas. The whole family soon joined him and worked in the restaurant too. My father and I would often stop into Bashas for lunch and meet up with the family after our early afternoon workouts together at the Y. Dad prepared all of the Najjar boys' income tax returns too.

Although I was grateful for the Najjar's thoughtful visit and genuine concern for my well-being, you can imagine how shocking and humiliating it was for all of us to be meeting up

213

in a "nut house." (I mean these were guys that I used to run with). As the four of them sat aimlessly conversing with me, I saw tears running down Simon's face - the most genuine and sentimental of the four brothers. I hated being the object of pity, and damn it there was no good reason for it!

Finally, two days before Christmas, psychiatrist - Levine saw fit to release me. Upon discharge, having no money and no place else to go on a cold winter's day, I was again forced to move back in with my parents. This pattern was getting painfully old. Dad, for his part, unwittingly hailed my return back home as *"a great Christmas present."*

Chapter 17:
A Life-Threatening Drug Reaction

Late in the afternoon on Christmas day, I had one of the most humiliating and frightening experiences of my life. In front of about thirty relatives who were celebrating the holiday at our house, I suddenly began urinating heavily in my pants and all over the kitchen floor. It came on before I was aware of it, and I was powerless to stop the process once it had begun. It felt almost as if it were happening to someone else. I witnessed the event with the same mixture of horror and distress that I saw in the faces around me.

Ho, ho, ho. Merry Christmas, everyone!

I retired to my bedroom and spent the rest of the day in self-imposed isolation. I knew my relatives would be understanding and would do their best to pretend it never happened, but I couldn't peel myself off the bed to rejoin them. Instead, I read a bad old mystery novel as the sounds of Christmas music and holiday laughter wafted under my door. Occasionally, there would be a tentative knock and then light retreating footsteps when I failed to respond.

The peeing incident proved to be the first signs of a "pseudo-parkinsonian" (i.e., drug-induced) reaction to the prolixin medication Dr. Levine had prescribed for me to continue taking as an outpatient. A few days later, the reaction worsened further. I began salivating and drooling uncontrollably, lost nearly all strength in my arms and legs, and couldn't keep my head up for the life of me. It felt like my forehead was attached to a cord being pulled from below.

I walked around the house moaning involuntarily, hunched over like a demented lab assistant in a '40s horror movie. My hands were so weak and uncoordinated, I couldn't navigate a glass of water to my mouth. My younger brother George details my helpless condition is his signed affidavit.

"Please be advised that during a brief holiday home vacation trip from California to Lawrence at the end of the year 1983, I frighteningly observed my older brother Charles in the worst physical condition that I have ever seen him in. Specifically, Charles was:

1. Physically incapacitated, unbalanced and disorientated.
2. Almost completely devoid of strength and coordination.
3. Maintained a glassy eyed, drugged appearance.
4. Unusually, pitifully overweight (40-50 pound estimate).

"During this extended period, Charles was so helpless and dysfunctional that my father and I had to carry him in and out of bed, wipe his face after he would drink because he would spill the fluid all over himself, and help him change his clothes and shoes."

At this point, I believe it appropriate to point out what I learned in a college ethics course. The ancient Greek physician and "Father of Medicine," Hippocrates, stated in 500 B.C. that the first rule of medicine is "to do no harm." Every medical school graduate since then has been required to swear to this 'Hippocratic Oath.'

216

Research into Parkinson's Syndrome indicates that it is caused by the death of brain cells that produce the neurotransmitter dopamine, which plays a key role in the nervous system's control over body movement. The syndrome is often irreversible. In some cases, it can even be fatal. Antipsychotic drugs are notorious for causing the disorder because they toxify the brain's delicate natural chemistry and, in the process, kill off the vital dopamine. The following excerpt from Psychotropic Drug Treatment - Possible Side Effects Information Sheet gives further insight into the pseudo-parkinsonian reaction:

"One of the more common side effects of the antipsychotic and anti-depressant drugs, it occurs most frequently in patients on high dosage treatment. The symptoms look like Parkinson's disease - tremors of the hand and face; lack of facial expression; robot-like, stiff posture and gait. In severe cases, symptoms usually are akinesia (physical immobility, either total or partial) and emotional indifference. The symptoms usually quickly disappear after dosage is withdrawn or concomitant administration of an anti-parkinsonian agent is begun." ...

That same handout also gives insight into Dyskinesia:

"Symptoms of the syndrome include habitual movements of parts of the body, particularly the face, mouth, tongue and jaw. The pattern is usually chewing movements, mouth puckering or something of that nature. There can also, in more severe cases, be involuntary movement of the extremities. The symptoms are persistent, often irreversible."

In the days following Christmas, the drug reaction wasn't showing signs of abating and was, in fact, growing worse. And so, around 9 p.m. on December 30th, my brother George and my cousin Doug, who was visiting George, literally carried me out of the house to Doug's car and drove me to the Holy Family emergency room. My mother and my younger sister Pamela, who were both frantic, followed us to the hospital in Pamela's car.

The ER wasn't very crowded - just a couple of guys who looked like they'd been in a barroom brawl, probably with each other. Within twenty minutes, I was seen by an intern who looked so young he could have passed for a high school sophomore. He seemed thorough and professional, however, as he checked me out physically and asked questions of my mother (who was in only slightly better shape than I was to respond to him).

"How long has Dr. Levine had him on the prolixin, Mrs. Ead?"

"Two months I believe, doctor."

"I believe your son's reaction is occurring because Dr. Levine neglected to prescribe the prophylactic Cogentin to counteract the side effects of the large dosages of prolixin. I do not like to criticize the practice of other physicians, please understand, but this really seems to be a gross oversight. Nearly every patient who receives prolixin is given Cogentin along with it as a matter of course. It is the only way to avoid these kinds of problems."

Accordingly, the following morning, my parents took me to the Merrimack Valley Mental Health Center in downtown Lawrence, where psychiatrist Levine operated an outpatient clinic. After a cursory glance at me, Levine told my parents,

"There is nothing wrong with your son. He's just faking the drug reaction. You see, Mr. and Mrs. Ead, he's immature, doesn't want to help himself, and is looking for attention from you."

An Oscar-worthy performance on my part if I do say so myself, since at the time I knew nothing about tardive dyskinesia or pseudo-parkinsonian drug reactions. I was perfectly faking a reaction I knew nothing about - bravo doctor! Levine had hardly finished speaking when I collapsed to the floor in agony. Levine heaved an exasperated sigh as if to say, Tsk, tsk, here come more theatrics. Totally horrified, my father tore into the psychiatrist:

"What the Hell's wrong with you, doc? This kid is sick. Look at him, for God's sake. Let's get him to a hospital!"

Levine's response: he allowed me to remain on the floor unconscious and unattended for another ten minutes, while my parents watched, now totally besides themselves, and repeatedly pleading with the doctor for some type of remedial action. At last, the psychiatrist finally broke down and called for an ambulance. It arrived moments later and under Levine's direction, I was promptly taken to Danvers State Hospital and then admitted upon my arrival.

I'm not sure what protocol was being observed here - commitment to a state mental hospital to treat an obviously physical, and potentially life-threatening, convulsive drug reaction caused by the man's own negligence and oversight? Dad, alas, okayed the move, citing the fact that I couldn't be sent to a general hospital because his insurance coverage for me had run out. Could we have descended any further into the abyss?

Dr. Ronald Pies, a staff psychiatrist at New England Medical Center whom I hired many years later to review all my medical records, strongly disapproved of psychiatrist Levine's actions:

DR. PIES: "With respect to the "prolixin reaction" you suffered in January, 1984, the following may be said: failure to recognize such a reaction, or at least document clearly that one has considered it and ruled it out, would constitute a substandard level of psychiatric care. Moreover, the appropriate treatment facility for such a reaction is a medical unit or emergency room, not a standard psychiatric facility. You should understand that the so-called "acute dystonic reaction" (muscle spasm of tongue, neck or other region) in response to medications like prolixin is not a life-threatening condition, though it is uncomfortable and frightening. However, since one of the conditions under consideration at the time of your reaction was neuroleptic malignant syndrome (NMS), immediate medical evaluation was called for, since NMS can be fatal if untreated. Finally, all patients receiving medications such as prolixin should be warned about the possibility of such reactions."

The gothic, Big House at Danvers was decked out for the holidays in crepe paper and discount-store cardboard decorations. The Santas and Rudolphs had that off-kilter look as if they'd been designed and printed in a sweat shop in China. It made my heart ache for the people who called this place a permanent home. My first night back at Danvers was a real "dark night of the soul." I had never felt so physically desperate. The muscles of my arms and legs kept contracting and releasing spasmodically with a deep discomfort that was somehow worse than even severe pain. My body felt as if it was trying to turn itself inside out. I wanted badly to escape it. After an hour or two I couldn't stand the feeling anymore. I began to yell and scream like the classic mental patient everyone seemed to believe I was. Hurray, I was finally living up to expectations! But it felt better than enduring the misery in silence. I smashed my head and shoulders against the painted brick wall repeatedly, trying to drive the discomfort out of my body like an evil spirit.

"Hey, pal, you can't get out of here that way," said a weary male voice.

I was dragged to the quiet room by two tall male staff members who looked as if they'd been on shift for thirty-six straight hours. I actually felt bad for them, having to deal with me. I imagined what I must have seemed like to them - a wild-haired, shrieking madman hurling himself against a brick wall. Just another day in paradise for them, I guessed.

Once within the small, locked, quiet room, I continued to launch myself against the thinly padded walls, trying to supplant my horrifying discomfort with actual pain. I screamed myself hoarse and mute. Someone must have finally given me an injection because I eventually crashed to sleep; there was no way I could have done so on my own. I slept curled up on the cold concrete floor of the quiet (solitary) room until late afternoon of December 31st.

The second night of my Danvers State hospitalization was New Year's Eve, and a holiday celebration was scheduled on the ward. Yay! I was released from solitary confinement and invited to "join the party," which I actually tried to do. I must say, the staff had gone to considerable efforts to create a festive atmosphere for the patients. There were tables full of soft drinks and supermarket pastries, even non-alcoholic champagne.

A hired piano player was working the old upright in the corner, hammering away at traditional Christmas songs and Auld Lang Syne. Patients' friends and families had been invited to the gala as a sort of open house. A few of them actually showed up. Surprisingly, the old place did feel sort of merry. I was determined to eke some enjoyment out of this, if only for the sake of a couple of the older patients I had come to like during my last stay.

221

But before another half-hour had passed though, my muscles began to rebel again. A terrible feeling of physical wrongness started coursing through my body. I tried to make it go away by pacing, but it quickly escalated. The muscle contractions seemed to be emanating from some mysterious place deep inside me. This episode was shaping up to be even worse than the previous nights.

If that became the case, I would choose death. No joke. I would simply find a way to end it. I'd grab keys from an attendant and inject myself with an overdose of something; anything. Or I'd use the convenient "open door policy" of the New Year's party to slip out of the unit, steal a car and drive it off a bridge. These thoughts were racing through my head as my pacing became more and more intense, more and more driven.

Although my faith had grown markedly while at Maclean's, I failed to pray for my Creator's help this time however. Being honest, I was too fucked-up to pray. The doctor on duty, though busy greeting guests and doing party duty, alertly noticed I was circling the ward, hunched over, drooling from the mouth and moaning uncontrollably. He alone had the good sense to finally realize what was going on and in turn immediately, Thank God, rushed me by ambulance to nearby Danvers General Hospital.

I moaned and thrashed against the leather restraints of the transport ambulance like a captive wild animal, even though I desperately wanted to go where it was taking me. I was completely out of my own control. If there is such a thing as demonic possession, I have an idea what it must feel like.

Shortly after my arrival at the medical hospital, staff physician Cornelius Driscoll, a competent-looking man, promptly administered the anti-parkinsonian agent Benadryl intravenously. In his medical notes, Dr. Driscoll attributed my

Parkinsonian reaction directly to the 'prolixin medication.' And because I had just been shipped in from a mental hospital, he ordered a psychiatric consultation too.

Records of that evaluation reveal me as a patient whose "speech in general was responsive, coherent, relevant and goal-directed," and who "showed no overt evidence of delusion, hallucination, formal thinking disorder, suicidal ideation or intent." The staff physician readily concurred with the drug-reaction diagnosis. An excerpt from the Danvers State Discharge Summary (which, by the way, is stamped: "CONFIDENTIAL AND PRIVILEGED: Not to Be Shown to the Patient!" - And why not? What are you hiding folks?) sums up the horrifying ordeal:

"The patient was admitted to the locked ward with orders of prolixin 10 mg. b.i.d., Cogentin 2 mg. q.d., lithium carbonate 600 mg. b.i.d. and sugar free and wheat gluten free diet. During the middle of the first night here he was noisy and was put in the quiet room. He became agitated and hit himself against the walls. Staff then put him in restraint to stop him from harming himself. He continued to moan most of the night. In the afternoon, he complained of helplessness, asking the staff to help him out of a chair. He was incoherent of urine twice and was showered but could not stand up in the shower."

"The patient's father reported that the patient had had no bowel movement for ten days. In the evening, the patient was observed on his hands and knees allowing his face to hit the floor, injuring his nose. He was found to have a temperature of 101.2 orally. The doctor on duty transferred the patient to Danvers General Hospital for

223

treatment of possible Neuroleptic Malignant Syndrome. At the hospital, all medications were stopped and the patient was started on Benedryl 50 mg. IM. q. 6 hours. His Parkinsonian signs gradually improved."

As outlined above, after two full days of benadryl treatment by Dr. Driscoll at the medical hospital, the convulsions, thank God, subsided. Instead of just being released back to my parents' house however, as one might have expected (since the original presenting problem was now under control), I was transferred back to Danvers State Hospital, where I was forcefully and inexplicably confined and treated with neuroleptics again for four additional weeks. Once again, my history of past psychiatric hospitalizations, not my present drug-reaction condition and diagnosis, was steering the course of events.

As an interesting side note to the above, about twenty years ago, I picked up by chance a copy of the Lawrence Eagle Tribune and saw photos of Dr. Levine and his wife, also a practicing psychiatrist, on the front page. The article below the pictures stated that the Levine's were being investigated for "criminal wrongdoing" by the FBI. I believe, although I can't recall for sure, that the issue at hand was Medicare fraud.

Finally, on the morning of Monday, January 28th, the day after the Super Bowl, which I vividly remember watching on the Danvers ward TV, because my long-time favorite NFL team - the L.A. Raiders and their Pro Bowl running back at the time - Marcus Allen were playing in it, I was finally released from the state psychiatric facility - a good fifty pounds overweight and obsessed with the idea of catching what the license plate number of the NEXT Mack truck that was going to run me over would be.

Chapter 18:
"My Escape to the West Coast"

About a week after being released from the state hospital, still feeling demoralized, I asked the Higher Power, whom I had just recently come to know, this question before bed one night:

"Lord, they just let me out of the Big House. I've lost everything - my fiancée, my reputation in the community, the respect of my friends and my family. I'm beaten down so bad that I feel I'll never be able come back. Tell me, where do I to go from here?"

This may seem crazy, even delusional. I can assure you, however, it was quite the opposite. Only moments after my short prayer, I heard a still voice within me say:

"Pull yourself together. Tomorrow morning, I want you to go to the Andover Bookstore. There are a few books I want you to pick up there. Trust me on this."

The following morning, I did as I'd been told and drove the old model beat-up Chevy Pacer that Mike Abodeely had given me six months earlier to the bookstore. Once inside the store, I was immediately *led* to the Self-Help section. There, at sheer random, I picked out three classics. They were The Power of Positive Thinking by Dr. Norman Vincent Peale, *The Greatest Salesman in the World* by Og Mandino, and *Think and Grow Rich* by Napoleon Hill. All have been multi-million sellers over the years. What strange force motivated me to select these three particular books over the many others that were on the self-help rack, I still don't know.

I took the books home and that night and began first reading *The Power of Positive Thinking*. After finishing that one in about a week, I went on to read the other two. At about the same time, I joined the Y with some of four hundred dollars a month in Social Security Disability my father had arranged for me to receive, unbeknownst to me, while I was in McLean's Hospital. (What a shot in the arm and a lifesaver this payment would turn out to be in the troubling years ahead. A guaranteed income every month, mining though it was, for life! Thank you, Dad. And thank you, God and FDR 43 well.

Now a fully paid member of the Y, I began running on the indoor track above the small gym. As I mentioned earlier, it was a small track - thirty-two times around constituted a mile. I started out by running a mile. Within two weeks' time, I had worked it up to two. Then, after about a month, I was running three miles with ease and began to notice that the huge amount of weight I had packed on while in the psychiatric hospitals slowly starting to melt away.

Also, while running around the track, I began repeating to myself, ten times each, from memory, about thirty or so of the positive, faith-inducing, and self-confidence-building affirmations I had taken from the three self-help books I had purchased - as well as some affirmations Norman Vincent Peale had suggested borrowing from the New Testament. This method of mind-servicing is referred to by most psychologists today as "autosuggestion." The affirmations included, from Dr. Peale:

"I can do all things through Christ that strengthens me"; "If God be for me, who dare be against me?"; "So long Thy power has kept me; sure it still will lead me on"; "I don't believe in defeat"; "God is with me and nothing can defeat me"; "Without God, I can do nothing; with God, there's nothing I can't do"; "and finally, 'According to your faith, so shall it be unto you.'"

From Og Mandino: "Yesterday is buried forever, I will think of it no more"; "Persistence will always be rewarded"; "The prizes of life are at the end of each journey, not near the beginning"; "It's not where you start, it's where you finish that counts"; and one I found especially pertinent to my life at the time: "When you think you haven't got a prayer, He's there."

And from Napoleon Hill: "The whole course of things goes to teach us faith, we need only obey"; "When one is truly ready for a thing, it puts in its appearance"; and "Nobody is ever defeated until defeat has been accepted as a reality," which the author took from a previous Helen Keller quote."

Diligently repeating these affirmations to myself over and over each day while I ran on the track proved nothing short of miraculous, just as Dr. Peale had promised it would in his book. After about two months of this "daily mind-servicing," new life suddenly 'burst upon me.' I found myself suddenly filled with a new spirit of faith, optimism, and confidence that I had never experienced before. And that spirit became apparent to people around me. In fact, just about all of my buddies at the Y noticed it and commented positively on it.

Apparently, as these three authors had stated in their books and from what the field of positive psychology has come to understand, these self-motivating statements enter through the *finite mind* and eventually find their way, through continuous repetition, into the deeper and more powerful *subconscious mind*, from where all human achievement supposedly emanates.

According to Dr. Peale, positive thought impulses that are deliberately fed to the subconscious mind lead to "success" results, while negative thought impulses, which, through indifference or passivity, are allowed to make their way into the same subconscious mind, produce "failure" results. I found out firsthand that the philosophy is as simple as minister Peale and both the other two authors claimed it to be. The subconscious mind, according to Hill, in fact, makes no distinction between positive or negative thoughts. It responds only to the information we feed it.

Upon reflection, I realized I had been the victim of "negative thought impulses" fed to my subconscious mind when, years earlier, I had that physical altercation with my Dad. My mother had unintentionally placed negative thoughts about my father in my mind and I eventually acted upon them. The building of positive faith, and self-confidence according to authors Peale, Mandino, and Hill, is accomplished through the same autosuggestion principle.

In fact, Hill states in his book that faith is the "head chemist of the mind." Millions of people, he says, believe themselves to be doomed to poverty or failure because of some strange force over which they have no control. According to him, however, they are the creators of their own "misfortunes" because of this "negative *belief*," which is picked up by the subconscious mind and translated into its physical equivalent-bringing understandably failure and defeat.

All through the ages, Hill further claims, religious leaders have admonished struggling humanity to "have faith" in this or that dogma or creed but have failed to tell people how to have faith. They have not stated, perhaps through lack of knowledge, that faith is a state of mind and it may induced by self-suggestion. Like the wind that carries one ship east and another west, the law of autosuggestion will either lift you up or pull you down according to the way you set your "sails of thought." I had miraculously stumbled upon this powerful truth through these three self-help books, just at the exact time I needed to.

In early March, still believing my health issues to be psychiatric in origin, my father made it a condition of my living with him that I participate in outpatient treatment every day at the Greater Lawrence Day Treatment Center. The head social worker at Danvers State Hospital had strongly recommended this program at the time of my January discharge.

The Day Treatment Center was a "psychosocial" rehab program located in the basement of an old downtown Lawrence department store that long since closed its doors. Various group sessions were held there, like classes, all day long, and attendees were also screened for compliance with their medication programs. Old man lithium was administered to me daily at the DTC. Also, as a crucial part of my "therapy," I was required to take such life-essential classes as needlepoint, arts and crafts, and current events, which consisted of reading the sports section of the local newspaper.

Most of my fifty or so fellow "clients" (the staff made a big point not to call us "patients") had, like me, been confined at some time to Danvers State Hospital. The central purpose of the DTC was to be a daytime holding tank for former inpatients who were now living in "less restrictive environments" due the Commonwealth's de-institutionalization policy (brought on by the state's lack of funds).

229

"Boy, I often would say to myself. I had clearly come a long way since Business School."

Around mid-May, feeling the positive results of my daily running/affirmation repetition and having sufficiently mastered the art of molding clay ashtrays, I stopped going to the Day Treatment Center. My father was not happy about this. He began telling me that if I refused to go back to there, he'd throw me out of his house and even worse, I felt that he really meant it.z

In early June, I visited with prominent medical practice attorney Neil Colleran at his Boston Office to see if I had any legal recourse on the mistreatment I felt had undergone with psychiatry. After listening to my story, including Dad's threats of imminent eviction, Colleran's advice to me was to get the hell out of town immediately, the next day if possible. He felt my father, legal guardianship papers in hand, might be working behind the scenes with the psychiatrists at McLean's or Danvers State to get me re-committed because of my refusal to go to Day Treatment.

I told the attorney that I was in no position to relocate or even to move out of my father's house, as I had very little money. The Boston lawyer then immediately pulled his wallet out of his back pants pocket, opened it, and pulled out three crisp one-hundred-dollar bills.

"Here, take this, kid. It will be enough to at least buy you a plane ticket out west. You've been screwed over big-time son, and I can see that you're a good guy. I want to help you out. We'll talk more about suing these pricks after you've situated yourself out there. Call me after you've done so."

Following my meeting with Colleran, I took a bus from downtown Boston back to my parents' home in Lawrence. That same night, after listening unattentively to an hour-long moral lecture from my father on how I was "neglecting my health" by refusing to attend Day Treatment, I went into my room, shut the door, and packed some clothes and toiletries into an old suitcase.

"Life is either a bold adventure, or it is nothing at all."

- Helen Keller

The next morning, after slipping out of the house unnoticed and then later on borrowing two hundred additional dollars from local Lebanese bakery owner and close family friend Nemer Korbani, a good soul that I'd known since childhood, I drove my beat-up Chevy Pacer to nearby Cosmopolitan Travel Agency and bought a one-way plane ticket to Las Vegas. That act set me back two hundred dollars.

Thanks to the money attorney Colleran had given me the day before, I had three hundred dollars in my pocket left along with my rapidly growing faith in both God and myself and the vague hope that an old girlfriend living in Vegas, whom I had met while on vacation to Sin City four years earlier and stayed in touch with, might take me in. The flight to Vegas was eventless (no emergency landings due to my disruptive behavior, in case anyone is taking notes).

With only carry-on luggage in hand, I trudged from the airplane through the air-conditioned, hermetically sealed environment of the airport terminal, with its mini-casinos and chain restaurants, and out the distant exit door. The hot desert air of mid-afternoon hit me like a wall. For a moment my body went into a panic, thinking it had been deposited back in the

231

Persian Gulf. But I calmed myself and made an attitude adjustment. I was going to enjoy this "vacation" and see where it led. I was in "adventure mode."

Once out of the terminal, I took a cab to my old girlfriend's apartment. On the way there, for some unknown reason, I got into a lengthy conversation with the cab driver. Out of nowhere, without even knowing my name or anything about me, he asked me if I needed a place to stay. I hadn't mentioned to him that I might be facing a housing crisis. I took his phone number, just in case things didn't work out with my ex. They didn't.

It turned out my ex-flame now had a live-in boyfriend - and a big and burly one at that. Accordingly, she told me I could only stay a couple of days at her apartment. Right after I left her place, I called the cab driver. He promptly came and picked me up and brought me to the house he was sharing with another male roommate; (A mere coincidence I ask you?)

I stayed with the cab driver and his roommate for three weeks, doing odd jobs around the house like cutting the grass and doing dishes to make at least some contribution to the household. Then, after borrowing thirty dollars for bus fare from him, took the five-hour bus ride through the desert to Los Angeles, where my younger brother George was living. When I arrived at the bus station in downtown L.A., I gave him a jingle. He showed up an hour later with a bewildered look on his face:

"Chuckie, what the Hell are you doing out here? I didn't know you were coming."

It was true. I hadn't called beforehand, just as I hadn't called my friend in Vegas either. Why not? Well, I guess a big part of me knew, in both cases, that I would have been discouraged or prevented from actually coming. My need to make a speedy move was more important than my need to be accepted once I got there.

George reluctantly brought me to his Manhattan Beach home that was owned by his very attractive blonde female roommate. Over the course of the next four days, the woman behaved quite standoffish, more than likely because George had told her I was a former mental patient. My fate was sealed on day four when I overheard her say to George:

"I don't want that psycho brother of yours living here anymore! Tell him to get out or else you get the Hell out yourself too! He scares the shit out of me."

I guess it couldn't have been spelled out any more clearly. That evening when George got home from work, he promptly confronted me:

"The witch tied my hands. I have no options left. I am sorry brother but you gunna have to find yourself another place to stay."

So, I gathered my belongings and hit the L.A. streets, and I hit them hard. I was broke and out of options. I was now officially a "homeless person."

Street life proved to be a punishing and shocking experience, certainly the most difficult thing I've ever gone through in my life, even more difficult than being confined in the mental hospitals. The closest thing that I can compare it to is the experience of a Navy Seal being dropped into a jungle with only a knife with which to survive.

When you're on the street, your priorities immediately shift. The most important goal in your life becomes simply finding a safe place to be during the shifting hours of each day. Your life revolves around the work shifts and habits of the police. As a homeless person, you see, you are an enemy of the state. No one wants you around. Everybody you encounter dismisses you as an eyesore and an irritant and wants you out of their face.

It seems as if the main function of the police is to find new ways to make you move from point A to point B and then from point B to point C. They know you have no ultimate destination; they just want you to "keep moving." It feels as if they want you to suffer and feel shame too, though I admit this might not be their true motivation. After finding a safe place to plant yourself, your next immediate priorities are, of course, eating, sleeping, and bathing.

My first night on the streets, I slept in the wooden lifeguard's chair on the beach two miles from George's apartment. (Where else do homeless dogs go?) I eventually somehow got comfortable in the hard chair and actually got a few hours of sleep that night. The following night I slept under a Roman 405 bridge in West LA. I awoke in the middle of the night to the sound of snoring only a few feet away in the pitch black. It scared the Hell out of the sun but also gave me a weird sense of comfort. At least I was not alone. Someone else was in the same straits I was.

I considered moving on into the night, but instead went back to sleep with the sound of my "companion's" ragged snoring filling my dreams and nightmares. When I awoke, my companion was gone. Whoever you were told by God bless you, my friend, if you ever read this.

Hunger changes a person. I went without eating the for next few days. I had no money at all and refused to resort to begging for spare change or carrying a cardboard sign claiming that I was homeless. as many homeless people are prone to do. I felt I was above that; guess I still had some pride left in me. Meanwhile, a pair of pay telephoned, phone calls to my two sisters back east requesting meager, short term financial assistance proved fruitless as both of them sadly told me to take a hike.

By day three, after a second night under the bridge, I found myself lurking in an alley near an outdoor burrito café, grabbing uneaten food from departed customers' plates when the waiters weren't looking. Sometimes entire tacos or burritos were left untouched! I never realized just how much food restaurants throw away. This one little place could have fed a dozen homeless people on an ongoing basis, just on its refuse alone. I did the "café lurk" for two full days. I think one of the waiters was on to me but was trying to help me out. He would conveniently disappear whenever a particularly juicy morsel was left on a plate. I'm sure I caught him looking right at me once as I "brushed by" a table and snagged a cold chimichanga.

On day four, the police caught on to my behavior and persuasively kicked me out of the neighborhood. The days and nights soon began to roll together in an indistinguishable blur. I'd often fall asleep in an alley and the police would come by at two in the morning, wake me up, and throw me back onto the streets.

Often times, just to get some sleep, I got creative and rode the L.A. transit bus all night. If the driver had a good heart, he'd let me curl up and doze off for a spell in the back of the bus. I would like to mention that I was able to keep going during this perilous time solely because I felt the continuous protective presence of a Higher Power. I guess you could say, in the words of Saint Paul that "I preserved because I saw Him who is invisible."

I couldn't look for work, though I wanted to, because I had no phone number and address by which a prospective employer could reach me. I still refused to panhandle though. Instead, whenever I felt above eating at a soup kitchen, which was often, I'd go into a McDonald's or Burger King and ask the manager if I could do some menial work (i.e., stacking boxes in the back room) for a few hours in exchange for something to eat - maybe a Big Mac or a Whopper. People are much kinder than you might believe. Most of the time, the managers let me do it and later fed me.

After about a month of this, desperately wanting a roof over my head, I called about a dozen friends and family members back east and asked to borrow some money - just two hundred bucks from each - that's all. Having always held a job and been self-sufficient since I was fourteen years old, it was the first time in my life I ever had to ask anyone for money. As you might gather then, I found the experience to be totally humiliating.

Even worse, everyone I called said NO. These folks included two female first cousins, whose entire families my parents had sponsored to come over from Lebanon in the early seventies, my very well-off godfather, and a highly accomplished and well-healed friend of mine (I thought) from the YMCA. These unanticipated rebuffs were enormously hard to swallow. It was now plainly apparent that I wasn't even worth two hundred bucks to anyone. I think those I asked for help believed they would have been "enabling me," whatever that means, or that I should "just get a job," or that "they'd never get their money back" if they said yes.

236

Street life was taking its expected toll, but almost every day I went to the Westside YMCA and tried, at the very least, to get in a run and a workout. If the staff wouldn't let me do this, I'd ask if I could just take a shower. The Y had a five-dollar guest fee, and most days I couldn't pay it. Quite a few times, the guy on duty let me in to at least shower. But not always. I wore the same jeans and shoes every day and carried all my worldly possessions around in an athletic bag. One of these was a woolen blanket I found on the beach. It came in handy whenever I was forced to sleep outdoors.

Meanwhile, back home, Dad remained intractable. Whenever I'd phone him for moral support or to ask him to wire me the proceeds of my monthly disability check (he was my "representative payee"), he'd urge me to return home, serving up platitudes like:

"You can't run away from your problems, son, you take them with you," and urging me to "come home to your mother and I, where you'll at least have a place to lay your head. Wandering the streets alone in a strange city like you're doing is no way to live."

You're preaching to the choir on that one, Dad. I'm the one out here suffering though.

As bad as things were, I did not want to return home. Why would I? So that my parents could re-hospitalize me? No, thanks!

After about three months of living on the streets, I was physically and emotionally drained. Late one Friday night, and after not having slept a wink for three days, I sensed I was about to crash and maybe even die out there. I knew I had to "do something" right away. I had no place to turn for help except to my Higher Power:

"Lord Almighty, I've come to trust you. You saw me through all this crap for a reason. I don't know what that reason was but I'm sure it wasn't to let me die and become another homeless statistic out here on the streets. Please help me like you did when I called on you before, and please help me NOW or I'm not going to make it!"

You might not believe what I'm about to tell you, but about a half-hour after I blurted out that simple prayer in desperation, a middle-aged stranger pulled his car up out of nowhere and stopped beside me on Santa Monica Boulevard. He rolled down his passenger window and said to me,

"Son, do you need help tonight?"

In happy shock and without giving it another thought, I responded:

"Yes, sir, I do. I'm homeless and have nowhere to sleep and am fearing for my life."

"Well then, get in."

The man drove me about twenty miles from West L.A to a rundown section of downtown Los Angeles. There was little conversation between us during our ride there. He never asked me my name, and I never got his either. All I said to him as we were riding to our still unknown destination to me was:

"Who are you, mister? Where did you come from and why did you stop for me?"

He responded, "Oh I'm just a Christian man just trying to do the right thing. I heard a strange voice in my ear which I don't often hear, telling me to stop; this young man might need help."

When we arrived at our destination - a run down, shabby-looking hotel - a large number of homeless and down-and-out folks were congregating on the sidewalk outside. The man parked in front of the hotel and said:

"Come on in with me, son."

We walked into the hotel together and up to the service desk in the lobby. The stranger then promptly reached into his back pocket, pulled out his wallet, and took out three one-hundred-dollar bills. He handed them to the innkeeper and said,

"This should be enough to cover the cost of one of your rooms for this fine young man for about a week, right?"

The clerk hammered away at his calculator, then responded,

"Yes sir, I think you're right. It will."

As you might know, "Los Angeles" means "City of Angels." I ask you, was this just a stroke of "luck" or else an answer to a desperate prayer?

I stayed in that hotel and rejuvenated myself for a whole week. About a week after that, I finally found a little job for myself in a West L.A. restaurant and a one-room place to live in a rundown rooming house. Once I got on my feet, I had myself examined by prominent West Los Angeles psychiatrist Clinton Montgomery for an "independent evaluation." He had been referred to me by the UCLA Medical Center.

Unlike the psychiatrists I'd met with before, Dr. Montgomery was a caring and compassionate man who looked me in the eye as if I were an actual human being. Montgomery saw me four times in or around October of 1984. Following his extensive evaluation, the psychiatrist gave me an opinion letter: It read as follows:

"I evaluated Charles Ead for four one-hour sessions at my office because of a history of mental illness. During my sessions with Mt. Ead, he showed no evidence of mania or depression and was not psychotic, and more importantly, contrary to his history, I found no evidence of mental illness in him. I instead, find Charles to be an energetic, resilient, and tough-minded young man who appears to be coping with the difficulties of establishing himself in an unfamiliar city quite well. I have agreed to meet with him periodically as he so chooses."

In addition to providing me with this letter, Dr. Montgomery voted great alarm with the psychiatric treatment I had received back home.

On a Friday afternoon in early October, I visited the Beverly Hills Hilton, hoping to find more profitable work there and struck up a conversation with a blonde-haired woman working there by the name of Dawn. She was about my age and quite lovely. Dawn took a liking to me, as I did to her, and invited me to have lunch with her the next day at a restaurant called Gladstone, which she said was "where Sunset meets the beach."

A little romance perhaps? Long overdue. Great, I thought; life in time city was indeed looking up. The next day around noontime, I took a bus down Sunset Boulevard to the beach and met Dawn at the sunny, open-air restaurant that had lots of greenery and featured seafood and salads. I wore clean clothes that had just come out of the laundry and did not feel out of place at all as I took my place at a booth beside that of a well-known female soap opera star. I didn't want Dawn to have a large bill so, I just ordered a salad. Dawn on the other hand, ordered a full-course meal - Surf & Turf with the works.

We were talking and having a stimulating conversation, and everything seemed just fine. Suddenly, after she cleaned her plate, without saying a word, Dawn picked herself up and marched out of the restaurant and never looked back. I was highly confused. Shortly thereafter, the waiter brought the check over to my table. It was for thirty-five dollars. I didn't have much money in my pocket, maybe five bucks at the most, so I told the waiter what had just happened.

"I'll wash dishes to pay the bill, sir," I offered.

"You just stay right here," was his firm response. Then two men in three-piece suits came to the booth, flanked me, and told me to stay with them.

About twenty minutes later, two police officers entered the restaurant. One of them spoke briefly with the maître-D', then the pair walked right up to my table. Without a word of explanation, they cuffed my hands behind my back, and, in front of two dozen or so of staring eyes, muscled me outside and shoved me into the back of their cruiser. I was utterly humiliated, to say the least.

The officers then drove me to the Santa Monica police station, where I was placed in a cell with another guy and told I would have to remain there until Monday morning, when I could go before a judge. Having no money for the fifty-dollar bail, I was forced to spend the entire weekend locked up in jail.

My "roommate" was a slight, bespectacled Hispanic man with a disarmingly gentle demeanor. Fit to be tied, I was in no mood for company, though. Doing my best to ignore this man, I paced back and forth like a caged panther. Every time the guy looked at me, I glared at him, trying to get the "leave me alone" message across loud and clear. He just smiled knowingly with

241

a gap-toothed grin and appeared to be not in the least bit intimidated. There was a strange peacefulness about this fellow though that made it impossible to be really angry at him. He seemed to find me funny for some reason, and it seemed like hours before either of us spoke:

"You seem to carry a lot of anger my friend," he finally said in his soft Latino accent after I had kicked the barred, cell door about four times.

"Were you born with these powers of deduction or did you have to learn them on the streets?" I asked.

"I'm Manuel. God loves you, my friend. You need to stop being so hard on yourself. You need to stop fighting with the world. You need to accept God's love and just Surrender to everything that's happened to you, as it was all God's Will."

"What the Hell would you know about what's happened to me?" I snapped.

"The more you keep fighting and thinking the world is doing you wrong, the more your nightmare will continue. Just like two boxers, you and the world - barn, barn, barn. The world punches, you punch back. It never ends. Just accept God's love. Accept that life is funny. God made a funny joke for us all to laugh at."

"Right. Ha, Ha."

"Look, my friend, this is you."

Manuel jumped up and started growling and pacing back and forth, imitating me in a comical manner. He actually did a very credible Chate. Each impression. I should have been enraged, I should have punched him out, I should have screamed in frustration at being stuck for the weekend in a four-by-eight cage with Manuel the Mad Prophet and his Traveling Comedy Show. But instead, I laughed, hard and long. Harder than I had ever laughed in my entire life.

Manuel laughed too. Nothing draws two human beings together faster than laughter. For ten solid minutes, we laughed so hard we were falling on the floor. The duty cop came by to check on the situation once or twice and rattled his baton against the bars. It only made us laugh even harder. When I finally stopped laughing, Manuel asked me:

"Are you ready to stop fighting the world?" Strangely, I was.

For the rest of the weekend, Manuel spoke to me about the Bible and its lessons. He was an endless font of knowledge and wisdom. Although he always known in my heart there was a God, I had never been a churchgoing person and had never given spiritual matters much attention before. Now, I had no choice. I was locked in a cell with Manuel - The Mad Prophet.

For a street guy, he really was an enlightened man. I am now quite convinced that Disappearing Dawn showed up in my life only to put me in that jail cell with Manuel that weekend. I eventually viewed our meeting as gift from God and Manuel as yet another angel, and this completely changed my perspective and became a major turning point in my life.

I felt resistance slip away as I did what Manuel suggested. I fully accepted my life circumstances. I "surrendered." In my heart I said Yes instead of No. At Manuel's urging, I forgave everyone I felt had wronged me- Dr. Denapoli; my parents; the hospitals; Paula - the head nurse from Hell. I felt the sixty-ton weight I had been carrying around since my first psychiatric hospitalizations lift off of my shoulders.

Monday morning arrived, and I was taken to a large room with about thirty fellow inmates. One of them claimed to be the older brother of the famed actor Charles Bronson. He looked very much like Charles, and I believed him. Instead of projecting bitterness and anger, I joked with everybody including Mr. Bronson and tried to make them all feel better.

It seemed to work. With me playing the clown, I could feel the room lighten up. I waited for several hours then went before a middle-aged, black, female judge. After telling her my story in detail with a smile on my face, she laughed heartily and I promised to pay the restaurant the thirty-five dollars as soon as I got my check from work the next week. The judge then said to me:

"I think you're a cool guy, Mr. Ead. So, just forget the thirty-five dollars"

She then immediately ordered the magistrate to release me. As I left the courthouse, I felt a sense of moral victory.

In the days that followed, I continued where Manuel had left off. For example, about a week later, I purchased a small blue book from the Hope Chapel in Hermosa Beach. It contained the New Testament as well as the complete and highly powerful, King David's faith-building, Old Testament Book of Psalms. Life took on a much lighter tone. My anger dissipated. I laughed often. I approached people I met with love in my heart, just as my new Master Jesus had taught. People automatically treated me the same way.

Surely, I was now in possession of a new world.

I'm happy to report that the faith I developed during that period of my life (mostly due to my daily reading of the Psalms) has grown stronger over the years and sustained me until this day, while completely changing my life perspective. Rather than focusing on "poor me," for reasons still unknown to me, I began for the first time, to develop a social conscience and a concern about the plights of others. It wasn't all about ME anymore. This newfound concern for others, especially those who were marginalized in society, like I had been, felt like liberation rather than a burden.

Chapter 19:
Now Back East Again

One day, I heard "the still voice" speak to me again:

"I want you to take the next step and leave L.A now and fly back east to Washington, D.C. There are some important things I want you to learn there."

"What kind of things?" I asked back.

"I'll let them be known to you when you get there."

"But how will I survive in D.C.? The only person I know there is my older sister. I don't really get along with her too well. Maybe she won't let me stay with her. I'll just end up homeless for a long stretch like I did here in L.A."

"Fear not and take courage. You'll be well taken care of there. Haven't you learned yet, That you're not alone down there on Earth? And where I guide, I provide."

Using some of the money I had earned by working at the restaurant and some of my monthly disability allowance, that my father had just a few days earlier faithfully Western Union-ed me as had been his policy on the third of every month when my check arrived at his house in the mail, I booked a one-way flight to our nation's capital, where my older sister Marion was living with her long-standing boyfriend. With my sense of social duty and my faith both growing, I said goodbye to L.A. A personal goal in moving to D.C. was to get involved with social policy. I didn't know how yet, but I figured D.C. was the place to start.

About 11 o'clock at night, I arrived at Marion's apartment in Alexandria, Virginia. The same thing that had happened with my brother George happened with my Marion however. Her live-in boyfriend Craig, a pothead and prodigious beer drinker, didn't want me to stay with them. Craig knew from a previous encounter with me that I didn't like him and I knew he didn't like me as well.

This guy thought so highly of himself in fact, that he made Donald Trump and Bill Clinton look like two men who suffered from deep-seated inferiority complexes. Needless to say, shortly after serving me a ham and cheese sandwich and a hot cup of coffee, my sister threw me out onto the streets.

Jesus correctly prophesized that in the last days, (The time Bible scholars tell us we are living in today), that a man's enemies will be members of his own household.

I now found myself in a housing crisis again. This time, though, I didn't let it panic me or crush my spirits, because I knew that my Creator had my back. I could sense that things were going to work out. Just twenty minutes after being thrown out by Marion, I stumbled into a homeless shelter just three blocks from her apartment. The staff person who answered the door took me in and told me I could stay for a full week. I was well fed and taken care of that entire time period.

One week later, almost immediately after I was asked to depart the shelter, I met up with a middle-aged, Middle Eastern looking stranger on an Alexandria, Virginia street corner, just three blocks from the shelter where I had been staying. Right out of nowhere, he started up a conversation with me in broken English.

"You Arabic sir?" he asked.

"My roots are Arabic, yes. Why do you ask?"

"Allah just told me talk with you. And I always do what Allah tell me."

"Are you Arabic too? You look Arabic." I then inquired of him.

"No, I not. I Afghan!"

"What are you doing here in D.C.?"

"Me and fellow countrymen flee war with Russians. We Muslims stay together in big complex down the street. You nice man, I can tell. Are you Muslim too?"

"No, I'm Christian," I answered.

"Would you like come with me and meet my people?"

Homeless and having no better options at the time, I responded:

"Sure. Let's go."

I followed the man to the housing complex he had just mentioned, which he now informed me housed roughly sixty fellow Afghani refugees. After I told the Imam who greeted us at the front door that I was homeless, he invited me, without hesitation, to stay with him and his countrymen for as long as I needed. Next, he led me to the one-room makeshift mosque he had set up in the building complex where I was told I could sleep.

The Imam then told me that I would be staying in the mosque and that he would ask his wife to prepare meals for me each day and deliver them on schedule. These meals, it turned out, were usually combination plates containing healthy portions of varied meats and chicken, white rice, and beans. I never went hungry during my three week stay with these highly generous and accommodating Muslim people. Needless to say, my respect for Muslims from that point on, started to grow by leaps and bounds.

I would later learn that almsgiving and caring for the destitute are two of the five major pillars of Islam. Would I have been treated so hospitably if I had knocked on a Catholic Church door instead? I have often wondered that to myself. After spending three weeks under the care of the Muslim refugees, I didn't want to burden them anymore so, I decided to move on. To where, though? I had no idea. Something unexplainable told me to I get on the metro and venture into the Foggy Bottom section of D.C.

Once again, I mysteriously met up with a stranger who showed up out of the blue. He led me to the George Washington University fraternity house of Theta Delta Chi, which was located just three blocks from the White House. Right after we arrived there, I was inspired to knock at the front door and was greeted by a young, welcoming apparent fraternity member who behaved as if he was expecting my arrival.

Quickly sizing me up, the member welcomed me in. After I told him I was homeless, he said I could stay there with him and the other fraternity members rent free for as long as I wanted. A week later, during a short initiation ceremony, I was actually indoctrinated into the fraternity as an honorary member.

True to my Creator's promise, I didn't have to spend even one night on the D.C. streets. Was all this just a series of strange coincidences? A well-respected Catholic priest I recently saw on the EWTN Catholic Television Network insightfully made the point that a coincidence is just "God trying to hide Himself."

During the ensuing year I spent in D.C., I worked as a waiter on weekends, joined a health club, and ran four miles, five days a week. After I got myself on my feet and left my friends at the fraternity, I moved into a third-floor, one-room loft close by. There I lived a self-imposed Bohemian existence and contented myself with only "sustenance and covering," the words of Saint Paul.

I did a great deal of reading, though - newspapers, magazines, political books, and Amnesty International reports, as well as my self-help books and the Bible and frequented several of the wonderful political bookstores that were located downtown on K Street. I was like a kid in a candy store. I completely immersed myself in the study of social issues, world affairs, and comparative religions.

A new and fascinating world was opening up to me, one in which making money and living the supposed "good life" no longer had any hold on me. I no longer wanted to be Warren Buffett. I wanted to be Martin Luther King instead. I eventually picked up a video copy of Dr. King's "I Have a Dream" speech, played it on my home T.V. several times, and thought it was the most inspiring peace of speech-making I had ever encountered, except for Christ's majestic "Sermon on the Mount" of course. Whenever I listened to it, which was often, goose bumps would run down my spine.

Among the many global issues I became passionately hooked into were: racial and economic inequities in America; growing world poverty and hunger; geopolitical fallouts from the Cold War; the senseless arms race and accompanying maddening, nuclear proliferation; the growing phenomenon of homelessness in our country; inter-religious conflicts; the negative and lasting effects of

250

colonialism on the developing world - most especially on my native Middle Eastern lands; the impending dangers of climate change; the seemingly intractable Israeli-Palestinian conflict; and the ongoing plight of the nomadic Kurdish people - forever struggling, but never succeeding, to secure a safe homeland for themselves in the harsh and unwelcoming middle east..

As the weeks passed, I kept up my daily running regimen. I ran around the Mall and the Lincoln Memorial, still faithfully repeating my memorized list of daily self-motivators. Running nearly every day allowed me to shed the pounds I had put on while hospitalized. By the following summer, I was trim again and feeling very fit mentally, physically, and emotionally. I began to feel homesick and longed to see my parents, my cousins, and my many good friends back home again.

I had a great deal of ambivalence about returning home however. I wanted to see my mother and father, whom I still loved deeply and held in high regard despite what they had needlessly put me through, and I still had the belief that if I could develop into half the man my father was, I'd be somebody. On the other hand, I didn't want to re-open the psychiatric Pandora's box.

As I pondered my folks' situation, it hit me for perhaps the first time, that being a parent is a totally thankless job, one done out of love alone and without any expectation of financial or other rewards. The immense responsibility placed on a mother or father I reasoned is like putting a thousand-pound rock on their backs. It's a weight that eventually chokes you to death before your time.

As the young actor Charles Bronson said in The Magnificent Seven, when confronted with several young boys from the village that he and six other gunslingers were trying to liberate from a band of thugs about their supposed cowardly, farmer fathers, who refused to fight:

"Being a parent requires more genuine courage than any warrior ever had to summon up on the battlefield, including me."

With these words in mind, I take my hat off to "any man or woman" who has the balls to bring children into this upside - down world today. I know that I myself never had enough gumption to do it.

I had known deep down, all throughout my ordeal, that my parents were doing the best they knew how and had only my well-being in mind. They had also provided me with the greatest and richest childhood any young boy who ever walked the face of the earth could have hoped for. Accordingly, I felt I owed them a great debt and held no lasting animosity toward them. In full faith that my Creator promised to protect me from harm, I returned home, despite some deep hidden reservations about possibly being psychiatrically re-hospitalized. I mean anything could happen - right?

To my surprise, neither of my parents made any mention whatsoever of anything related to psychiatry. They were just elated to see me again. It was as if nothing bad had ever taken place between us. The fourteen months that I'd spent away from home had worked wonders for me. I was happy again, in great health, and focusing on the state of the world and not on the petty issues of my past. I also could sense that my spiritual life, through continuous effort on my part, was improving exponentially.

While at home with my parents, I felt the desire to do some creative writing. Seeing myself as a social activist and no longer as a shallow-minded mob of corporate America, I also developed a desire to enter the media and/or political fields. I wanted, more than anything, to serve my newfound Creator in any capacity He wanted me to and to do something - hopefully something big that would make this world a better place.

So, after spending six positive months at home with my parents and doing some writing, I flew back to Los Angeles, partial scripts in hand. Initially I stayed on the UCLA campus with the same Theta Delta Chi fraternity I had lived with in D.C. A week after my arrival, I secured a job waiting tables at a West L.A. Lebanese-American restaurant coincidently named Byblox. I soon saved up enough money to get my own place - a single room in an elderly woman's house in West L.A., three blocks from where I was working. Not an ideal situation, but at least my own. I was learning to appreciate the small things.

The elderly woman with whom I found lodging confided to me the day after I moved in that she chose me for the apartment ahead of thirty other UCLA student applicants because she sensed I was honest and would pay the rent on time. Also, as she put it, there was "something special" about me.

I loved L.A. as I had loved D.C. Unlike back east though, the weather in L.A. was always great. And unlike the last time I had lived in L.A., I now sensed it to be a city of unlimited opportunity where I could become anything I wanted to be. A month or so after moving into my pad, I enrolled in a screenwriting class at the UCLA film extension school. It was my strong desire back then - as it still is now, thirty years later, to develop the story of my psychiatric mistreatment into a book and possibly even a film in order to and expose psychiatry's ugly head to the public.

253

I named my story 'Snap Diagnosis' because I felt it accurately captured my psychiatric experience. About a month after I enrolled in the writing class, I also interviewed with the daughter of Lee Strasberg at her method-acting school in West L.A., which she had taken over from her famous actor director/and teacher father - Lee after his death. I was informed by the young Strasberg that numerous well-known actors had studied at her school including Marlon Brando and Al Pacino.

Miss Strasberg told me after only a half-hour interview that I was very good looking, had "great acting instincts" and was the perfect age for an actor. 30. In her view, I had what it took to make it in the movie industry. Miss Strasburg later said she very much wanted me as a student at her school and promised that if I attended it and successfully graduated two years later, she would aggressively use her contacts in the industry to open doors for me and help me get started. Take that Dr. Linden and McLean's!

Right before parting company, Ms. Strassberg asked me why I wanted to become an actor. I responded:

"Well, first of all, I think that I can be very good at it. And secondly, I figured that if I could achieve some notoriety in the film industry, I could use it as a platform to be the face for a great many hurting people out there by advocating for a progressive social agenda."

She responded by saying back to me:

"Charles, that's very high-minded of you, but you're going to be the exception to the rule. Let me tell you. I've been involved with this industry for over twenty years. Trust me. NOBODY involved in it cares the least bit about or does anything for anybody else except themselves! Get over it. This business, with just a handful of exceptions, is full blown hedonistic."

As I worked on writing the details of my personal story, a lot of negative emotions began to stir up inside me, and I wondered if this was even the right thing for me to be doing. I kept reassuring myself that it was, but I also came to realize there was something more that needed to be done. Although I had survived the nightmare of my psychiatric mistreatment and had forgiven in my heart all those I felt had wronged me, and although my Og Mandino book advised me to "bury the past and think of it no more," I was experiencing increasing internal conflict.

I fully realized that my reputation and good name had in fact been ruined, unjustly, by the psychiatric profession. There was no arguing that fact. I reasoned further that if I ever decided to run for political office or hold a job of political leadership, which I aspired to do in the future, this psychiatric crap of mine would inevitably come back to bite me in the ass, unless I did something to resolve it.

My screenwriting instructor at UCLA - Frank McAdams, was an understanding and practical guy. I talked with him at length about my concerns. He agreed with me that I should take some remedial legal action. After reviewing my two-page synopsis of 'Snap Diagnosis' five weeks into class, he told me my story was "very compelling", had "great potential" and was a mixture of 'Cuckoo's Nest' meets 'Midnight Express'.

His feedback gave me a great feeling of encouragement and made me believe I was on the verge of having lightning strike. Professor McAdams went on to say that if I felt that strongly about repairing my reputation, I should sue the doctors and hospitals that mistreated me - not for revenge or as an angry and/or disgruntled ex-patient but to make a statement and force people to accept some responsibility for their actions.

Following up on this, I talked with a couple of prominent medical malpractice attorneys in the Los Angeles area, one of them Century City lawyer Raoul Magana, who, after patiently listening to my full story, told me I might have a case but that I'd have to get a Massachusetts lawyer to file suit for me. Doing so, he said, most likely would require me to return to my home state and petition local lawyers to take my case. Now I was conflicted even more.

I didn't want to go back to Lawrence, Massachusetts, - a downward-bound, former mill city. I wanted to make to make my home in L.A. instead - a can make things happen, place where I saw a bright future for myself. After mulling the situation over for about a week, I decided to put my promising new career on hold and return home to "take care of business." This was not what I really wanted to do, but rather what I felt that I really had to do.

Chapter 20:
A Failed Lawsuit

I dropped out of the screenwriting course and told my employer at *Byblos* Restaurant that I needed some indefinite time off, then flew home. Both my parents met me upon my arrival at Logan. They were delighted to see me home again and in good spirits.

"That California sunshine really did the trick, huh, Chuckie?" beamed my mother.

The three of us had a pleasant ride home, chatting about this and that. When I entered the family home, it looked different, the way home often does when you've been away for a while. I settled in for a few days and found myself completely at ease once again with my parents.

The first local lawyer I contacted told me that before I could even petition lawyers to handle my case, I needed to have the permanent legal guardianship, which had been awarded to my father in 1983, vacated. Seeing me now in good health and good spirits, my father had no objection to this. In fact, he encouraged it enthusiastically. Local attorney Mike Stella, whom I knew from the Y, handled the paperwork at no charge and within a couple of weeks the guardianship was terminated. I was now free to call on lawyers about the larger case.

Before seeking counsel, I prepared a detailed, twenty-page typed up summary of what had happened to me throughout my negative encounters with the psychiatric profession. I was hoping to secure my medical records and read through them before I completed the summary. The four hospitals that I was confined in, however - Holy Family, Baldpate, McLean's and

Danvers State - all refused my phone requests for the records, stating they would only release them to me through an attorney. This run around, I later learned, was against the law.

Preparing the summary was a lot of work, given all the doctors and hospitals that had treated me. Once I completed it, though, I made an appointment with prominent Boston malpractice attorney Camille Sarrouf, a man of Lebanese ancestry and one of five top personal injuries lawyers in Massachusetts. Sarrouf had a plush and expansive office on the wharf of the Boston Waterfront. Nice digs for a contingency lawyer; I was optimistic. I handed Sarrouf my written summary, which he spent twenty minutes reading, and then detailed my story to him verbally. He proceeded to burst my bubble however.

"Your case, Charles, is a hot potato!" (He shook his hand in the air as if my prepared document was actually on fire and burning in his hand.).

"It's my experience that psychiatric disorders are a highly nebulous form of pathology. By this I mean you can always find an expert witness who will say the opposite. You can go to five psychiatrists and get five different diagnoses. Psychiatry is not an exact science, regardless of what many psychiatrists may claim. (*Amen to that*, I thought.). Due to this, it will be very hard to prove misdiagnosis in the courtroom."

"In addition, you're dealing with multiple doctors and hospitals here, not just one. It's going to be nearly impossible to prove that every one of them screwed up. I can see you're a fighter, Charles. I admire that quality in a man. But you're beating a dead horse. You have the will but not the way. I'm also concerned that the three-year statute of limitations on cases like yours may have already run out."

He concluded by stating that although it was obvious to him that I'd been screwed over and that he felt very bad about it, he could not represent me.

I probably should have listened to Sarrouf's seemingly sound advice, faced the fact that I was trying to achieve the impossible, thanked my lucky stars that I had at least survived the ordeal, and cut my losses. But because though of my headstrong nature and my determination to clear my good name and help other abused patients, I did the opposite. I made the decision right then and there while still in Sarrouf's office to forge on. To put things in accounting terms, being headstrong can sometimes be an asset. If the trait is not controlled, however, it can also be a major liability, as I would soon discover.

Mary Manzi - an elderly woman who had worked alongside my father in the city tax assessor's office for ten years and who knew my family very well tried her best to drill some sense into me:

"Chuckie, why don't you abandon this stupid lawsuit thing and spend your time finding a nice girl for yourself. You're not getting any younger, you know."

"Mary, no disrespect intended, but securing justice for myself is more important to me right now than having a mate."

Determined to have my day in court and feeling a moral obligation to go to bat for the tens of thousands of psychiatric patients who were currently being "imprisoned" and possibly abused in psychiatric hospitals each year, I continued to knock on lawyers' doors. Over the course of the next three months, I called on at least three dozen of them. To my dismay, none of them would take my case. Everyone I spoke with said basically

259

the same thing: - the case was too hard to prove in court, and the statute of limitations was too high a hurdle as well. Seeing no other seeming route to justice, however, I stubbornly shook off each rejection and fought on.

In early September, now feeling completely frustrated, I flew to Washington D.C. and sat down with Albert Mokhiber - the legal director of the Arab American Anti-Discrimination Committee (ADC). I had met Albert during my many visits to the ADC's K Street office while in D.C. the year before. I had visited the office to deepen my understanding of the Israeli-Palestinian conflict. The Mokhiber avenue, I reasoned, was my last hope. *If the ADC's legal head can't help me*, I told myself, *I'll give up the lawsuit angle and go back to L.A. and try to complete 'Snap Diagnosis.'*

After reading my legal brief, the ADC legal head told me that what had happened to me was terrible and surreal and gave me the name of Boston attorney Louis Massey, who was also an Arab - American and had done some earlier work for the Committee. When I arrived back in Massachusetts two days later, I phoned Massey and made an appointment to go into his office and present my case to him.

After reading my treatment summary, which he referred to as the best prepared legal case he had ever seen, Massey expressed outrage. A tall, heavy-set man with dark eyes, dark hair, and a dark complexion, he told me that in spite of the inherent difficulties of the case, we Arabs must take a lesson from the Jews and stick together and help each other, and so said his firm would take on my representation. Maybe author Og Mandino was right?

"Persistence will always be rewarded."

Massery however, failed to make known to me he specialized in worker's compensation law and had never tried a medical malpractice case before. He spoke only of the legendary legal skills the supposed super star, head partner of his firm - Earl Cooley was blessed with even going so far as to proudly confide that his co-attorneys at his firm often joked in heartful admiration that Cooley often walked to work every morning on the nearby Charles River.

The following week, Massery sent me a contingency fee agreement with instructions for me to read it and sign it. I promptly complied. Attached to the agreement was a one-page letter from him, the last sentence of which read:

"I have no doubt Charles that we will bring this case to a favorable conclusion for you."

After receiving my signed agreement through the mail, the Boston attorney called me and asked if he could meet with me and my parents so, I arranged for all of us to have dinner together at Bishop's Restaurant. Upon meeting my new attorney, my parents seemed a little apprehensive. Massery had a reassuring manner however, and quickly struck up a lively conversation with them. My parents soon relaxed and we had a constructive meeting.

We didn't talk too much about my psychiatric history. Massery touched upon it just briefly. After dinner, my attorney then thanked my parents for coming, and my always generous father picked up the check. Massery told me he was going to get started on the suit right away and would be in touch.

His first order of business was to secure all of my medical records. He sent me record request forms for all the doctors and hospitals that had treated me. I promptly signed them and returned them to him. It seemed I had done all I could do. My case now appeared to be in good hands and I started thinking about returning to Los Angeles and re-entering film school. I phoned Massery and spoke to him about this.

"Do you need me here in Massachusetts anymore, Lou? I want to go back to L. A."

"No, Charlie. I'll take it from here. Enjoy the swimming pools and movie stars."

Soon thereafter, I applied for the Khalil Gibran Educational Scholarship. To my delight, the foundation called and told me I had won it. A brief history on this: I had picked up by sheer chance a book of Gibran's entitled "Jesus the Son of Man" in a bookstore while living in D.C. I found it a fascinating read. It represented a new way of looking at the life and ministry of Christ. Later on, at my request, I phoned and befriended Khalil Gibran's nephew, also named Khalil, who was still living in the Boston home of the long-deceased poet. He took a liking to me and in turn invited me to his home.

While I was there, the younger Khalil strongly encouraged me to apply for the scholarship, which was awarded annually to three Lebanese - American students who showed academic promise. And so, a week before Christmas, with the $1,000 in Gibran scholarship money in hand, I flew back to L.A. I stayed again at the fraternity house at UCLA, and a week after arriving, I signed up for the spring semester screenwriting class at UCLA Extension again.

In early February, attorney Massey sent me a letter stating he had gotten all of my medical records and was preparing to file a complaint "soon." Two weeks later, I received a copy of the complaint Massey had filed. To my great dismay, it named only my mother's psychiatrist, Denapoli, as a potential defendant. The document I felt was ambiguous and poorly written. I had initially hoped that my lawyer, working for a prestigious firm as he did, would have done a better job on it.

It was my strong belief that for my suit to be successful, all of the doctors and hospitals who treated me should be named as defendants. If only one doctor was named, he would call the other doctors into court to back him up. If, on the other hand, all the parties were named, they'd be preoccupied with defending themselves and couldn't pull such a move. I've since spoken with a reputable personal injury attorney who told me my legal logic back then was spot on.

Further angering me was my lawyer's two-paragraph cover letter accompanying the complaint, which stated he was no longer "that optimistic" about my case because the records of Dr. Denapoli's first hospitalization indicated that a medical exam had been performed on me while I was in the Holy Family Hospital. To me it seemed that Massey was developing cold feet and splitting hairs - and that he was missing the whole two major themes of my case: those being misdiagnosis and false incarceration.

Meanwhile, the evening screenwriting class was going well. I also signed up for Strasberg's acting school for the following fall semester and found work as a part-time accountant during the day, which helped pay the time hundred-dollar monthly rent at the frat house. My health was still excellent and I ran and exercised five days a week at the West-L.A. YMCA, which was just a short bus ride from my living quarters. Although still displeased with the way my attorney had prepared the complaint, I put my case it in God's hands, which eased my mind a bit, and all systems seemed to me to be a good.

In late March, however, things unraveled quickly. I awoke one morning with a massive and overwhelming headache. It seemed even worse than the severe migraines my brother George would get during his high school and college years, which often rendered him bedridden for days. Later that week, I began to suffer from severe muscle, chest, and joint pain and overpowering mono-like fatigue. I was so tired I couldn't wake up to go to work in the morning. Damn! What the Hell was this all about?

After being sick like this for a full week, I went to a West L.A. internist. He examined me, drew blood, and told me to return in a week. When I went back to see him, he told me I could very well be suffering from an undetectable virus. Still unable to work, I depleted my finances rapidly. In mid-April, nearly broke and sick as a dog, I was forced, at the internist's recommendation, to drop out of film school again and fly home where I knew I could live back with my parents without expense. I hated intensely to have to do this though.

Once back home, my cognitive functions deteriorated and I began to slip into the angry, confrontational mode of my L.A. street days. In this state I rashly wrote a letter to the head partner of Massey's firm, Earl Cooley, supposedly one of the most respected lawyers in Massachusetts, and complained that I felt that there should have been multiple defendants named in Massey's complaint against Dr. Denapoli. After receiving my letter, Cooley called me at home and told me to come into his office and on the morning of April 25th I complied with his wishes and did just that.

I began the meeting by brashly telling the chief partner I was disappointed we couldn't broaden our legal assault. I realized, only upon later reflection, that perhaps I should have been more diplomatic in my manner with Massey quietly present in the room. Cooley responded:

"I reviewed your case, Charles. You think this is a good case? I don't think this is a good case. We've done the best we could for you, and it appears you're not satisfied. I'm sorry, but we're no longer going to be able to represent you. So please take your file with you and leave."

"But Mr. Cooley, your firm signed a legal contract with me last October to provide representation in this matter. Aren't you going to honor your contractual obligation to me?"

"Maybe you didn't hear me the first-time son. I said: LEAVE!"

As I disappointedly grabbed my file from Cooley and got up to leave, he at least alerted me to the fact that the complaint Massey had filed with the probate court needed to be "served" as soon as possible. Having no legal experience and not knowing what the legal term served meant, I just dismissed Cooley's statement as unimportant and abruptly left his office.

Totally discouraged and feeling that Cooley had ripped the heart out of my chest, I strolled the three blocks to Fancuil Hall Marketplace. I recall that it was a cold, dreary, rainy spring morning, and I was under-dressed with only a light, alligator. spring jacket on. Shivering, I marched into Hoolihans Bar and ordered myself an Irish Coffee to warm me up before the dispirited, forty-five-minute bus ride down Route 93, back home to Lawrence.

Luckily, I was able to remain at my parents' house for a while, because I was too sick to work and pay rent. Still not wanting to give up on my malpractice case, I began talking to attorneys again. My efforts proved futile. Now that I had messed up with Massey and Cooley, no other attorney would touch the case with a ten-foot pole.

265

Suddenly, everything seemed hopeless again. Here I was, back at my parents' house in Massachusetts, gravely sick again and unemployed, with little apparent hope of putting my legal case or my health back together again - a sickeningly familiar-feeling. I realized then how quickly the cards can turn against you.

In early June, I encountered an article in the paper about a Dr. Anthony Komoroff, the head of the Infectious Disease department at Brigham and Women's Hospital in Boston. He was involved in the treatment of an illness unfamiliar to me called Chronic Fatigue Syndrome - (CFIDS). The article was a revelation. The symptoms seemed to exactly match those I was experiencing!

I promptly made an appointment at Brigham and Women's and evaluated by an associate of Komoroff's, - internist Jean Schaffer. Unlike the psychiatrists who claimed to have "examined" me, Dr. Schaffer took a detailed medical history, which included my trips to the Persian Gulf and the disabling symptoms I had experienced upon my return home. She also drew blood and told me to return in a week. A week later, I met with Schaffer again:

"Charles, your past medical history, current symptoms, and blood work clearly indicate that you are indeed suffering from Chronic Fatigue and Immune Deficiency Syndrome (CFIDS). It is a relatively new disease, and it's viral, and there is currently no cure or treatment for it. I want you to brace yourself for this: you're going to be sick and debilitated with CFIDS for a very, very long time."

After listening to Schaffer's dismal prognosis, I became angry with my Higher Power for dealing me yet another bad straw. Hadn't I been beaten down enough in the Persian Gulf, in the psychiatric hospitals, and on the streets of L.A.? This grim diagnosis really put my faith to the test. When if ever was I going to get a good break?

"I'm a good guy, Lord," I pleaded silently. I believe in all the good stuff - social justice, human rights, loving your neighbor, the dignity of human life. I'm on YOUR side. Why then are you beating me up again like this? Wasn't my psychiatric ordeal and the half-year I spent living on the streets enough for you?"

On the other hand, I recalled the many times God had miraculously intervened and saved my hide in the past. And I recalled the words a wonderful, black, and devoutly Christian man I had befriended on the campus of George Washington University in D.C. once shared with me:

"If I complained Charles, I wouldn't be grateful."

I was deeply conflicted for the umpteenth time. After a discussion with my highly astute parish priest, I eventually came to understand that although we might rack our brains, we humans with our only three-dimensional, finite minds, can't possibly understand the Divine purpose being worked out in our lives. He claimed that there are hidden mysteries in this vast, thirteen-billion-year-old universe that we aren't even "mean" to understand. As examples: Why did God take my younger brother Mark from my life? And why is there so much unjust suffering in the world?

At the behest of this same priest, for solace, I read the account of the life of the Biblical figure Job, who was plagued inexplicably, with multiple and repeated setbacks, illnesses and calamities. The renowned French author and novelist - Victor

Hugo (*'Les Miserables' and 'The Hunchback of Notre Dame'*) paid homage to the still anonymous author of 'The Book of Job' (the oldest known book in the world), by dubbing it:

"The greatest masterpiece of the human mind."

If you haven't read Job's account yet in the Old Testament, I suggest that you do so. You'll be in for a rare treat. In a nutshell, the tale plays out like this.

God says to the Devil:

"Have you taken note of my loyal and just servant Job, a man who is so good you can hardly believe it? Job is rich, healthy and loved. God says that he has a spirit of excellence; he's blameless, and that there are surely none like him in all of the Earth."

The serpent duly takes note. He sees that Job, a God-fearing man, is prospering greatly then craftily responds to the Almighty,

"Virtue pays, the serpent charges. You Almighty buy loyalty with goodies. Your servant Job honors and remains loyal to you only because you bless him with everything he wants and needs. Hand him over to me and let me smite him and take away everything he cherishes, and I promise you he'll turn against you and curse you to your face."

Confident of his servant's loyalty, the Divine takes up Satan on his dare and accepts the fallen angel's challenge:

"You're on Satan. Do whatever you want with Job, but just don't take his life."

And it's away we go. ...

Shortly thereafter, as you might have guessed, the bottom falls out on Job. Following a series of nasty calamities and misfortunes, appearing one right after the other, including the loss of his home, the loss of his business, the death of all of his livestock, the death of his children and his grandchildren, and finally his affliction with a terrible disease that produces immensely painful and smelly boils all over his body, Job is left totally overwhelmed and dumbstruck. Mystified as to why these disparaging things have happened to him and struggling to find answers, he summons three of his closest confidants to console him and provide him with some spiritual insight.

Wrongly, these overly self-righteous buddies, in their misguided attempts to comfort their innocent and beleaguered friend, tell him that nothing happens in a vacuum and that he must have done something bad in the past that pissed his Creator off. When Job protests that he hadn't done anything wrong to deserve this treatment, his friends denounce him further for calling God unjust. Adding insult to injury, Job's fair-weathered wife weighs in negatively as well:

"Job, why are you wasting your time with this? You're finished. Just give up; curse God and die!"

Job, however, isn't swayed by any of these folks. He maintains his faith and rebuffs his friends and disloyal wife, refusing to turn on his Creator:

"My Redeemer still lives!

What" he says, with the minimal energy he has left.

"Shall we receive only good from the hand of God and not bad? I came into the world 'naked' and 'naked' I shall return. Leave me you fickle people. You've all done me no good."

Then, at that exact moment, Job's wife mysteriously drops dead.

Looking down at this unfolding drama from Heaven along with his adoring angels at His side and greatly pleased with His servant's awe-inspiring display of patience and loyalty, God mocks the serpent and proceeds to reward Job by first restoring him to full health and then blessing the latter part of his life even more richly than He did the first part.

Job ends up with double the livestock he had before; a more beautiful, loyal, and God-fearing wife; eight new children; two dozen of new grandchildren; and a more spacious house than he had before for all of them to live in. In fact, it was said of Job's new granddaughters that none were more beautiful in all the land. Job ends up living out his many remaining years on earth in great peace, good health, and with an even deeper devotion to his Creator.

In addition to this faith inspiring story, I also found comfort in King Solomon's Biblical admonition:

"Trust in the Lord with all your heart and lean not on your own understanding." (Proverbs 3:5)

And in the epistle of Saint Paul in the New Testament wherein God says to Paul after an uncharacteristic bout of complaining from the apostle:

"Stop with your unbecoming self-pity Paul. My Grace is sufficient for you. My "strength" is made manifest in your "weakness."

I realized then that I needed to abandon the self-pity, dig down deep, draw on my faith, and hunker in for the long haul because with the debilitating CFIDS, I was now facing what would turn out to be the most uphill and formidable challenge of my life.

Chapter 21:
Living with Chronic Fatigue Syndrome (CFIDS)

The news from Dr. Shaffer was of course, devastating. How was I going to function? Unable to work, how was I going to survive financially and provide for myself? Was I now in need of someone else to take care of me? Was I destined to spend the rest of my life helpless and in a nursing home? CFIDS had no treatment. Surely, I could at least do something to help myself.

In early June, broke and needing money, I landed a temporary nine-to-five accounting job with Merrimack Paper Company in Lawrence. Looking back, I don't know how I did it but I somehow toughed it out and lasted three months on the job. My life consisted of going to work, coming home at 5 o'clock, eating supper, taking a shower, and going directly to bed at 6. On weekends, I slept the entire day. I'd get up to take a shower about 6 at night, have a bite to eat, and go back to bed.

By mid-July, I was so fatigued I could no longer go into work, so I called the accounting manager at work and requested some time off. He said it would be okay, provided I furnish him with a doctor's note to support my claim. After getting a medical workup by my primary care physician, I mailed the doctor's two-paragraph letter confirming my diagnosis to my boss and was granted a two-week reprieve. I took the following two weeks off and just slept and slept and slept.

I eventually went back to work but found it was even harder to function than before my hiatus. At the end of August, my temporary three-month assignment at Merrimack Paper finally ended (thank God) and I stopped working. The idea of trying to find another job now seemed patently ridiculous.

What is *Chronic Fatigue and Immune Deficiency Syndrome (CFIDS)?* Infectious disease specialists say it is a stress-induced, immune system disease that also adversely affects the central nervous system. The aforementioned Dr. Anthony Komaroff - Director of Internal Medicine at Brigham and Women's Hospital and an expert on the disease has this to say:

"The syndrome is characterized by varying degrees of chronic fatigue, sore throat, aching muscles, aching joints, sharp shooting pains in various parts of the body, headache, depression and difficulty concentrating. The onset of the syndrome seems to be in young adulthood. Some toxin or possibly even stress could theoretically be the cause of activating the virus. By definition, patients with this syndrome have been evaluated for a variety of chronic illnesses which produce similar symptoms, including both physical and psychological disorders."

In Jane Meredith's Boston Globe health article, CFS researcher Dr. Paul Cheney expounds further:

"Because the first reported cases were in affluent high achievers, the illness became known as the yuppie flu. And because depression was a frequently mentioned symptom, many doctors dismissed the illness as a trendy, psychologically induced ailment. Most now firmly reject that idea. Several new manifestations of chronic fatigue have emerged."

273

"Cheney, in what was considered a major report at the conference, said he was finding an abnormal number of unexplained white lesions, or areas of damaged tissue, in the cortex of the brain's outer layers of gray matter of chronic fatigue patients. Abnormalities in the brain's temporal lobes, where vision, hearing, memories and emotions are processed, he said were found in persons with chronic fatigue in much greater frequency than in the control group."

In late fall, while aimlessly browsing around the Andover Book Store, I came across a book entitled" *"Chronic Fatigue Syndrome: The Hidden Epidemic"* which was written by doctor Jesse Stoff, an infectious disease specialist. The book indicated that Dr. Stoff's office was in western Massachusetts, so I drove out there and had him evaluate me. Based on his physical examination and blood work, Stoff concurred with Dr. Schaffer that I was indeed suffering from CFIDS. In his book, Stoff sheds additional light on the syndrome:

"If acute infection is delayed until adulthood (as is often the case in wealthy, industrialized nations) the patient is in for a very difficult battle. If the infection persists long enough and penetrates deep enough, the immune system may ultimately turn against the patient. Chronic patients sometimes experience peripheral nerve pain, numbness, seizures, paralysis and even encephalitis (a swelling of the brain). The liver is one of the primary targets for the infection. The liver is one of the major powerhouses of the body and when it is badly infected, disruption of both metabolism and the immune system results, followed by fatigue - a main hallmark of the disease, and depression. Thus, it is essential that the liver be treated. Liver-based fatigue produces a terrible sense of lifelessness and a loss of will. With the sapping of the will comes impairment of the ability for forethought. Exhaustion can become so overmastering that getting out of bed to begin the day requires monumental effort, let alone planning ahead for the next week."

"Less visible, but no less important is the doing will function of a person. Doing will is what provides the oomph to get out of bed in the morning. Owing to the tremendous drain on the body's energy reserves by the immune system as it battles the virus, a sinister feeling of lethargy creeps in. The overwhelming fatigue destroys the victim's stamina and with it the energy to work and to lead a normal life."

"Finally, we come to the paramount level of human function, that of cognitive activity. Here the processes of memory and the ability to concentrate and think linearly are often compromised. The virus can attack the brain and in so doing will impair the cognitive functions."

One afternoon while I was reviewing my medical records, which Attorney Massey had secured for me, my Aunt Elsie and her husband, my Uncle George, stopped by the house to visit with my father and me. Seeing me alone at the kitchen table, my face buried in the medical records, Aunt Elsie innocently asked me what I was doing:

"Oh Auntie, these are the medical records of my psychiatric hospitalizations. I was wronged, so I'm trying to get a lawsuit going. I'm finding it very hard to do so, though."

"Chuckie, let me give you give you some good advice," she responded.

"What's that Auntie?"

"BURN those medical records."

Right after Auntie said those words to me, Uncle George, now sitting at the kitchen table with us, threw his two cents in as well:

"Stop living in the past Chuckie! Why are you still dealing with that crap? Just put it all behind you and go out and get yourself a job?"

As you might guess, I didn't take either of their recommendations; just the opposite. A week later, I contacted North Hampton psychiatrist Ronald Carino, who was referred to me by a patient's rights advocacy group, briefly explained what had happened to me and asked him to review my file and issue a medical opinion. He kindly agreed to do so free of charge.

Two weeks later, I borrowed Dad's Lincoln, drove out to western Massachusetts, met with Carino, and left my medical records with him. Two weeks after that, I received a two-page letter from the psychiatrist summarizing his findings. It fully supported my beliefs and contentions. The last sentence stated that in the doctor's professional opinion, not only was the psychiatric treatment I received "malpractice" but it was also "criminal" as well.

In June of 1988, I received a notice from the Essex County Probate Court in Salem, Mass. that the complaint attorney Massey had filed against Dr. Denapoli had to be served. Now lacking the benefit of a lawyer's protection, I ran the risk of angering Denapoli and having him punitively re-hospitalize me if I in fact served him myself. Undaunted, I arranged with the sheriff's office to have the complaint served on the psychiatrist.

About a month later, I received papers from Denapoli's Boston defense attorney Linda Leffert asking the court for a motion to dismiss the case for both "statute of limitations" and "delay of service" reasons. I then meticulously prepared and filed a motion with the court, citing past case law (which I had researched at Suffolk Law School) arguing against the dismissal of my case.

In early the fall of 1988, a hearing was held in front of the Probate Judge in Salem Probate Court. Present at the hearing were attorney Leffert and myself as well as two young, legal upstarts from attorney Cooley's law firm. The two had showed up solely to ask the judge to formally allow their firm to be dismissed as my attorneys in the case. (*Why the overkill from Cooley?* I wondered. *Wouldn't ONE attorney have been enough to handle this petty matter?*)

The judge, without argument, granted their request, and they promptly left. I then handed the judge my brief arguing against dismissal. Handling it as if were used toilet paper, he threw it to the side of his desk without even pursuing it. Then, following an oral hearing in which I was allowed to speak, the judge dismissed my case "*with prejudice*," meaning I could never bring suit against Dr. Denapoli or anyone else involved in my medical treatment again. The game was over. I was "forced" to "give up." Well, better it be left to fight in another way.

About a year later, I was still living at my parents' house, which I now shared with my father alone. Ma had moved out, as her Boston divorce lawyer Delibrio had instructed her to and was living at her sister Nemra's house in anticipation of an impending divorce settlement. Because Dad lacked sufficient funds, his longtime attorney - Iggy Piscitello, (remember him?) who was not a divorce lawyer, agreed to represent him in the divorce - pro bono. Using Iggy as his divorce lawyer proved to be the wrong move for Dad as the much more experienced divorce attorney cleaned Piscitello's clock in court.

Prior to the court proceedings, Dad rarely slept at home. Instead, he stayed nearly every night at the Salem, New Hampshire condo of his new love interest, a forty-year-old, fairly attractive Korean immigrant named Ann Kim, who was twelve years younger than him. Never married, this woman was anxiously looking forward to tying the knot with Dad right after his divorce with Ma was final.

Not to be judgmental, but the best this woman had done with her life was to work as a piecemeal assembly-line worker in a local factory. She spoke broken English, which was very hard for everyone except for Dad to understand. Perhaps I'm being too hard on the woman. Maybe she really loved my father, but the whole deal smelled fishy to me and my three siblings. We thought it was probably nothing more than a standard gold-digging play.

Around noon on an early fall Sunday, Dad, Ann, and her whole family including all five of her younger, immigrant sisters as well as one of her two younger brothers burst through the front door of my father's house. I was eating lunch at the time at the kitchen table:

"Get yourself ready, Chuck, we're moving in right now," Dad bellowed as he and the others charged in.

278

Despite the fact that my parents' divorce was not even final yet, the next thing I knew, Dad's fiancée and her family were moving furniture, couches, chairs, a kitchen table, and numerous suitcases filled with clothes and other items into the house. My Aunt Elsie and her husband my Uncle George, who for reasons still unknown, worshiped the ground that Ann walked on, soon arrived and joined the hullabaloo as well. It all took place so quickly and with such force that it seemed like a live re-enactment of the D-Day - Omaha Beach Invasion.

Stunned and still severely debilitated by the CFIDS, I nonetheless did not want to appear selfish or indifferent, so I joined in the hoopla and started moving Ann's stuff into Dad's house too. I recall working nonstop from noontime till around six that night (without a thank-you from Ann, her family, Dad, or my Aunt or Uncle). Around eight that night, I fell into bed, totally exhausted.

Now sharing the house with Dad and Ann, I felt like the odd man out. Moreover, Ann proved to be very difficult to deal with. She would often get angry with me or Dad over some petty little thing and then throw an emotionally charged fit that would last for ten or more minutes, her voice screeching just like that of a prisoner being tortured in a Damascus jail. What, I thought to myself, did cerebral and easygoing man like my father see in this woman? Couldn't he have found a nice, laid back and more sane, Lebanese woman with whom to spend the rest of his life? There was certainly no shortage of them in the greater Lawrence area.

One morning, about a month and a half after my father and Ann moved in, Dad's fiancée charged into my bedroom right after I woke up, clutching a vacuum cleaner in her right hand, and said to me in a caustic voice:

"Chuckie, vacuum your rug. It's filthy."

It was voiced as a command, not a request. With a facetious smirk on my face, I responded:

"No, not right now, Ann, I haven't fully woken up yet. I'll do it later."

Expecting me instead, to act on a dime, Ann dropped the vacuum cleaner on my bedroom floor, charged out of my bedroom in a fit of rage, stormed to the nearby bathroom where my father was shaving, and started yelling at him so loudly her voice must have nearly ruptured his eardrums. He responded:

"Sweetheart, please calm down. Don't bother Chuckie like that. This doesn't sound like a really a big deal honey."

Later that afternoon, still in a rage, the Korean immigrant approached me alone in the kitchen and I immediately sensed trouble.

"You have to leave MY house by tomorrow afternoon. If you don't get out, I call police and they come and drag you out. You hear, Chuckie?"

I guess the house no longer belonged to our family; it was Ann's. At least in her mind.

I responded by calmly telling Ann that I was very sick and had nowhere else to go except the streets. I warned her that due my ill health, I wouldn't last even a night on the streets or in a shelter. I asked her to have a little compassion and reconsider her decision. But there wasn't even a molecule of sympathy in the woman.

"You sick, Chuckie? I not going to take care of you. No! I want you out of here!"

I felt sorrier for my father at that moment than I did for myself. I didn't escalate the matter or discuss it with Dad, as, in hindsight, I probably should have. If I had done so, I'm sure he would have put the woman in her place and let me stay at HIS house, but I felt he had enough problems at the time. Not only did he have to deal with his upcoming divorce, but the new, young punk mayor of Lawrence - Kevin S., was obsessively trying hard to get Dad fired from his tax assessor's job just months before his retirement in order to screw him out of most of his well-deserved city pension and I definitely didn't want to add any more stress to his life.

In the early evening of that same day, just to relieve some stress and unwind, I walked the two uphill miles to the Starbucks in Andover center. While sitting at one of the tables there, sipping on a latte, I remember saying to myself:

"This nutty woman means business. She's actually going to force me out onto the streets." What the Hell was I going to do? I had to act quickly. I was staring at the unforgiving streets of Lawrence, which I felt, that due to my debilitated health, certain would finish me off in short order. Seeming to lack any viable options, I bowed my head, closed my eyes, and prayed once again for God's immediate help.

Believe it or not, only about twenty minutes later, a very attractive, middle-aged woman walked up to my table, uninvited, and said to me:

"You're a very handsome young man, sir. May I join you?"

"Sure you can Miss. And would you like a drink or a piece of pastry? I'll be happy to get either of them for you or both of them if you'd like." I answered.

"You're a very generous man too. Thank you, but no. I'm Louise Marshall, a recent widow, and I own a house three blocks from here on Chestnut Street - right next to the Andover Common. You seem like a very nice man. I'm glad to meet you. What's your name?"

"Chuckie," I said. "I'm from Lawrence." (I should add that folks in upscale Andover are often standoffish toward those from my much less affluent neighboring city.)

"Chuck, I can see you're also a gentleman, and there aren't too many of them to be found anymore. For some strange reason, although I just met you, I feel I can trust you. If you ever need a place to stay, I have an extra room in my house that's un-occupied. (Where did that come from)? Once again, I was being offered lodging out of the blue at a critical moment.)

The rent at my place is cheap - three hundred a month. Here's my number, (She wrote it down). Call me if you're ever interested. I have things to do right now so I can't stay. Well, goodbye Chuckie. It was great meeting you today."

Marshall then stood up from her chair and left the coffee shop. The next morning, right after I got out of the shower, I phoned Marshall and told her I'd take her up on her offer. I said I was in a pinch and asked if I could move into her place as early as that as that afternoon:

"Sure you can. That's great news. At about what time three or so?

282

"That sounds about right." I said.

"Good Chuckie. I'll be expecting you then."

My father was playing golf and wasn't home at the time so, I asked Ann if she would give me a ride over to Marshall's house. Seemingly in a better frame of mind now, she agreed to do so. And so, early that afternoon, with a suitcase full of clothes in hand, my father's fiancée and I drove peacefully together over to Marshall's Andover home.

I stayed with Louise Marshall for the next three months until my mother got her share of the divorce settlement from Dad. It was for $150,000. Ma used it immediately to purchase a single-family house in a quiet residential neighborhood in neighboring Methuen. A week after the papers on Ma's new house were signed, per her invitation, I left Marshall's home and moved in with her.

In early November of 1992, about a year later, while still living at my mother's new house, disaster struck again. Due strictly to the CFIDS, my health condition took a turn for the worst. Specifically, I failed to eat or sleep for ten days and ran a continuous 102 - degree temperature. That tenth night, believing strongly that I was not going to make the morning, I prayed nonstop throughout the night. I didn't care that my prayer was so loud my mother could easily hear it in her adjacent bedroom. It went something simple and to the point like this:

"Jesus, please help me. I'm up against it again! I don't think I'm going to make it till the morning. Help me, Jesus! Help me, Jesus! Please help me, Lord!"

I ask now honestly; how many times can you go to the well with the Almighty?

My mother awoke early the next morning to find me rolling on the living room floor, perspiring profusely, groaning uncontrollably, and in apparent, tremendous agony. Totally petrified, she called my brother George and told him to go get my father and have both of them come over to her house, right away.

Roughly twenty minutes later, George and Dad arrived at Ma's house. I was now sitting stooped over on the living room floor, hallucinating and swearing like someone with jungle fever. My father tried to talk to me about going to the hospital but I was incapable of decision-making. Dad, always a man of action just like his lifelong hero FDR was, acted quickly and decisively once again. Seeing me in that helpless state, he promptly grabbed the phone in my mother's kitchen and called 911. George told me later on that I became a little violent with EMT's when they arrived so, they were forced to put me in restraints before loading me into the ambulance. I don't remember any of this taking place.

The next thing I remember was waking in up in the ER of the Holy Family Hospital, strapped tightly to a bed with an IV needle in my arm. I remember seeing my mother in the room with a string of rosary beads in her hands, praying feverishly for me. She was elated when I came to, as were both my father and brother. The attending physician, - a Dr. O'Neil, as I later learned from Dad, had given me a strong shot of Haldol upon my unconscious arrival at the hospital. The medication apparently had worked.

Right after awakening, I politely asked Dr. O'Neil to remove the wrist restraints, as they were cutting into my skin and making me feel severely uncomfortable. He responded by firmly stating:

"No, Charlie, the restraints are staying on and you're not leaving here."

This was turning out to be the most horrible day of my life - and if you've read my story thus far, you know there's a lot of competition for that honor. I was recently told by a prominent psychiatrist that I could have choked to death lying there alone tied to the bed with no health worker to watch over me. All that would have needed to happen he said was for me to vomit with no way to turn my body and spit it out. Without any explanation whatsoever, I was forced to remain tied to my bed and in hand restraints for twelve more hours.

Roughly an hour after his first visit, Dr. O'Neil approached me in my treatment room. This time he was armed with my complete file of medical records from Holy Family, which included my previous hospitalizations for alleged manic-depressive illness (Bi-polar disorder), errantly made ten years earlier.

"You arrived at this hospital this morning in a psychotic state Charles. Accordingly, I'm going to transfer you to McLean's Psychiatric Hospital again. They'll have a bed for you there sometime later tonight. I'm sorry but we don't have one available for you in our psych ward at this time."

"Well, I'm not psychotic now, so just release me back to my mother's house. You don't understand doctor. All that's happened today was caused by *Chronic Fatigue Syndrome*, not a psychiatric illness. I've been sick with the disease for a long time. Please contact my former doctor - Jesse Stoff, or my current treating physician at Lahey Clinic - Dr. Wu. Either of them will verify this."

He countered with, "You have a history of manic depression Charles. It's clear what's happening here. What do you think I am, stupid? You're headed to McLean's as soon as a bed becomes available there, and that's final!"

Around eleven o'clock that evening, some twelve hours after I was admitted, O'Neil transferred me to the Belmont psychiatric hospital, strapped down in an ambulance like Frankenstein's beast. Rod Serling, are you logging all of this in? Just prior to my transfer, the wrist cuffs were finally removed.

Once admitted to McLean's, my old psychiatric records again dictated my treatment. I kept telling the doctors and the staff there that I had been diagnosed by three prominent physicians as having CFIDS. I begged them over and over again to call either Dr. Shaffer at Brigham and Women's, Dr. Stoff in western Mass., or Dr. Wu at Lahey. No one, however, would listen.

Regardless of what I said, I was placed, as I had been years earlier, on a mixture of neuroleptic medications. Clearly, the initial, false psychiatric narrative was prevailing once again. The only thing that kept me going was my faith. I remembered Manuel in the prison cell in Los Angeles. He would have told me with a twinkle in his eyes to stop fighting with life, to *roll with the punches*, and to recognize that everything has a hidden purpose, even suffering.

My ensuing six week stay at McLean's, according to my medical records, was quiet and uneventful. The fact that they were treating me for the wrong disease I somehow managed to endure with humor and good grace. I kept repeating to myself; "this too shall pass." At least the meals were good and the curtains matched the bedspread. I passed my time offering a gentle presence to my fellow patients and trying to be cheerful and supportive wherever I could. Maybe I did some good. Maybe that was the reason I was forced back there. What do you think Manuel?

286

At my request, my Uncle George Faris showed up with Dad one afternoon at the hospital to visit me. With tears running down his face, Uncle quietly said to me:

"Chuckie, we all love you."

What else could the uninformed man say? Dad then sounded the General Patton alarm:

"Chuckie, this is do or die for you right now. You've got to MAKE IT this time."

On or around January 1st, I was finally released from McLean's and, having no other place to go, returned to my mother's house. It was rough for quite a long period. I often stayed home alone all day while my mother was at work and especially during the cold and snowy winter months found myself getting deeply despondent. Then, as if by a stroke of magic, the lights mysteriously came on and some good things began to happen.

Chapter 22:
A New Stability

Sick and tired of being sick and tired, I finally responded to a want ad for seemingly lucrative part-time employment in the local newspaper, got off my butt, and snagged myself a telemarketing job during the evening hours.

At around this same time, my younger brother George bought a new car for himself and sold his old, beat-up Toyota Celica to me for fifty bucks. This was a great break for me as prior to this, I hadn't had a car for two years because I couldn't afford to buy one and was thus relegated to taking buses everywhere. This proved to be a tough go during the winter. Now, with a car, I was able to drive back and forth to work, as well as drive to the golf course and the Y and meet up with my old friends on weekday afternoons before going to work.

Also, at five o'clock on Friday nights, my night off from work, I volunteered at the soup kitchen in the basement of the local Salvation Army building. There I met up with four or five older, devoutly Christian, co-volunteers who also attended church services every Sunday morning at the Protestant Assembly of God Church. One of these volunteers, eighty-year-old Armand Michaud, headed the operation. He was the sweetest, kindest, most loveable man I have ever met. In fact, he gave me the Bible I still have today.

Now long since retired from the successful insurance business he founded, Michaud spent every weekday -all day, visiting nursing homes in the Merrimack Valley, giving hope and encouragement to old folks facing the tail end of their lives. What a man this guy Armand was; and what a role model he became for me too.

Another elderly volunteer at the soup kitchen was a man by the named of Jerry. He would often play the piano upstairs and would lead folks in Christian hymns and songs before we all sat down and ate. Always upbeat and smiling, Jerry, like Armand, was a remarkable man. I still remember a few poignant words of spiritual wisdom he imparted to me and which have stuck to this day such as:

"Charlie don't put your faith in money. Don't put your faith in people. Put your faith in God!"

Seeing many of the poor, down-and-out souls who came for a simple meal at the Army, most of whom were probably homeless drug-users, made me realize things weren't as bad for me as I often imagined they were. While serving coffees and sodas to these folks (my assignment at the kitchen), I often thanked the Good Lord for the many blessings that I felt that I still had left. At about six-thirty, right after we were done at the soup kitchen, I often headed over to the Methuen Knights of Columbus, where I would unwind, and have a few cokes at the bar, and watch the older guys play high-stakes poker. (I wasn't then, and still am not, a drinker.)

Often at about ten o'clock, the players would take a break and put together a list of coffees and pastries they wanted from the Dunkin Donuts which was conveniently located directly nearby. They'd pitch in ten bucks each, even though the cost of their orders was much less than that much and ask me to go to the donut shop and pick up the goods. When I would return twenty minutes later and present their filled orders along with the change-often thirty dollars or more, one of them would say,

"Just keep it, Charlie." - A few much-needed extra bucks for myself.

289

In spite of being severely ill, I had come full circle. I was finally having some fun for myself again. I remember Houda - my cousin Nadim's wife, telling me with some admiration during this period:

"You're very tough Chuckie."

I worked the part time job four hours a night, Monday through Thursday in a phone room raising funds for police charitable organizations. Working at night was the perfect fit for me. It allowed me to stay home and rest up during the day before I went into the office to make phone calls at five o'clock. After many years of drought, things seemed to be going my way again. Things remained OK for a good while.

Several years later however, I encountered another severe bump in the road. My mother loved to keep the house very cool at night, especially during the winter months. I preferred the temperature to be warmer at night in the winter. Her insistence on keeping the thermostat low each evening caused me to develop bronchitis twice during the two previous winter seasons. I went out and bought an electric blanket and an electric heater for my bedroom in the hopes of solving the problem. They failed to do the job however.

One night I was feeling especially chilled, and after Ma went to bed, I raised the temperature to 72 degrees. This really pissed her off. Sensing the warming temperature, Ma charged out of her bedroom and told me to leave her house. Where was I supposed to go, I asked her:

"I don't care, Chuckie, just get out!" she said sharply in reply.

The following afternoon, I came home from the golf course to find that the locks on the front and garage doors had been changed. Now staring at the streets and a sure and quick death again, I instinctively did what I always did when I found myself up against it.

"You must be sick of hearing from me by now, Big Fella," I said, holding onto the wheel and looking upward from the driver's seat. "But what would you have me do now?"

The inner voice I'd heard several times in the past "spoke" to me again. This time it said:

"Chuckie, drive back to the golf course right away."

I had learned over the years to recognize and trust this voice. Delusional, you say? Well, let me tell you. When I got to the golf course and walked into the players' lounge, my high school friend and fellow Lebanese - American, - Greg Hyatt was sitting at a table by himself drinking a beer.

"Hey Charlie. How are you? Long time no see. Grab a drink and come sit with me."

So, not being a drinker, I ordered a Coke from the bar, then went over and sat with Greg.

"Chuckie, you don't look good buddy; you seem kind of anxious and worried today."

"I am Greg. My mother just threw me out of her house and now I have no place to live. I'm looking at the streets now. And I'm very sick to boot. I'll never make it out there in the poor condition that I'm in." Greg responded:

"You poor fellow. I think I can help you. I have an empty bedroom at my condo. So, I'm going to solve your problem by letting you come and live with me."

"God bless you, Greg, You're a a life saver." I told him.

I moved in with Hyatt that evening and didn't have to spend even one night in a shelter or on the streets which, in my state of health, probably would have finished me off quickly. I kept my telemarketing job too and didn't have to take a single night off from work. Undeniably, my faithful Maker was watching out for me again.

After I'd return to Hyatt's apartment from work at night, the two of us would often play honeymoon whist and poke friendly fun at the many colorful misfits that both of us knew at Bishop's and the Knights of Columbus. After three months of this, however, Hyatt changed completely and the good times suddenly ended.

He started staying up till three or four in the morning, partying and getting drunk with a pair of younger male residents of his complex. Whenever I mentioned to Greg that I couldn't sleep because of all of the noise, he shot back, like a nasty drunk does:

"I'm doing you a huge favor by letting you stay here, Charlie. If you don't like it, you can get the fuck out."

I realized I was in danger of being thrown out over the next provocation. And I knew it would be best for me to start looking for another living situation - ASAP. So, I started pricing apartments in the area. Everything I looked at however, was seven hundred dollars a month and up. On my limited budget, I could afford the three hundred a month I'd been paying Ma but couldn't swing seven. I found myself once again in a housing crisis. Not wanting to be thrown out onto the streets by Hyatt, I went to my Almighty Father once again for help.

As "fate" would have it, two days later, my brother George's wife Hanna phoned me at Hyatt's condo and, without my even telling her I was facing a homing crisis, said:

"I saw you outside Greg's yesterday Chuckie, and I could tell you weren't happy living there with him, so, last night I called a friend of your mother's and mine - Vickie Anton. She is very close with Dave Burke, the housing manager at a subsidized housing complex in Lawrence. Vickie thinks she can help you and wants us both to meet her at Mr. Burke's office this afternoon at three o'clock. Will you come and meet us there?"

"Of course I'll come, Hanna!"

My sister-in-law generously baked a huge tray of baklava and a full tray of kibbee and brought them with her to Burke's office. I barely knew Miss Anton and had only heard from my mother that she was a thoughtful and kind Lebanese - American woman who relished going out of her way to help other people out who were up against it - especially young Lebanese folks.

The three of us summarily met at Burke's office as Hanna had arranged, and Hanna gave Dave Burke the trays of food, which he graciously accepted. During our ensuing, one-hour meeting, the stand-up Anton minced no words:

"Dave, this good boy here is desperate. He's sick and needs a place to live right away. Now, are you going to step up to the plate and help him or not?"

"Vickie," Burke responded, "I know Chuckie's father - Fred very well from our Mayor Buckley years. And I knew his grandmother Mary Ead too. She loved me and used to cook me kibbee and grape leaves when she lived in our complex many years ago. The sweet taste of that food is still in my mouth. Yes, of course, I'll help Chuckie. There is currently a five-year waiting list to get in here, but I'm going to move him to the top of the list on "*an emergency status*."

Burke then turned to me and said:

"Congratulations, Charlie. You're in. My laborer crew is currently cleaning and refurbishing a second-floor apartment. It's centrally located, it has windows in every room, and it's just about the finest one we have in our hundred-unit complex. I've been told by my maintenance staff that it'll be ready by tomorrow afternoon. So, get your belongings together tonight at your friend's house so that you can move in with us sometime early tomorrow evening."

Wow! I seized the opportunity. Burke started me off with a monthly rent of only two hundred dollars, which represented 33 percent of my six hundred dollar monthly Social Security Disability check. And this included heat, electricity, and hot water. Winter snow shoveling and summer grass-cutting were also provided by the Housing Authority at no additional charge. As I mentioned earlier, I was looking at apartments for seven hundred a month without electricity and heat.

At a move-in celebration party that I hosted a month later (for Hanna, Vickie Anton, Burke, my mother, as well several of my new fellow housing residents I had come to befriend), Anton, the God-sent angel, interrupted her meal, looked me directly in the eye and said:

"Chuckie, I got you an 'apartment for life.' You'll never be thrown out of here. All you need to do is pay your rent on time and don't cause any trouble for the other residents and you'll be fine."

Ma then interjected with an unusual spiritual twist:

"Chuckie, this apartment is a gift to you from God."

"You're telling me something I don't know, Ma?" I retorted.

I'm glad to report that I've lived in this same subsidized apartment for the last twenty-six years and have never had to face a housing crisis again, and hopefully won't in the future. Although my monthly rent has increased a little bit each year with the annual cost of living increases in my Social Security check, it's still an unheard-of deal, and I thank my Maker every day for this timely and lifetime blessing.

After moving into the housing complex, I kept working nights as a telemarketer. The work was simple and non-stressful. I just sat at my desk and talked to people for four hours. Although well below my educational qualifications, I found that I actually enjoyed telemarketing much more than I did accounting work. Over time, by blending my successful peers' sales pitches into my own, I became quite a proficient telemarketer.

Then disappointment suddenly struck uninvited, again. At or around 9:30 Am, on September 11th 2001, I felt a strong compulsion to turn on the TV, did so, and immediately witnessed two planes crashing - one right after the other, into the World Trade Center in New York City. Both planes were emitting high levels of fire and smoke. Highly confused as to what was taking place, (as even the television announcers were), I phoned my father at his house and asked if he too was also watching the debacle on TV. He said he was so, I then asked him if he could provide any insight into what was taking place:

"The information I just got Chuckie says that your Aunt Nemra's son, your first cousin - Peter Hashem, was on one of those two planes." Oh my God!

A phone call that I made over to Aunt Nemra's house several hours later confirmed that what Dad had relayed to me about Peter a little while earlier was in fact true. Apparently, from what one of Nemra's daughters told me, poor Peter had canceled his early evening flight out to California the night before in order to attend his oldest son's soccer game and had in turn rescheduled the flight out for the following morning.

My first cousin subsequently left seven, middle aged siblings, a stellar, Lebanese-born wife - Rita, (also a Hashem), and two prized, young sons - Christopher and Patrick. In the weeks that followed, I remember asking myself, over and over again:

"Good Lord, how could you have allowed such a horrible thing to have happened?"

Needless to say, our entire Hashem clan, numbering in the hundreds, - those both in Greater Lawrence and those back in Lebanon as well, were totally shocked and for the longest time, mortified by the nightmare.

Now, back to my telemarketing job. The owner of our fundraising company Mike Q. liked me very much and gave me "great material" most nights (call sheets of affluent neighborhoods, where residents were able to donate more to police charities than folks in poorer neighborhoods could). As a result, I earned some good money for myself - often 250 to 300 dollars a week - solely on commissions. Not bad for a sixteen hour a week job, and I felt extremely lucky to have it.

I made a good friend at work too - a fellow telemarketer named T.W. - the nephew of a well-known, past, Boston political figure, he had been raised in a privileged household, but had met with a few bumps in the road, just as I had. A true gem in the rough, T.W. spared me a lot of stress by driving me the thirty or so highway miles into work and back each night. Although not college-educated, the guy knew vastly more about how the world worked than I did, and I looked up to him for this. While driving the long ride into work, he would often talk international politics to me as he knew I had a social conscience and a thirst for knowledge in this area. I learned a lot from T.W., and he became a close, trusted, and lifelong friend.

Mike Q. - the millionaire owner of our fundraising company, who claimed he started from humble beginnings, was familiar with T.W.'s privileged life history. I remember one night he walked up to T.W., rapped him hard on the head with his knuckles, and said to him:

"You know the difference between you and me, T.W.?"

"No Mike what." my friend instinctively responded.

"You were born at the top and are on your way down. I was born at the bottom and am on my way up."

T.W. then quickly stood up fearlessly, looked Mike in the eye, and replied:

"You're wrong on all four counts, Mike."

I admired T.W.'s strength and principles.

Some of the other guys working the phones weren't quite as principled. One night for example, I distinctly heard the caller next to me say to a potential donor:

"If you can do the big one tonight (a hundred-dollar donation), I promise we won't call or bother you again for another five years."

Mind you, this guy had absolutely no control over whom we did or didn't call as a team in the future. Another time, when asked by a perspective donor if he was a policeman making the call (we at Mike Q's raised money for police charities), this same fellow answered with:

"I'm glad you asked that, sir. No, I'm not currently a member of the force, but I am on the waiting list to become a cop and the chief promised me that if I make these calls, I'll move up the list faster. ... Total bullshit!

I'm happy to say that T.W. and I never played these deceitful, head games with our potential donors. I guess we weren't prepared to sell our souls for chump change. But T.W., unfortunately for me, quit working for Mike Q. in 2005, and I was then forced to drive the thirty highway miles into the Norwood office and back by myself. I was okay with this for about a year or so, although I often found it hard to navigate the long Route 128 stretch in rush-hour traffic by myself.

The evening ride home in the pitch dark out was equally treacherous as I often found myself sandwiched between huge tractor-trailers, which, because of my CFIDS induced fatigue and my tiredness from work, made me feel unsteady and disoriented behind the wheel.

The situation finally climaxed when one night, shortly after starting my drive home, I began suffering what I can best describe as a severe panic attack. My body froze up and I started getting dizzy. I knew I wouldn't make it even to the entrance ramp for Route 128 - three miles down the road, so, I drove cautiously to the nearby Holiday Inn, a mile away, and checked myself into a room for the night, hoping I'd wake up in the morning feeling better. After spending about an hour resting on my back on my hotel bed, I actually started to feel worse, so I summoned an ambulance to take me to the nearby Norwood General Hospital ER.

When I got to the hospital, I was told by the ER triage nurse to "just sit down and be patient." It was after ten o'clock by this time, and I was concerned about what I was going to do with my car, which I had parked in the hotel parking lot. Would the hotel tow it if I just left it there? In a "panicky" state, I phoned my father at his home thirty miles away and filled him in on what was happening. Never one to ever abandon me, Dad, as usual, responded right away:

"Just sit tight son. Ann and I are leaving right now to get you. Just be patient."

About ten minutes after my call to Dad, still feeling panicky and dizzy, I walked up to the triage nurse again and said,

"Miss, I feel like crap. I'd like to be see a doctor right away!" She responded,

"Just sit down and relax, Mr. Ead. We're very busy tonight. It's going to be a little while longer."

I went back to my chair and tried unsuccessfully to relax. Twenty minutes later, feeling even worse, I went to this same nurse again:

"Please Miss, get me in to see somebody will Ya?"

By now I could see she was getting annoyed, and I feared if I continued pestering her, she might conclude I had an emotional problem and answer instead for me to go to McLean's, which was located just ten miles down the road. About a half an hour later, to my delight and relief, Dad and Ann confidently marched into the E.R. I still hadn't been seen by a physician yet. Dad spoke briefly to the triage nurse then turned to me and said:

"Come on, son. We've been given the green light. We're going home."

I felt instantaneous relief and a lessening of my panic symptoms. Dad and Ann then walked me out to Dad's car and drove me the long tide back home. The whole experience was so traumatizing, that I made a promise to myself that night that I would never drive into work in Norwood again.

The following day, my father and my good friend Andy G. helped me retrieve my car in Norwood. That night, I phoned Timmy C., the night room manager at Mike Q.'s, told him what had happened the night before and said I needed to resign from my job. He responded:

"I hate like Hell to lose a good phone man like you Charlie, but the more important thing right now is your health. Good luck fella. Know that we all love you here."

My telemarketing days were over. Early the next day, I phoned T.W. and told him what had transpired.

"You lasted at the job for ten years, Chuckie. Don't feel the least bit ashamed of yourself. Given your depleted health state, which we all knew about in the office, we all held you in high esteem for even attempting the job and for showing up every night. So, give yourself a huge pat on the back. If anyone deserves one, it's you my good buddy."

T.W. went on to say:

"I probably won't see much of you in the future. I know you have a strong appetite for knowledge, and I won't be able to 'tutor' you anymore. So, take my advice. Start watching the PBS News Hour with Judy Woodruff and Gwen Ifill (now deceased), at six o'clock every weeknight. They'll help keep you well informed and up to date."

I took my good friend's' advice and for the last fifteen years have watched the program religiously. By doing so, I've greatly expanded my knowledge of world events and have developed a strong moral compass, and I believe a healthy value system too. Perhaps because of my own taste of what mistreatment feels like, I have also developed a soft spot as well in my heart for folks who suffer abuse, injustice, and mistreatment, throughout the globe.

Having for a longstanding interest in the goings on in the Arab and Muslim world, I continually enjoyed the insightful reporting of PBS Middle East investigative correspondent - Jane Ferguson, the blonde lioness who often bravely put her life on the line as she reported as a white, American, outsider from such rough and tumble places as Afghanistan, Syria, Yemen, and Gaza.

301

I was also especially fond of the ten-minute, Friday night, closing episodes of *Shields and Brooks*. Mark Shields, now retired, was a pro - life Catholic and liberal Democrat like me, as well as a long-time syndicated columnist, and became my political hero. Mixing it up every week with Republican reporter David Brooks and host Woodruff, the man continually astounded me with his in-depth knowledge of U.S. political history. And, unlike most other "news" channels, the News Hour gives extensive time to every issue it covers, instead of just one-minute sound bites.

Back for a moment to my job; The money I earned during the ten-year period I was able to work in telemarketing allowed me to buy a good used car, save half my income each week, and put some money in a 401(k) for a rainy day. Equally as important, the job helped me to restore some semblance of self-reliance, self-respect, and dignity to an otherwise broken life. And I'm happy to report that I'm still able to pay the rent for a subsidized apartment and pay all of my bills and living expenses as well. From where I was for a long time, I think I've come a long way. Although I never "made the big leagues," like I always wanted to, I'm proud of myself for what I've been able to achieve under tenuous circumstances.

This CFIDS disease is tough. Every day I awaken to a condition of extreme fatigue and discomfort. In addition, because CFIDS slows down the metabolism, I've put on about forty pounds. I try to walk for about twenty minutes, three days a week, but that's all I can do. It's not enough to counteract the added weight gain.

I hope and pray that a cure for CFIDS will arrive someday soon. There is currently a research organization working on it, and they are encouraged by what they are finding. The head of the National CFIDS Foundation - Al Cochetto, a former college Professor of Engineering, and a lion of a man, who, like me, contracted the disease over thirty years ago and is still completely disabled with it, is a man of strong faith who has also been blessed with a positive and upbeat personality.

Over the years, I've come to really admire Al and we've become great friends and soulmates. A can-do, "man's-man" and a straight shooter, he uplifts my spirits every time I call him in order to find out where the research stands. He unfailingly reminds me there's a purpose in all this and thanks me for my own positive and hopeful attitude toward him (which makes me feel good and lifts my spirits even higher). He also often sadly tells me about other CFIDS patients who call him for emotional support, some of whom "can't take it," and actually commit suicide, while alone and often bedridden in their apartments. "This CFIDS," Cochetto more than once has told me is *a real bitch.*"

I have made it my dual purposes in life to do what I can to publicize this insidious CFIDS disease and to try to prevent further abuses of my fellow human beings by what I have come to view as an unprincipled and draconian psychiatric establishment that simply wields too much unregulated power. I realize this sounds like the end of my story, but it isn't. Not quite. Please stick with me just a little bit longer.

Chapter 23:
A Dark Night

"The Agony in My Bedroom"

CHAPTER PREFACE: In his much-acclaimed book, *"The Greatest Salesman in the World,"* author Og Mandino elaborates on the "effectiveness" of prayer's:

> "Who is of so little faith that in a great moment of disaster or heartbreak has not called to his god? Who has not cried out when confronted with danger, death or mystery beyond his normal experience or comprehension? From where has this deep instinct come which escapes from the mouth of all living creatures in moments of peril?

> "Move your hand in haste before another's eyes and his eyelids will blink. Tap another on his knee and his leg will jump. Confront another with dark horror and his mouth will say "My God" from the same deep impulse.

> "My life need not be filled with religion in order for me to recognize this greatest mystery of nature. All creatures that walk the earth, including man possess the instinct to cry for help. Why do we possess this instinct, this gift?

> "Are not our cries a form of prayer? Is it not incomprehensible in a world governed by nature's laws to give a lamb or a mule or a bird or man the instinct to cry out for help lest some Great Mind has also provided that the cry should be heard by some Superior Power having the ability to hear and answer our cry?"

At around 11 p.m. on September 15th of 2019 and several decades after the events I described in earlier chapters, I was lying peacefully asleep (or so I thought) in my bed, when the mattress and box spring inexplicably slipped off together and fell into the two-foot space between my bed and my large desk. I landed in the cramped space too. (I won't even conjecture here on how such an "impossible" accident could have happened.) Expecting to just get up from the floor, I was shocked to find I lacked the strength in my legs and arms to pull myself up. I tried and tried and tried, but to no avail, I was trapped.

After a long and frustrating series of failed attempts, I looked to my right wrist, which I presumed held the emergency alarm band I had been furnished a year earlier by Medicaid. To my great dismay, it wasn't there. I suddenly recalled that I had uncharacteristically taken the band off before climbing into to bed and placed it on top of my desk, which I now couldn't reach. I knew right then I was in serious trouble and began to panic. My cell and landline phones were in the adjacent kitchen. Wow! I seemed to be up shits creek for sure.

A hopeful thought arrived after a time: my close and trusted friend, retired local attorney Arthur Khoury- the younger brother of my previously mentioned, fellow waiter at Bishop's - Sam Khoury (now deceased), was scheduled to come pick me up at 10:30 the following morning and take me to Holy Family Hospital for an 11 a.m. colonoscopy exam. My only hope of survival, I soon came to realize was to hold it all together and try and keep myself alive until Khoury eventually arrived.

The ensuing fourteen hours that I spent awake and helpless on the floor proved to be a horror show as I tried dozens of times, unsuccessfully, to grab hold of the top of my desk and lift myself up. There wasn't adequate room in the tiny space to turn my body over, so, I was forced to lie there on my back the entire time. I tried also to get the attention of my good Spanish neighbor across the hall by yelling out every ten minutes or so throughout the night at top of my voice: - help!. help! help, but apparently not hearing my cries, he failed to respond to any of these pleas. After about four hours, my lower back started to hurt intensely and, due to the stress of it all, I began to swear profusely from the head, face, and neck - so much so that at times it felt like I was actually sweating blood.

And then the real fears began to creep in. Khoury might knock at my door at 10:30, fail to get a reply back, think I forgot the appointment, abort the mission, and leave. My fears turned more and more ominous, and I now became convinced I was going to expire there all alone on the bedroom floor with nobody to find me until my body began to stink. The only recourse seemingly available to me was, for the umpteenth time, to turn to the Almighty for help. So, I began praying feverishly, with words to the effect of:

"You're not going to let it all end like this are you, Father? I don't want to die here alone. You've never let me down before, so please don't now, dear Lord."

Over and over and over I prayed, all night long and into the following morning, with sweat pouring from my head and tears flowing down my face. Somehow, I miraculously held on until daylight, but as 10:30 arrived, there was no Arthur Khoury. Knowing I couldn't hold on much longer in the severely depleted condition I was in, I finally threw in the towel and now began petitioning God to at least grant me a bit of leniency in the next life. In this surrendered state, I must have drifted off to sleep.

A short while later, maybe fifteen minutes or so, I awoke to the sound of two men chatting in my kitchen. One of the voices was that of my good friend Arthur. The other I quickly recognized belonged to the Head of Security at the housing complex where I was living - Robin Monroe, a middle-aged fellow who I had over the years, come to know very well.

"Is that really you Arthur?" I yelled from my room as the lights miraculously came back on in my life. The two men then marched into my bedroom and Khoury, seeing me completely drained and helpless on the floor, immediately pulled his cell phone out of his jacket pocket and phoned 911. I guess that both men were reluctant to pick me up off the floor themselves for fear they might injure me even further.

Ten minutes later, two paramedics arrived. After quickly assessing the situation, they lifted me up off the floor, loaded me onto a stretcher, whisked me out of my apartment, and proceeded to drive me straight to the Holy Family Hospital's Emergency Room - My Lord and God, how magnificent You are!

As Khoury told me several days later, he had arrived at my place at the appointed 10:30 time and knocked at my apartment door. Receiving no reply, and now gravely concerned, he promptly called my brother George and alerted him to the situation.

George then promptly called Monroe at the Housing Authority and put him in touch with Khoury. After the two spoke briefly with each other, Monroe correctly grasped the seriousness of the matter and agreed to meet Khoury at my apartment and open my apartment door with his master key and see what the deal was.

Upon my subsequent arrival at the hospital, the ER physician on duty diagnosed me with shock, severe kidney damage, and dehydration. He administered intravenous therapy and formally admitted me for what he said would be a few days. Toward the end of his evaluation, he confided to me that in all his years at the ER, he had never heard of anybody surviving totally helpless on the floor for as long as I had:

"Thank your Lucky Star today, Charles." he said. "All I can say to you is: somebody up there likes you."

ACT III: MY CONVERSION

Chapter 24:
Roll Back the Stone!

About a month and a half later, towards the tail end of November of 2019, Joe Bonacorsi, my best friend in the world at the time and an older and much wiser man than me (now deceased), who over the last twenty years that I've known him, acted as my spiritual mentor - my Socrates, began telling me during our evening coffee get togethers at McDonalds that I looked terrible - gaunt and dehydrated Joe specifically said. Needless to say, he was very worried about me and in turn told me repeatedly to schedule an appointment to see my doctor and go in for a workup as soon as possible.

I finally relented and on October 30th made an attempt to schedule an appointment with my primary physician. Because of my primary's booked - up schedule, however, the earliest I could get an appointment with him for was November 14th. The Omniscient Creator, however, knew that time was of the essence and that He'd have to orchestrate something miraculous to ensure I got help sooner.

Just two nights later, at about 11 o'clock, while I was asleep, I awoke quickly then immediately started throwing up all over myself. (This was the first miracle, though I admit it doesn't sound very miraculous.) Alarmed at this unanticipated turn of events I pressed the emergency button on my right wrist. Ten minutes later, two paramedics arrived at my apartment and marched into my bedroom together.

"You look terrible, Mr. Ead. Why don't you let us take you to the hospital?" one of the two men said.

"No thanks guys; I'll be all right, sir. I already made an appointment to see my primary in two weeks. Let me just clean myself off and rest here for a few minutes. I'll be alright." Seeing the situation differently, the paramedic repeated his concern. This time however, it wasn't phrased as a polite request.

"Charles, you look very sick to me. I feel you need medical attention NOW! And I'm not taking no for answer. So, come on, let's go."

I eventually relented. (This was the second miracle, in my view. I hope that you can see the Divine Hand as I did, quietly at work in this scenario.)

Shortly after my arrival at Holy Family ER, the attending physician thought my condition was serious enough to admit me and promptly did so. A week later, after a failed second blood transfusion, and still gravely ill, I was visited at the hospital by my older sister Marion - a registered nurse.

"Chuckie, I'm not going to mess around here," she said. "They're not doing anything for you here at this glorified first-aid station. It's clear to me that you're not getting any better. I have a contact at Mass. General - MGH - widely recognized as perhaps the best hospital in the world. I'm going to call him right away and ask if he has a bed available for you." - (This, I believe, was the third miracle.)

As "fate" would have it, a bed WAS uncharacteristically available right away at MGH and I was summarily shipped to the Boson Hospital there at Marion's insistence by ambulance early the next morning. Upon my arrival, a team of staff physicians and nurses promptly attended to me in my room. One of the doctors who did so was a rheumatologist by the name of Dr. Dau, a relatively young looking, Asian man. Blood was drawn from me by one of the staff nurses and Dr. Dau assured me that a diagnosis and prognosis would shortly thereafter follow the work up.

Early the following morning, Dr. Dau came into my room and told me the blood tests that were taken evidenced that I was suffering from "a dangerously low red blood cell and platelet disorder," most probably caused by an adverse reaction to the sleep medication - Thorazine I had been taking for the CFIDS, for many years and that my condition was "critical." He said the blood work further evidenced that I had somehow contracted the highly debilitating auto-immune disease Lupus as well. Add that to the autoimmune disease CFIDS that I had already been suffering from for some thirty years and you can get an idea of how grave my condition was back then. When I asked Dr. Dau for his prognosis, he answered with:

"Well, it's not good, Charlie. You'll be very lucky if you even make it. In fact, if you had arrived here a day later than you did, we'd be calling in the undertaker (the fourth miracle). We're going to start you off with a round of experimental medication with the small hope of getting your low red blood cells and platelets up to the levels where they should be. Even if it's successful, this medication tends to take a long time to work, sometimes several months, so, prepare yourself because you're going to be in for a long and perilous ride. Our prayers for you here are that our hospital are that medication somehow does kick in and does the trick."

Ten minutes later, the hospital chaplain came into my room and administered my last rites. You can imagine the negative effect this had on my spirits. Later on that day, my sister Marion and my brother George visited me together at the hospital. Marion spoke first:

"Chuck, I just spoke with Dr. Dau. They're going to do everything they can for you here. You're in the best possible place you could be. The rest is up to that God of yours that you've told us about so often. But I'm afraid to say, it's not looking good for you right now. So, although I don't believe in your God or in the merits of prayer, if you think that it'll be of help to you, my advice to you is that maybe you should start praying." (Marion is an agnostic. She claims she needs "proof.")

George then interjected, "Brother, we all love you and we're rooting for you. I've got everybody praying for you. Just hang tough and keep your chin up like you always have done and keep putting one foot in front of the other. I'm sure you're going to be OK."

As I've detailed in this book, I've been gravely sick before, but never had I ever been as sick as I was then. In addition to the overpowering fatigue, I was now highly hopeless to the point of even being suicidal at times. I would like to state emphatically that, prior to this experience, despite my many misfortunes, that I had never been suicidal. The hospital staff assured me this was the result of my very low red blood cell and platelet levels.

As Dr. Dau explained it to me, red blood cells transport oxygen to all the bodies organs, including the brain. He claimed that I was feeling so acutely hopeless simply because I wasn't getting enough much needed oxygen to my brain. Moreover, because Dr. Dau had ordered the thorazine stopped immediately, but mysteriously failed to replace it with another, less damaging sleep medication, I was forced to remain fully awake every night during my ensuing ten day stay at the hospital. This added to my already severely fatigued condition each day. What a clusterfuck! God help me (again).

On about the tenth day of my MGH hospitalization, the head would worker on the floor walked into my room and told me that due to insurance reasons, the hospital couldn't keep me any longer and that I'd accordingly have to be discharged by the next day. This didn't sit well with me as I knew I was still too sick and debilitated to make it all alone by myself in my apartment. Needless to say, the hospital booted me out anyway. The following afternoon - (on a Friday) my brother George picked me up and brought me home.

Still unable to get a wink of sleep due to lack of an effective sleep medication, I stayed awake all that night while in my apartment. Around ten o'clock the following morning, my knees buckled under me and I collapsed on my living room floor in agony. Luckily, I was able to make it to my last line phone, called Marion, detailed to her the condition I was in, then stated that I wanted to return to Mass General right away. She agreed this was the right path to follow.

About an hour later, Marion and George picked me at my apartment up and drove me to the Boston hospital's emergency room. Now if you can believe this, my forty - year-old psychiatric records from McLean's somehow popped up on the computer at MGH, so, while waiting for a bed upstairs at the hospital to be made available for me, I was, "ordered" by the ER trial, nurse to meet with a MGH staff psychiatrist for a psych evaluation in an adjacent treatment room. Obviously, the old, falsehood ridden, psychiatric narrative had somehow resurfaced once again to potentially bite me in the ass.

314

Now struggling just to keep my legs from buckling under me, I innocently entered the glass enclosed treatment cubicle where a well-dressed, middle-aged woman who identified herself as a MGH staff psychiatrist was waiting anxiously to meet with my two siblings and me. Almost immediately after introducing herself to the three of us, she threw a blow torch at me as she began peppering me with irrelevant, psych-related questions.

Then, without conducting even a shred of medical testing, she voiced her belief that my health problems were psychiatrically and not physiologically induced and were caused by "bipolar disorder" and NOT by a combination of a blood-platelet disorder and a simultaneous lupus infection, as the medical testing at her own hospital was conducted only 11 days earlier, clearly evidenced.

Oh boy! - Fantasy Land; Here we go again! - another 'Snap Diagnosis;' The misguided shrink then went on to state that her intent was to cancel my readmittance that day at MGH and instead to transfer me directly over to McLean's Psychiatric Hospital where I had been hospitalized and treated thirty-five years earlier, to be given a "comprehensive psych evaluation." How utterly galling and ridiculous.

Are you for real, young lady? Not over my dead body!

I then told this misguided doctor that she should:

"Go back to medical school and get it right this time."

I mean the utter audacity of this flimsy dame trying to sell me and my two siblings on the stale and outdated belief that I was somehow mentally ill and in need of psychiatric treatment again. Needless to say, she appeared highly angered by my aforementioned, counter offensive statement.

315

I then quickly got up from my chair and with the little strength I had left, hastily made my way out of the treatment cubicle and back into the ER waiting room and sat down again. George and Marion meanwhile, remained behind and spoke further with the psychiatrist for a couple of more minutes. Perhaps they bought into the misfit's bullshit. I don't know.

After finally managing to get admitted at MGH again, I remained at the hospital for an additional six days with no apparent improvement in my medical condition. My nephew Ronny, who was attending pre-dental school at Tufts University in downtown Boston at the time, was thoughtful enough to take the train across town after classes concluded every day and visit with me at the hospital. His continued heartfelt support, and daily encouragement were the only positive forces that kept me going back then.

When my insurance provider said that it was time for me to be released from the hospital again, the head social worker at MGH strongly recommended this time that instead of being released to my apartment, where I most probably fail again, that I spend some time at a rehab facility to allow for the medication to kick in and get myself stronger and on the road to recovery. This seemed to be the wise way to go so, I OK'd the move.

My brother George then to his credit, at long last, rose to the occasion and stepped up to the plate and personally checked out about a dozen rehab facilities in the Greater Boston and Merrimack Valley areas and finally settled on the Mary Immaculate Rehab Facility (MI), which, according to my brother, had a five-star rating and was conveniently located just three blocks from my apartment in Lawrence. With my permission, I was transferred there the following afternoon by ambulance.

The staff physician who examined me upon arrival at MI determined my condition to be critical, just as the MGH doctors had diagnosed previously. Thankfully, I was given my own spacious room and was attended to by a compassionate nurse who informed me that the rehab staff would give me my medication every day, help me take showers, check in on me frequently, and serve me my meals in my room so as to make my stay there as comfortable as possible.

Unfortunately, however, I spent the better part of my days at the MI however, just lying in my bed, and worrying myself to death about whether or not I would be well enough to make it at home alone upon my quickly upcoming, eventual release. Making things even worse, just like what took place at Mass General, despite my repeated requests of the MI staff physician, without any justification, failed to order an effective sleep medication for me to take so I was forced to remain fully awake throughout the twenty-five nights that I spent there. Because I couldn't sleep, I felt out of sink and exhausted during the subsequent mornings and afternoon each day.

Adding insult to injury, my nurse sister - Marion was of the opinion that I "wouldn't make it" alone at home and so started making arrangements, without my knowledge or permission mind you, to have me shipped to the downstairs nursing home floor at MI upon my release, where I would supposedly receive around the clock care. When I learned of this, I became even more disheartened than I already was, if such a thing were even possible.

Meanwhile, family and friends visited with and/or phoned me at the MI frequently, often expressing alarm at my totally out of character, hopeless and defeated spirit. On the plus side, I phoned my friend Arthur Khoury who lived nearby, around noon each day and being the good soul that he is, would drive over to MI as soon as he got showered and dressed and provide me with some much-needed inspiration. Khoury was a self - effacing man of few words but what words he did speak were always meaningful and on target.

317

He would also often go out of his way to pick up my mother at her apartment and bring her with him before visiting me and would generously bring along combinations of iced coffee, pizza, and/or pastries as well. Arthur and Ma would then typically stay and console me for hours on end. It was easy to see though that these visits were psychologically draining on Ma, who sometimes had to wipe tears from her eyes, wondering whether perhaps she was going to lose another son or not.

Without Arthur and Ma's faithful support, and that of my nephew Ronnie as well, I'm absolutely sure I wouldn't have come through it all. Khoury also asked all my friends from McDonald's - about two dozen folks, as well as several local religious organizations and our parish priest to pray for me. He also gave me a get-well card that he had all of my friends sign their name to, which served to lift my spirits - at least temporarily anyway. As for me, I could only summon the mental stamina to pray these simple words at Ronny's recommendation just once or twice each night before retiring to bed:

"Old Man, I'm in deep trouble here, help me please!

On a negative note, one evening, in total despondency, and for some desperately needed emotional support, for the first and only time, I phoned my younger sister - Pamela who has been living for the last forty years in Sarasota, Florida with her husband Jim and their two now fully grown kids: The call went something like this:

"Pam, I'm on the ropes. Can you say anything Sis that would boost my spirits. I'm feeling totally hopeless right now." She then responded as you might expect a loyal and loving sister should:

"Chuckie, stop acting like a little baby and start taking responsibility for yourself, and stand on your own two feet and start pulling your own weight for a change. Keep in mind that I had never asked for nor taken a dime from anyone before mind you - most especially from Pam.). Ma and all of us down here are sick of you. Don't call here anymore! Click."

The Master - Jesus of Nazareth once stated:

"Out of the overflow of heart, the mouth speaks."

This wasn't the first and only time that Pam had gone against the family. Six years earlier when my father passed away, claiming that it wasn't "her responsibility" to bury Dad, she openly refused the family's request that she chip in her $2500 share of his funeral expenses. Pam adopted this defiant stance despite the fact that she and her husband Jim, working side by side, had run a very successful food brokerage business in Sarasota for a good number of years and had become millionaires in the process. Providing our late Dad with a financial infusion in this way was necessary because due to a one sided and nasty divorce settlement, the highly accomplished man, following a long and unwinnable battle with leukemia, was unfairly forced to exit this planet without a penny to his name.

On a more promising note, my brother George's wife - Hanna, my nephew - Ronnie and my previously mentioned, good friend - Arthur Khoury, all kept reassuring me each day that I'd be OK returning home to my apartment. On the final Friday of my four-week stay at the rehab, a meeting was held in my room between George, the head social worker, and myself. My sister Marion meanwhile, phoned in to the meeting from her home through speaker phone.

319

The purpose of this meeting was to determine where I would be sent upon my discharge from MI, which was scheduled for the following day. Marion, as you might expect, argued forcefully that I was too debilitated to be sent home and that I should be sent instead to the downstairs, third floor, nursing home ward where I'd be properly cared for around the clock.

George - my health care proxy at the time, conversely argued that I was well enough to return home. Thank God, I kept saying to myself, that I'd been wise enough not to name Marion as my health proxy. After listening to both sides, the social worker told us the final decision was ultimately mine.

I finally spoke up and said that during the course of the meeting, I had made the decision to make an honest attempt to return home to my apartment and give it my best shot. This didn't sit very well with Marion who, most probably felt at the time that her supposedly vast medical knowledge and/or her lengthy nursing experience wasn't being properly respected. With her over-sized ego apparently now severely bruised, she abruptly took affront, angrily hung up her phone, and despite the fact that I was still severely sick and very much needed her emotional support, refused to speak a word to me and/or George for the entire next month.

Chapter 25:
My Total Surrender to The Almighty and Accompanying Redemption

The Sea Finally Opens for Charles Ead

The night I returned home from rehab, in the throes of a negative funk that had begun while I was hospitalized at Mass. General two months earlier, I phoned my nephew Ronnie and told him about the intense emotional and physical trauma I was experiencing. He said he felt greatly for me but from his years of dabbling with spirituality (Ronny had spent two years living in a Buddhist monastery in San Diego directly following his graduation from college), he could only offer this brief advice:

"As I see it, Uncle, all you have left is your faith. Stop relying on all the rest of us for help. We've all done all we could for you. It's just you and God now. So, start praying right now!"

Taken aback by Ronnie's "pull no punches" words, I followed his instructions to the tee and with what little strength I had left, managed to somehow pray continuously throughout the night. My prayers I'm embarrassed to say however, still reeked of self-pity and went something like this:

"God, why have you forsaken me? Why did you beat the living crap out of me again like this? What's up with You? Are you trying to finish me off? When will your great wrath end against me dear Lord? Come on Father, tell me. Who praises you from the grave?"

And on and on I went. ... You've probably heard of the Alcoholic Anonymous version of this dynamic which is widely referred to in AA circles as *"stinkin - thinkin."* It sounds like this:

"Poor me. ... Poor me. ... Pour me another drink!"

The following morning, I received my answer back from our tough-minded Creator as He, without showing even a speck of mercy, took me to the woodshed.

God now Speaking: "Stop it, Charles. Don't run away from me. I'm not done with you yet. Sit up in your bed and address me like a man. What I just did was to break you down to nothing, just like the military does with its new recruits so that they can rebuild them from the ground up exactly the way they want them to be. I let all this happen to you to humble you so that I can work with you, just like what I did with my faithful servant Moses."

"Now, don't get a big head and go thinking you're anywhere in Moses' league. You're not. In fact, you're a basket case right now. To even begin to shine My great prophet's shoes, even though you're still ill, you're going to have to work much harder than you ever have on improving your psyche, your outlook on life, your faith, and your character. All I want you to do is *to grab hold of my hand and just surrender completely to Me and let Me have My way with you*, and I'll take it from there."

"I want you to know, that you're still 'my boy' and that your well-deserved punishment has officially ended. Although I hurt you so that you would respect Me, the record shows that I never once abandoned or forsake you. Despite your seemingly advanced age (65), and your checkered past, you've come through all the heartbreaking tests and trials that I

322

subjected you to like a champ and in addition, your grave sin has been now fully atoned for with Me as well. So, accordingly, I'm going to start rewarding you now by putting together some big plans for you for the future. But before we get going on those, you're going to have to formally get fully right with Me and here's the deal. ..."

"There's still one thing that has up until now, been left unresolved. What you did to your father many years ago Charles greatly hurt and offended all of us up here, especially your beloved grandfather and your adoring younger brother Mark, both of whom shockingly watched it all play out. So, here are the hard facts. Although I was compassionate and merciful and saved your hide from jail back then, and I know it wasn't all your fault (your mother played a part in it too), 'the buck still stops with you.' Your father was top shelf so, your behavior that fateful Saturday afternoon was inexcusable and you should never have let things get that far - no matter what your mother was telling you."

"You were no longer a kid at the time and you should have known better. Shame on you for that. So, here is what I want you to do now. Go and confess this longstanding mortal sin of yours to a priest and get it off both your chest and Mine so I can wipe the slate clean and begin to work with you like I did before your ordeal took place. Do this as soon as possible. After you have done so, we'll talk again."

So, the next day, having been read the riot act by my Creator, I called my good friend - Ross, an elderly and devout Christian man who was the first cousin of my closest and most trusted friend in the world - Joe Bonacorsi, and asked if he knew of a competent clergyman that I could confess my mortal sin to. He in turn told me of a Father Joseph - a black African

Catholic Priest who pastored his own church in the town of Everett - a suburb of Boston, some twenty miles away. Ross said he was confident that Father Joseph would be willing to hear my confession. I then asked Ross to call the African priest and book a meeting with him right away, and he promptly did as I asked.

Before my meeting with Father Joseph, God's Holy Spirit helped me to recall many other sins that I had committed during my life. Nothing mortal like the one I had committed with Dad, but just venial sins - the disrespectful ways I had treated and /or taken advantage of others in the past. These, I figured, I should confess to Father as well.

One week later, Ross drove me to Everett and I met with this Father Joseph in the basement office of his downtown church. An avid runner like I was, this priest and I bonded right away. Still fairly ill, and in a somewhat emotionally troubled state, I did my best to first explain to the African born pastor exactly what had taken place many years earlier with Dad. In the midst of doing so, I broke down and wept uncontrollably for about a whole minute. Fully expecting Father to say that he had never heard of such a vile thing - a young man beating up his own father, and then accordingly throwing me out of the confessional room, I was completely taken aback when he instead, smiled warmly and then said to me:

"Charlie, contrary to what you might have been led to believe, we priests are not in the judgment business; but are only here only to listen and then offer the forgiving and healing power of the Savior. Trust me when I tell you that in my twenty years or so as a man of the cloth, I have heard many stories that are ten-times worse than yours."

324

"It's obvious from the way you explained it to me young man that you were caught right in the middle of an intractable, turf battle between your two folks, both of whom you loved and cherished very much. I fully understand this dynamic and so I believe does our merciful Creator. So, consider your sin like a piece of dirty clothing that has been put into a laundry machine. It's now snow white clean. Go in peace my good friend. In the name of our beloved Savior - Jesus Christ, your seemingly unforgivable sin, which I can easily detect has been a ball and chain around your conscience for a long time, is now fully forgiven."

Oh, what burning words: "Your sin is now fully forgiven."

What music to my long, guilt tormented mind and soul. ... Wow! What a release this was for me! In fact, as Ross and I entered his car and began the ride back home, I began to feel an overpowering and indescribable sense of freedom and inner peace that I hadn't experienced since young adulthood. As we drove off, I remember saying to myself:

"This experience was magnificent. Why hadn't I discovered this confession thing a lot sooner in my life?"

At around the same time, the medication that Dr. Dau had prescribed for me during my stints at Mass General now at long last, began kicking in and not a moment too soon, and my health in turn began gradually improving. About a month after my confession, while lying on my bed one night, meditating and trying to make some sense of everything that had recently transpired, I heard again the voice of my Creator, through the same communicative agent of his Holy Spirit, speak to me again:

"You did the confession thing as I told you to do Charles - Bravo! You want to expose the abuses of the psychiatric system? Well, so do I, for nothing that takes place in this universe escapes my eye."

"Does He who formed the eye not see? I am well aware my son that present day psychiatry has harmed multitudes of helpless folks like you and that the profession is still in its mere infancy stages with a lot of kinks to still get out."

"But I don't want you to blame psychiatry, your parents, or anybody else for what has happened to you over the years. It was I who crushed you and willed every bit of it to happen. So, don't be enraged at anybody anymore. Instead, look up and take heart because I'm also a Master of 'turning lemons into lemonade,' and I very much want to do that with your situation in order to demonstrate my love and my omnipotent power. It's just as my faithful Apostle Paul states in My Good Book:

'We know that all things work together for Good for those who Love God and are Called to His Purpose.' (Romans 8:28)."

"In addition, I'm going to help you out even further by confronting all those folks, including your family and your fair weathered friends, who have been quick to judge a book by its cover and have in turn been unjustly mocking and shaming you all these years because of your misfortunes. I want them to fully understand that you're still my boy and that it is Me who is going to avenge you."

From: The Book of Isaiah

"Do not fear for I am with you; Do not anxiously look about you, for I am your God. I will strengthen you, surely I will help you."

"My word states that 'not a single sparrow falls from the tree to the ground apart from my Will,' and that 'even the very hairs of your head are numbered.' And perhaps you've heard by now that all things in this universe are subject to 'My Providence.' It is I who create light and fashion darkness. My hands rule the world. I by MYSELF bring meal and govern misfortune. I'M in total control of everything. So, I don't want you to fear any bad outcome here or to worry about anything."

"I'm also a God of justice. Justice is my middle name and to prove it, I'm going to stand fully behind you on this one. I'm going to grasp hold of your right hand and we're going to go at this task as an undefeatable team. I want you to just relax and fully trust that I'm totally in your corner. Perhaps you've heard my famous admonition by now: 'Without Me you can do nothing. With Me there's nothing that you can't do.'"

"You have tried very hard by yourself to accomplish your twin goals of restoring your reputation and exposing the misdeeds of psychiatry instead of letting me do those things for you in my own time and in my own way. I hope you've learned your lesson by now. As you might have come to understand by now, the courtroom wasn't the proper venue for you to accomplish these goals. It's too limited an arena. I must admit that it was highly painful for me to watch your protracted legal fiasco run its predictable, failed course."

"I purposely instructed Attorney Sarrouf to warn you off, but you were stubborn, as you Lebanese folk by nature tend to be and refused to take the back off advice he gave you. As the Old Testament evidences, My Chosen People, your cousins -

the ancient Israelites, were stiff necked in the same way. Well, that's all in the dead past now. Let's look to the future and go forward instead."

"This time you're not going to fail in your two goals like you did before. I'm not going to let you fail. Now though, we're going to do it My Way! So, get out of the driver's seat and let Me run the show. Didn't my prophet Jeremiah say somewhere that:

"It's not for man even to direct his own steps."

"So, I'm asking you to surrender yourself and every single aspect of your life over to My 'Will.' But before we begin this mission though, you're going to have to get yourself a lot stronger, physically, mentally and spiritually. You're terribly weak in these areas right now. So, I want you to keep taking your medication as prescribed and start reading your three self-help books and your Bible, all of which have just been gathering dust on your bookshelf for the last twenty-five years."

"Also, start again to repeat to yourself the faith and confidence-building self-motivators, found in the self-help books, and in the Bible as you did during your successful years in L.A and D.C. In fact, I want you to type them all up so you won't overlook any of them. You need to be re-branded. I want you strong again. I'll feed you more affirmations to add to the list as we progress."

"And regarding finances. I know that you're presently low on funds. But I don't want you worrying about money at all in the future. I know what you're going to need to get by and I know how to get it to you."

"With my grace, your buddy Al Cochetto's CFIDS' research team along with the good doctors at Mass. General, will take care of the medical part of the equation. Don't give up on the belief that a cure for CFIDS can be found in the near future. I'm directly overseeing Cochetto's research work too. Nothing is impossible for me. Doesn't my Holy Prophet Isaiah say:

"Those who wait for the Lord will gain new strength. They will mount up with wings like eagles; They will run and not get tired. They will walk and not become weary."

"And I Myself am going to bind up and all of the wounds and emotional scars you have accumulated over the years. For your part, concentrate on just *"doing your job:"* - as the sure, future Hall of Famer and your favorite NFL coach - the Patriots Bill Belicheck is fond of imparting to his players. I'll take care of the rest of it. After you've done this for the next six months or so, get back to me - or better yet, I'll get back to you."

"Oh, and before I forget, I also want you to show me some respect and come and visit me in my house by attending church faithfully every weekend. And you can start loosening up with your money too. Don't be afraid to be more generous and charitable. It will go well with you. As I state in My Word:

"You can't outgive Me." and 'What you do give Me, I'll give back to you sevenfold.' (Malachi)."

"In this same vein, I want you to 'honor Me with your wealth' by gladly tithing ten percent of your monthly income to the needy and less fortunate (Almsgiving), just as this same prophet - Malachi admonishes you to do in the Old Testament.

Remember also that: 'Almsgiving covers over a multitude of sins.' (The Bible Book Of Wisdom). And didn't I also say somewhere in the Good book that: 'I love a cheerful giver?' Your future, new-found generosity will allow Me to open the door and to start 'pouring out blessings on you' (Malachi again), like I've purposely backed off doing for a long time. I promise you that these blessings will numerous, so much so in fact that there going to literally chase you down."

Despite being severely ill with the CFIDS and now the Lupus, I began to put into practice all that the Good Lord had instructed me to do and I could see that over time it was really working. Just three months into it, my good Christian friend Ross spontaneously phoned me with the suggestion that I insert the Eternal Catholic Television Network (EWTN) into my cable TV mix.

He said that by doing so, I'd be able to watch the Daily Mass, which the network broadcasts three times a day, as well as other Catholic programming such as documentaries on the lives of the saints, episodes of the late Bishop Fulton Sheen's legendary show 'Life Is Worth Living,' and talks by the station's deceased founder and hopefully soon-to-be-canonized saint - Mother Angelica. When I asked Ross why he had called me with this idea, he said 'a hunch' to do so had inexplicably came over him suddenly.'

After I added EWTN to my cable service, in order to feed my soul, I've watched the Daily Mass faithfully and have additionally tuned in to an hour or two of other Catholic programming most evenings as well. I have also taken in dozens of Billy Graham's past crusades episodes on the U-Tube channel as well as numerous segments of the Bill Gaither Gospel Hour and the Gospel Tenor George Beverly Shaw's recordings, all of which I found to be immensely stimulating and spiritually helpful.

Then, when I have the desire to be spiritually fed, I turn on the TV preachers, and then Joel Osteen, Craig Lauri, David Jeremih, and the legend Graham. In my humble opinion, these are the only TC legitimate televangelists out there who I respect and care will even listen to them. From what I view regularly on television, the great majority of the remaining prosperity gospel preaching others I maintain, are not in it to sincerely serve God, but instead, are mere, glorified snake oil salesmen who do their thing just for the naked pursuit of the massive amounts of money they shamefully solicit and then take in from their sincere but unwitting followers.

Further on this subject, it's a huge mystery to me as to why our US Attorney General's Office and/or our Congress haven't clamped down on these charlatans yet. Make no mistake about it though, they're all going to have to answer someday to the Almighty Himself for their blatant mockery of Him even though they presently don't believe that they will be forced to. But we'll let this slide for now as it's a very involved discussion that is better left for another book.

In addition, I follow all of this TV viewing up by reciting an Our Father, three Hail Mary's, and a Psalm 23 of King David each morning right after which I recite the two following prayers to myself as Og Mandino eloquently penned them in, 'The Greatest Salesman in the World.'

First From Mandino:

'Lord, this day is all I have and these hours are now my eternity. I greet this sunrise with cries of joy as a prisoner who is reprieved from death. I lift mine arms with thanks for this priceless gift of a new day. So too, will I beat upon my heart with gratitude as I consider all who greeted yesterday's sunrise who are no longer with the living today. I

331

am indeed a fortunate man and today's hours are but a bonus, undeserved. Why have I been allowed to live this extra day when others, far better than I, have departed? Is it that they have accomplished their purpose while mine is yet to be achieved? Is this another opportunity for me to become the man I know I can be? Is there a purpose in nature? Is this my day to excel?"

And secondly, again from author Mandino, for daily guidance and direction, I recite the following:

"Oh Creator of all things, help me. For this day I go out in the world naked and alone and without your hand to guide me I will wander far from the path which leads to success and happiness. I ask not for gold or garments or even opportunities equal to my ability; instead, guide me so that I may acquire ability equal to my opportunities."

"You have taught the lion and the eagle how to hunt and prosper with teeth and claw. Teach me how to hunt with words and prosper with love so that I may be a lion among men and an eagle in the marketplace."

"Help me to remain humble through obstacles and failures; yet hide not from my eyes the prize that will come with victory. Assign me tasks to which others have failed; yet guide me to pluck the seeds of success from their failures. Confront me with fears that will temper my spirits yet endow me with courage to laugh at my misgivings. - (For, God Himself, 'gives' courage!)."

"Spare me sufficient days to reach my goals; yet help me to live this day as though it be my last. Guide me in my words that they may bear fruit; yet silence me from gossip that none be maligned."

"Discipline me in the habit of trying and trying again; yet show me the way to make use of the law of averages. Favor me with alertness to recognize opportunity; yet endow me with patience which will concentrate my strength. … (For nature never acts in haste)."

"Bathe me in good habits that the bad ones may drown; yet grant me compassion for weaknesses in others. Suffer me to know that all things shall pass; yet help me to count my blessings of today. Expose me to hate so it not be a stranger; yet fill my cup with love to turn strangers into friends.

"But all these things be only if Thy will. I am a small and lonely grape clutching the vine yet Thou hast made me different from others. Verily, there must be a special place for me. Guide me. Help me. Show me the way!"

"Let me become all you planned for me when my seed was planted and selected by you to sprout in the vineyard of the world. Help this humble salesman (or servant). … Guide me, God!"

And then from Dr. Vincent Peale's long time classic: "The Power of Positive Thinking," I recite the following faith building admonitions - one right after the other, and just as the enlightened preacher instructed:

"I believe. I believe. I believe. I believe!"

"This is the day the Lord had made. I will rejoice and be glad in it (repeated four times)." - The psalmist.

"I believe that today is going to be a wonderful day. I believe that I can successfully handle all problems that will arise today. I feel good physically, mentally, emotionally. It is wonderful to be alive. I am grateful for all that I've had, for all that I now have, and for

all that I shall have. Things aren't going to fall apart. God is here and He is with me and He will see me through. I thank God for every good thing."

And again, from the enlightened, Protestant minister, I pray:

"I place this day, my life, my loved ones, my work, my health and my future in the Lord's Hands. There is no harm in the Lord's Hands only good. Whatever happens, whatever results; if I am in the Lord's Hands it is the Lord's Will and it is good."

"Lord, the first thing I am going to ask you for is good health: give me a strong body. Then give me the ability to think clearly. Give me honest to goodness courage so I can keep going when the going is hard. And give me real confidence. Finally, just let me know that You are with me - that I'm not going it all alone. Lord give me these five things and I will do the rest myself."

And Then I recite the following five short prayers:

"Lord, lift me above my own narrow horizons that I might fulfill your true vision for me."

"Lord, give me the grace to see what I have to do, and the strength, the courage and the ability to do it."

"Lord, help me to know you better and to love you more each day."

"Lord, have your way with me."

"Lord, help me to always do what pleases You."

334

"And Lord, let it done to me according to Your will."

And then after that, I recite the following prayer to the valiant, young, French warrior - Saint Joan of Arc that was sent to me at my request by an EWTN staff member:

"Dear St. Joan, in the face of your enemies, in the face of harassment, ridicule and doubt, you held firm in your faith. Even in your abandonment, alone and without friends, you held firm in your faith. Even as you faced your own mortality, you held firm in your faith. I pray that I may be as bold in my beliefs as you, St. Joan. I ask that you ride alongside me in my own battles. Help me be mindful that what is worthwhile can be won when I persist. Help me hold firm in my faith. And lastly, help me believe in my ability to 'act well and wisely.' Amen."

And lastly, I quite often meditate on the prayer that was penned by Saint Mother Teresa that can still be found on a poster on the wall of her Children's home in Calcutta: It goes as follows:

- *"People are often unreasonable, irrational and self-centered. Forgive them anyway.*
- *If you are kind, people may accuse you of selfish, ulterior motives. Be kind anyway.*
- *If you are successful, you will win some unfaithful friends and some genuine enemies. Succeed anyway.*
- *If you are honest and sincere, people may deceive you. Be honest and sincere anyway.*
- *What you spend years creating, others could destroy overnight. Create anyway.*
- *If you find serenity and happiness some may be jealous. Be happy anyway.*

- *The good you do today will often be forgotten. Do good anyway.*
- *Give the best you have, and it will never be enough. Give your best anyway.*
- *In the final analysis, it is between you and God. It was never between you and them anyway."*

I'd like to mention that I live in a relatively small city where everybody knows everybody else's business, especially within the Lebanese - American community. Although many of the people who knew of my psychiatric history have passed on by now, those who are still here with us often shun me like a leper and/or treat me in a condescending manner. No, I'm not imagining this; it's real. And I have to admit, it greatly angers me whenever it happens.

When I see folks I knew from the golf course, the Y, or Bishop's Restaurant at the supermarket or out on the street, or even some relatives at family gatherings, they often purposely avoid eye contact with me. And also, many of my old and close friends fail to call me anymore to check up on me. Weddings and wakes are often disasters as well. My natural inclination is to strike back - at least in my mind, and say to these folks something along the lines of the following:

"Why you two-bit, garlic eaters; if you were forced to endure even a tenth of what I've had to go through in my life, you probably would have squealed like pigs and blown your brains out a long time ago."

But I've since been told by an insightful priest that this angry, internal response is self-defeating. He said it would be more spiritually beneficial for me to adopt a more Christ-like response such as:

"Forgive them Father, for they not what they're thinking."

Although I always try my best adopt this more beneficial attitude, I must admit I often find it very difficult to do. This priest further advised that if I can't forgive these folks to just ask God to *"make me forgive"* and pray hard that these people will someday *"see the light."* I'm hoping that perhaps after reading this book that they will. Father promised that this approach would, at least for the short term, do the trick. To my credit, I believe, I try not to get too discouraged by what other people think or say about me.

I guess that perhaps because of my past experiences, I've developed a thick skin over the years. I've learned that it's only God's and my opinion of myself that truly matter. What's also has been of great help in dealing with this negative dynamic has been to occasionally review a dissertation on the subject of *"Attitude"* that was authored by the famed, 19th century, social scientist - Karl Menninger that I've had pasted to my bedroom wall for some time. It was initially handed to me by a local psychologist whose help I sought out in dealing with the problem some years ago and reads as follows:

"ATTITUDE"

"The longer I live, the more I realize the impact of 'Attitude' on life. Attitude, to me, is more important than facts. It is more important than the past, than education, than money, than circumstances, than failures, than successes, than what other people think or say or do. It is more important than appearance, talent or skill. It will make or break a company a church a home. The remarkable thing is we have a choice every day regarding the Attitude we will embrace for that day. We cannot change our past. We cannot change the fact that people will act in a certain way. We cannot change in inevitable. The only thing we can do is to play on the one string we have, and that is our Attitude. I am convinced that life is 10 percent what happens to me and 90 percent how I react to it. And so, it is with you. We are in charge of our Attitudes."

In addition, I now have a deeper and more abiding faith in my Creator since my Conversion and believe wholeheartedly that even though I am at an age when most folks consider themselves too old to achieve, that my Father in Heaven may still have plans for me in the future, and maybe big ones at that. And I am assured, based on my past experiences coupled with His Word, that He's NEVER going to *"forsake or abandon"* me. So, despite everything, I just put one foot in front of the other and *"keep on keeping on."* I have also learned to take things one day at a time, to live every day, at author Og Mandino's urging, like it's my last day, and to try and make each day count.

And, having been through all that I have, and am somehow miraculously still here to write about it all, I have come to consider myself (without being blasphemous in any way), to be on par with the Yankee great - Lou Gehrig, who as you may know, upon his forced retirement from baseball due to an incurable bout with ALS nearly a century ago, claimed in front of 60,000 adoring fans at Yankee Stadium to be:

"The luckiest man on the face of the earth."

And although it's sometimes difficult, I try to keep love in my heart and I make it a point to thank God for the *"unearned and priceless gift of another day"* as well as for the blessings that I still have in life, which, when I count them all, are numerous. This gives me hope for the future, helps me

338

keep my chin up, and my head held high, and helps me to realize that all that has happened to me might well have been for God's bigger purpose, which I must admit, I haven't been able to fully grasp yet.

The saying is that cats have nine lives. Well, I've been blessed with twenty of them! Perhaps for this reason, not to boast or moralize, whenever I meet up with a less fortunate person who might be roaming the streets of my impoverished sanctuary city, I say to myself:

"There but by the grace of God go I." or "What you do to 'least of these,' you do to Me."

And hopefully not to appear any way to be self-righteous, instead of doing, believe it or not, what a lot of bozos, actually do of giving the poor, out of luck soul an address where he or she can get a voucher for some food, I instead, hand the person, not merely a dollar bill, but a five spot, if I have one on me. Enough so he or she can go out and buy a Big Mac or a Whopper and at least be able to fill their stomachs for the day.

And I don't care one iota if that individual is lying and is going to use the money to buy alcohol or drugs (many people seem to use this as a cheap justification for not giving). No, I just hand the poor soul the five bucks in good faith and say, *"God bless you,"* because I know firsthand from experiencing the bitter harshness of street life and poverty myself that they are most likely telling the truth. And if indeed they're not, it's strictly their business and none of my concern.

I also pray daily that my painful experiences have not been wasted. I pray that you - the reader, will be moved by them somehow, if only to open your heart a little more widely to a fellow human being struggling to get by in this upside-down world. And I pray also that our entrenched psychiatric establishment will gain a better understanding of how to treat its patients more humanely and therapeutically.

"Heavenly Father, please let it be so!"

Perhaps in answer to my prayers, my nephew Ronnie approached me a year and a half ago while I was visiting with him at his parent's home and said to me:

"Uncle, yesterday I had an interesting thought I'd like to share with you. From what I've witnessed firsthand myself and have also been told by others, you've led an extraordinary life, with a lot of interesting twists and turns and ups and downs. Why don't you write a memoir and see if you can get it published so that others might benefit from learning how your faith has helped you come through it all. I know that everyone in our family would love to read it."

I responded: "Ronnie, that's all very flattering, but I'm still very debilitated, not only with the CFIDS but with now Lupus as well, so, I'm out of commission for most of the day. Where am I going to get the time, energy, and stamina to complete such a daunting task? I'd have a better shot of successfully climbing Mount Everest with one leg."

"Just write for a few hours each day Uncle," Ronnie replied, "and on only days when you feel up to it. I've at least learned from my extensive college experience that small attempts repeated will complete any undertaking. Even if it takes you two or three years to finish your manuscript, what's the hurry? You'll have no pressing deadlines hanging over you.

Time is your friend. So, come on, give it the old college try; Will Ya."

"I'd like to order you a good computer and a printer for you through the internet with word processing software so you can get started. We can be in business for about seven hundred bucks. If you don't have the money to pay for it all now, I'll be happy to lend it to you."

I subsequently prayed daily on Ronnie's suggestion, and I have to admit his recommendation set up a challenge for me - and I've never been one to ever back down from a challenge. So, after much deliberation, I finally got the green light from the Holy Spirit and commenced my writing.

Despite my severe health limitations, I'm proud to say that I *'dug down deep'* as Ronnie further suggested that I do and worked hard and long on this endeavor, often staying up writing through the entire night and into the late morning hours of the following day and I'm sure much to the detriment of my already depleted health. I can honestly say that completing this manuscript has been a huge accomplishment for me, even greater I maintain than earning my MBA or completing the Boston Marathon, as it was something that initially I felt that I'd never be able to do.

I've tried to write from the heart. I've also tried my best to come clean and be authentic. Accordingly, I haven't sugarcoated or glossed over anything, even when the facts cast me and many others in an unflattering light. I hope that in doing so, although I might have lost your respect earlier in my life, I that now possibly have earned at last some measure of it back. And hope as well that somehow, I've aroused your interest and critical curiosity as well about the masked practices of our current, totally power driven and out of control, psychiatric establishment.

And not to be negative but I now have to report to you yet another tough setback. Two years ago, my sole remaining brother George was diagnosed with brain cancer. I'm happy to report to you now though that following successful brain surgery at a major Boston hospital, perhaps as result of all of our prayers, that George's cancer has miraculously gone into remission and that he is doing markedly better than all of us ever anticipated he would.

But what can we do? I guess all we can do is to continue praying and to roll with the punches, one day at a time. I most especially feel apprehensive about my still surviving mother who has already had to endure the painful emotional fallout of losing one son (Mark), and for this reason I continue to pray every day that George's cancer remains in remission for a long, long time.

And lastly, I would like to leave all of you readers out there on a more upbeat note with a prayer which I recite each morning along with my other prayers and find inspiring. It is anonymously entitled: 'An Irish Blessing,' and it goes something like this:

"May the road rise up to meet you. May the wind be always at your back. May the sun shine warm upon your face, and the rain fall soft upon your fields. And until we meet again, may God hold you in the Palm of His Hand."

Chapter 26:
"The Afterword"

What's Wrong with Psychiatry?

The currently practicing psychiatrist and distinguished author - Peter Breggin, who I previously quoted in this book, is a leading critic of psychiatric drugs and the "psychopharmaceutical complex" (as he dubbed it). He has been described as "the conscience of American psychiatry." Dr. Breggin is a graduate of Harvard College and Case Western Reserve Medical School and was formerly a teaching fellow at Harvard Medical School and a full-time consultant with the National Institute of Mental Health. He is director of the Center for the Study of Psychiatry and has been in full-time practice of psychiatry since 1968.

Dr. Breggin is also the author of "Talking Back to Prozac" and "The War Against Children." but is in perhaps is best known for his enlightening work: "Toxic Psychiatry" in which he most persuasively addresses the wrongs that are taking place in institutional bio-psychiatry. I heartily recommend this book to anyone who has been intrigued by the psychiatric aspects of my story. Please take a few moments to read these enlightening excerpts which I have selectively taken from it:

"Breggin: "I had learned as a college student that love and care and supporting the patient's self-determination were the most effective elements in helping people, even in rehabilitating "lost souls" on the back wards of state mental hospitals. I also learned that many of the inmates were simply homeless - disheartened, poor people with no place to go. But after I entered my medical and psychiatric training, I would never hear another word about the importance of love in helping people through their helplessness and despair. Even supporting the patient's sense of self-determination and personal responsibility would rarely be mentioned. And problems of poverty and homelessness would be wholly ignored. Instead, I was taught that the patients had diseases like schizophrenia, major depression, and manic depression or bipolar disorder. They needed pills instead of people. Shock instead of social reform."

"By 1966, when I had finished my training and become a full-time consultant at the National Institute of Mental Health, psychiatry was well on its way toward its wholesale conversion to biochemical and genetic theories and to the technological interventions such as drugs and electroshock."

"Ironically, the "new psychiatry" was not at all new to me, because it resembled nothing so much as the old state mental hospital psychiatry where patients were considered biologically and genetically defective and subjected to degrading and damaging treatments. Tragically, what was once the psychiatry of the poor was now becoming the psychiatry for everyone."

"In the past, there had been a double standard. In the state hospitals and public clinics, the vast majority of patients had always been treated as objects without concern for their feelings or the human causes behind their hopelessness and despair. They were blunted with drugs, insulin coma, electroshock, or lobotomy - the surgical mutilation of the highest centers of the brain. But a relatively small number of better-off people, especially those in major urban centers, sometimes received a more humane psychotherapy. Even though psychoanalysis never made up more than ten percent

344

of the profession, most educated people mistakenly equated psychiatry with psychoanalysis rather than with the much more dominant bio-psychiatry. Now the disparity between rich and poor was being eradicated and everyone was being diagnosed with genetic aberrations and "biochemical imbalances" suitable for drugs and electroshock."

Dr. Breggin goes on to give insight into the modern psychiatrist:

"Many people continue to think of the psychiatrist as the wise, warm and caring person who will help tackle their problems. But the modern psychiatrist may have no interest in talking therapy. His or her entire training and commitment is more likely devoted to "medical diagnosis" and "physical treatment." He or she may look at you with all the empathy and understanding of a pathologist staring through a microscope at germs, and then offer you a drug."

"The same is true if you are seeking help for a member of your family, such as your elderly mother who's getting more difficult to care for at home, or your son who's become supposedly hyperactive, difficult, or uncomfortable in school. You may want advice on how to be more helpful to your mother or your son; but the psychiatrist will explain that their problems are biological and treatable with drugs, electroshock or hospitalization. You may be relieved at the prospect of having the difficulty prescribed away by an expert. But beware; you are creating effects from which your mother or your child may never recover."

"Because this may be hard for you to believe, let me put it another way. The next time you go to a psychiatrist, you may find yourself in the office of someone who has never been taught how to talk with you about your problems or those of

345

your family. Nor has he or she been trained to understand personal and family conflicts. Instead, the doctor will listen, make some observations, jot down some notes, make a medical diagnosis and prescribe a physical treatment.

"Recently, while teaching a seminar at a mental hospital, I asked the assembled psychiatrists, psychologists, social workers and nurses if their recent training had dealt at all with the issue of caring about or loving their patients in the process of helping them heal. Among the fifty participants, only one person, a nurse, raised her hand."

"If you are educated in the humanities or have read a few good self-help books and if you think about yourself and others, you may have more insight into personal growth than your psychiatrist does; and if you've taken a few college courses or read a little in academic psychology or psychoanalysis, you might know more theory as well. If you've also shared feelings and personal problems with some of your friends, then you may well have more experience and practice in "talking therapy" than your psychiatrist."

"On the other hand, your psychiatrist will have more power than you. He or she can prescribe drugs or shock, lock you up against your will, talk behind your back with your husband, wife or parents and make plans for your future without consulting you. As a medical expert in malpractice and patients' rights suits, I have dealt with numerous cases of individuals who sought help for routine problems in living, such as sadness over the loss of a loved one, only to find themselves swept along the path of bio-psychiatry, ending up with permanent brain dysfunction and damage from drugs and shock treatment."

"We have found strong evidence of the efficacy of psychotherapy and social therapy with acutely disturbed people. So why don't bio-psychiatrists recognize that psychotherapy often helps? Indeed, why are they so insistent that it cannot possibly help?"

"There is a personal reason why most bio-psychiatrists cannot accept psychotherapy as something useful: they are not good at doing it."

"Why would so many young psychiatrists turn out to be poor therapists? In general, medical training is the worst possible way to select and prepare psychotherapists. To become a medical student, you undergo your undergraduate years as a lab mole and a bookworm, subterranean creatures most unsuited to working with people. The whole premedical and medical training is so competitive and authoritarian that much of the student's humanity is washed out. Indeed, the problem of producing too many stilted and socially inept physicians with narrow interests is now generally recognized in medicine and frequently discussed in professional publications. Even warm, loving, insightful people find themselves losing their humanity during psychiatric training."

Dr. Breggin details the need for havens within the psychiatric establishment:

"Many people could benefit from a haven or retreat in which to be safe while working through their psycho-spiritual crises. Many would seek such an alternative if they did not have to fear involuntary treatment and toxic drugs."

"At present, psychiatry provides no safe havens, although a number have proved successful in the past. Meanwhile, every psychiatric facility I know of in the country now routinely uses medication and subjects the individual to the risks of involuntary incarceration and coercive treatment. Each subjects the patient to rituals of humiliation that are demeaning and suppress personal growth. Each neglects the psychological and spiritual needs of the individual."

"Reaching out to others often becomes the first step back to human reality. When someone then responds with love and care, the recovery process is on its way. But this rarely happens in the psychiatric system. When the patient reaches out, the psychiatrist puts a pill in his hand."

"Sensitive, caring students are increasingly reluctant to enter psychiatry, and some already in the profession are dropping out. A young resident in psychiatry recently told me how she refused to give electroshock, only to be challenged by her department chairman, "Then why did you go into psychiatry?" She gave the treatment rather than be fired. Another young psychiatrist explained to me how he lost his job in a clinic because he refused to give everyone drugs. An older psychiatrist told me the same thing."

"One of my psychiatric colleagues - a "talking doctor" like myself, tells me, "I wouldn't do it over again. No, if I knew where psychiatry was going, I'd never become a psychiatrist.""

"Another psychiatrist spoke even more directly through his actions: he retired twenty years ahead of time and changed careers. He couldn't stand what's become of the profession. Still another colleague, who continues to teach psychiatric residents, explained to me "They have changed. Young physicians going into psychiatry are more aloof, less caring, less involved with people.""

In the September 1989 Clinical Psychiatry News, Lothar Goldschmidt laments that "opening any psychiatric journal of our times is like opening a textbook of chemistry," and "psychiatrists to a large extent have given up practicing psychotherapy and addressing themselves to emotional problems." Psychiatrists are not trained in the humanities or even "in basic psychology." He writes, "Residents in psychiatry know close to nothing about various fields that have contributed to our understanding of the human mind."

But in reality, psychiatry is much more than an academic discipline or a therapeutic approach. Psychiatry is the political center of a multi-billion-dollar psychopharmaceutical complex that pushes biological and genetic theories as well as drugs on the society. It is a political institution licensed by the state, financed by the government and empowered by the courts. Its diagnoses carry enormous legal weight and have vast political implications. Psychiatric labels allow parents to lock up their children in psychiatric hospitals and allow the state to do the same to homeless people.

Psychiatry's political power has permitted it to perpetrate the harm documented throughout this book, from drugging millions of children to shocking tens of thousands of the elderly. Its power has allowed the profession to go largely uncriticized and unimpeded while producing an epidemic of brain damage. There is no place for the political institution of psychiatry in a free society, and it should be abolished. The first step requires stripping the profession of its legal but illegitimate powers, including the right to lock up and treat people against their will.

The second step involves disempowering the psycho-pharmaceutical complex. Psychiatric organizations such as the American Psychiatric Association (APA) and individual psychiatrists must be stopped from collaborating financially with the drug companies while claiming to act as objective scientific bodies or scientists. The third step will be even more difficult to attain, because it strikes at the heart of the psychiatric viewpoint. Psychiatry and psychiatrists must not be allowed to make claims about genetic and biological origins of so-called mental illness. Such claims are unethical, if not fraudulent, and serve only to perpetuate the influence of the profession and individual practitioners.

Once psychiatry is separated from its illegitimate powers, its relationship with the drug companies, and its unfounded claims, then we shall see if people really want what it has to offer. Can psychiatry compete in a more free market with psychotherapy and psychosocial alternatives, as well as with all of the other ways people seek to heal their minds and their hearts and to grow? Would people rather talk through their problems and go to self-help groups, or take drugs? Would they rather think of themselves as struggling persons or as defective biochemical devices?

Would people prefer to seek the source of their personal problems within themselves and their lives, or within their genes? Would they rather go to non-medical havens for moral and spiritual support, or to mental hospitals for medication and electroshock? Would they rather provide the homeless poor with better, more affordable housing, or shut them up and drug them in custodial state hospitals? Would people prefer to provide the elderly with more love and better social services, or with electroshock? Would they rather offer the nation's school children smaller and more stimulating classrooms or Ritalin? Would people prefer to face the problems plaguing the American family, or drug and lock up its troubled members?"

THE END

www.ingramcontent.com/pod-product-compliance
Lightning Source LLC
Chambersburg PA
CBHW051257120626
46547CB00015B/1986